Rewriting Contemporary Political Philosophy with Plato and Aristotle

Also available from Bloomsbury

Cultivating a Good Life in Early Chinese and Ancient Greek Philosophy, edited by Karyn Lai, Rick Benitez, and Hyun Jin Kim
Health and Hedonism in Plato and Epicurus, by Kelly Arenson
Plato's Trial of Athens, by Mark A. Ralkowski
The Bloomsbury Companion to Political Philosophy, edited by Andrew Fiala

Rewriting Contemporary Political Philosophy with Plato and Aristotle

An Essay on Eudaimonic Politics

Paul Schollmeier

BLOOMSBURY ACADEMIC
LONDON • NEW YORK • OXFORD • NEW DELHI • SYDNEY

BLOOMSBURY ACADEMIC
Bloomsbury Publishing Plc
50 Bedford Square, London, WC1B 3DP, UK
1385 Broadway, New York, NY 10018, USA
29 Earlsfort Terrace, Dublin 2, Ireland

BLOOMSBURY, BLOOMSBURY ACADEMIC and the Diana logo
are trademarks of Bloomsbury Publishing Plc

First published in Great Britain 2019
This paperback edition published in 2021

Copyright © Paul Schollmeier, 2019

Paul Schollmeier has asserted his right under the Copyright, Designs and
Patents Act, 1988, to be identified as Author of this work.

For legal purposes the Acknowledgements on p. viii constitute
an extension of this copyright page.

Cover design by Maria Rajka
Cover image: The Pnyx; or Place of Assembly of the People, Fulleylove, John (1847–1908) /
Private Collection / © Look and Learn / Bridgeman Images

All rights reserved. No part of this publication may be reproduced or
transmitted in any form or by any means, electronic or mechanical, including
photocopying, recording, or any information storage or retrieval system,
without prior permission in writing from the publishers.

Bloomsbury Publishing Plc does not have any control over, or responsibility for,
any third-party websites referred to or in this book. All internet addresses given in
this book were correct at the time of going to press. The author and publisher
regret any inconvenience caused if addresses have changed or sites have ceased
to exist, but can accept no responsibility for any such changes.

A catalogue record for this book is available from the British Library.

A catalog record for this book is available from the Library of Congress.

ISBN:	HB:	978-1-3500-6617-5
	PB:	978-1-3502-4450-4
	ePDF:	978-1-3500-6618-2
	eBook:	978-1-3500-6619-9

Typeset by Integra Software Services Pvt. Ltd.

To find out more about our authors and books visit www.bloomsbury.com
and sign up for our newsletters.

*To our Progenitors
And our Progeny*

... ἀλλὰ λέληθέ σε ὅτι ἡ ἰσότης ἡ γεωμετρικὴ
καὶ ἐν θεοῖς καὶ ἐν ἀνθρώποις μέγα δύναται·
σὺ δὲ πλεονεξίαν οἴει δεῖν ἀσκεῖν·
γεωμετρίας γὰρ ἀμελεῖς.

– Σώκρατες

Contents

Acknowledgments — viii
Preface — ix

Part 1 The Cave: The Turn to the Intelligible

1 Rational Animals — 3
2 Political Animals — 23

Part 2 A Eudaimonic Polity: An Opportunity Overlooked in Contemporary Political Thought

3 Liberty and Slavery — 49
4 Rightness and Fairness — 71
5 Public and Private — 93

Part 3 The Cave Again: The Daunting Prospect of Political Tragedy

6 Poetical Animals — 121

Notes — 140
Select Bibliography — 203
Index — 205

Acknowledgments

I would be remiss not to thank my many philosophical colleagues scattered hither and thither at various universities throughout the world. With electronic communications as well as more traditional conferences and conversations, the community of scholars is more alive and thriving more than ever. Without their critiques and encouragements, my book would not be what it is. I thank also my editors and copyeditors, who offered many suggestions and comments during the publication process. Their helpfulness does not go unappreciated.

I presented, to the consternation of my audience, a paper gleaned from the last chapter of this book at the second Interdisciplinary Symposium on the Hellenic Heritage of Southern Italy held in Syracuse, Sicily. The paper was entitled "Plato, Politics, and Poetry," and it has since appeared in *Politics and Performance in Western Greece*, edited by Heather L. Reid, Davide Tanasi, and Susi Kinbell (Sioux City, IA: Parnassos Press, 2017), pp. 253–264.

Preface

With this volume I offer an apology for political philosophy. Who among us, philosopher or no, could not be aware that political philosophy in our day has gone awry? Contemporary philosophers who theorize about politics have become little more than mouthpieces for the status quo. They preoccupy themselves with developing and explicating theories to justify political societies of the kind that we presently inhabit.

But we live in political societies considerably less than just, I dare say. Our societies consist of both prosperity and poverty in the extreme. Some people succeed in amassing fortunes beyond fantastic, and some people struggle to get by on less than a pittance. Is a distribution of wealth so disproportionate likely to be just? Today one percent of the adult population owns one half of the household wealth in the world.[1]

That some more fortunate persons among us are philanthropic souls who use their wealth to do well by others, I would not deny. But I would also ask, Should those less fortunate among us have to depend on kindnesses?

I propose to discourse more on how one might restore to political philosophy her proper dignity and less on how she might have fallen into her present plight. My intention is to develop a philosophy of what a political society in our era ought to be rather than another theory of what a society happens to be. My hope is that the philosophy proposed will inspire my colleagues and companions with a new purpose for their political inquiries and endeavors and ultimately alleviate the disparities of privilege and privation so evident today.

I shall advance a novel principle for my instauration of political philosophy. Actually, the principle only appears novel to us. I could hardly pretend to have invented a principle entirely new for an endeavor as longstanding and as enduring as politics. Unfortunately, political philosophers have recently subverted this principle if they have not ignored it altogether. They exhibit a distinct tendency to subordinate the principle to other, less worthy, principles.

My principle is happiness. This principle will appear novel to many because I wish to take this concept in its ancient sense—albeit with appropriate modifications. I shall advocate political happiness in the sense of a rational activity and not in the sense of an emotional passivity. We are happy, I shall argue, when we engage in a rational activity primarily for the sake of itself and not primarily for the sake of something else, usually our profit or pleasure. I defer to Plato and Aristotle for an exposition and defense of this definition (see esp. *Ethics* 1. 7.).

I would thus ask you to entertain a simple and, I should think, evident hypothesis, that each and every human being who wishes to be happy, and who does not, ought to have an opportunity to be happy. Each and every one! I do not say, nor can I say, that every human being who wishes to be happy ought to be happy. No, happiness we can no more grant to one another than we can grant one another wisdom or virtue.

Happiness in the classical sense requires that we not only wish to be happy, but that we also choose to take the appropriate measures to become happy. If we are happy, we are performing an action for its own sake and acting from virtue, which is simply a good habit. If we are to become happy, we must accordingly choose to perform an appropriate action, we must choose to perform our action for its own sake, and we must choose to perform our action repeatedly until it becomes habitual.

But we cannot act without resources. These resources include, at a minimum, a function to fulfill within a society, an education appropriate for a function, and the material means requisite for its fulfillment. No one can provide another with the aspiration or the dedication to take proper advantage of the necessary resources. But one can offer others who possess the desire and the ability an opportunity to avail themselves of these resources. Surely, one ought not to hamper or to hinder another by denying them an opportunity of this kind.

Please take note that this volume concerns happiness in a political sense and not in a personal sense. I shall mention personal happiness only by contrast. We too often neglect to consider our happiness within political society. Our society can, paradoxically no doubt to a contemporary ear, be an end in itself and not a mere means. Happiness in a political form consists of participating in a political society—participating, I mean, for its own intrinsic public value and not for private instrumental value.

What is at stake is the very idea of a political community. We human beings can find happiness by participating in a community, I shall argue. One might think of political society as if it were a choreography of human activities in which we can participate and enjoy as an end in itself. We ought also to afford our companions an opportunity to participate. Why disregard their potential? When we give others an opportunity, we are likely to make our society the better for it and to enable others to make themselves the better.

I wish to argue, then, that contemporary political philosophers overlook an important human good when they fail to give due consideration to our political happiness. Indeed, they overlook, I shall claim, the most important political good of all. With my endeavor I shall question the most basic assumptions of contemporary political thought. My contention shall be that a political society ought itself to be a moral end and not a moral constraint, so-called, on private ends.

Our contemporaries for the most part gussy up current economic theory in an attempt to make it seem moral. They apparently deem economic considerations paramount. We live in what we euphemistically call a consumer society. We preoccupy ourselves with producing and consuming material goods. But do we not have all the devices and appliances that we could possibly want? Indeed, we are throwing away gadgets and gizmos at such an alarming rate that their disposal presents serious problems.

I wish suggest that we have burdened ourselves with fallacious thinking of an embarrassingly elementary sort. We appear to be of the opinion that the more material resources we possess the better persons we will become. Good persons do require resources, but resources do not make a good person. Not even a good producer or a good consumer.

I would that I could also advocate specific policies for the attainment of our political happiness. But I am, alas, a humble philosopher and not a politician. This fact is not laudable, I admit. Even Plato and Aristotle lament the fact that theory and practice were far more often than not separated from each other. They thought that any one who might be possessed of both philosophical acumen and political ability would be nothing less than a godsend.

I shall not, then, make any pretense to go beyond a formulation and a defense of principle. What I set out in theory I can only hope that others more experienced than I might deem worthy to pursue in practice. Indeed, what little experience I have gleaned in matters political suggests that policy matters ought best to be specific to a given situation. Those more versed in their own circumstances would most likely be best suited to develop and to implement policy.

My hypothesis about our happiness rests on a prior assumption that we ought to be cognizant of our humanity. Our humanity, I assume, provides a foundation for our happiness. What is a human being? A rational animal, I should think. I hope that this answer is unproblematic. What is our rationality? This answer might be problematic. We shall see that our rationality, when we exercise it, is our happiness. Even when we exercise it in a political arena.

We deny our rational nature if we exercise it not for its own sake but for the sake of something else. A rationality exercised for something else would most likely be employed ultimately to procure satisfaction for our desire. Our happiness, so-called, would no longer be a rational activity but an emotional passivity, and we would not be rational but passional animals. We would be less than fully human. We would be human beings in potentiality only and not in actuality.[2]

I would also ask, What is a human being if not a political animal? Our humanity can find an expression within a political society. We best exercise our political nature when we engage in political activity for its own sake though we tend to forget this fundamental fact. We can be happy, in a word, when we participate together with others in political activity without an ulterior motive. Not to engage in political activity of this kind would also be to deny our nature.

I intend, then, to draw attention to our political functions and roles though I would not deny private roles and functions. If we are political animals, we ought to perform a political function. Or else we forsake our happiness and our nature. At least, in part we do. The political, I shall argue, is a *res publica* to be held in common, not a *res privata* to be held in contention. We are surely less than happy and less than human when we utilize our political activity for private ends. We live without a community though we live within a society.

My antagonists in this endeavor are, as always for a eudaimonist, if I may use the term, the sophists. We live in an age of sophistry, I make bold to say, and we are now reaping its rewards. I do not speak of intellectual sophistry, though it, too, is surely present. I speak rather of moral sophistry, and in particular I speak of its political variety. The moral sophists seek happiness not in a rational but in a passional sense.

Sophistry we usually think to be fallacious reasoning. We can see why one might so think if we ask why anyone would indulge in fallacies. The most likely explanation is that we permit ourselves to rationalize about our conduct when we seek to indulge our appetites. Our rationalization takes for its principle whatever notion might seem to justify our indulgence. A rationalization of this sort can obviously pervade political theory and economic theory as well.

Protagoras is probably the most famous exponent in the ancient world of sophistry in the intellectual sense. Man is the measure of all things, he declares. Though less well known for it, he also expounds sophistry in a moral sense. Man is apparently the measure of all things moral, too. Ironically, Socrates with a theory of deferred gratification best explicates this sophistical position for us and apparently for Protagoras himself. At least, Plato so argues in an eponymous dialogue.

Plato also portrays other ancient sophists in his dialogues. Perhaps Callicles and Thrasymachus are the most famous of these. Callicles argues brashly that those with political ability ought to be manly enough and brave enough to satisfy all their desires, and that they ought to make their desires as many and as strong as possible. Thrasymachus bluntly contends that those who have political ability ought to use others solely for their own satisfaction.

These poor souls and their ilk Plato imprisons for all eternity in the lower class of his ideal political society. This class comprises the artisans and the farmers and herders. A guardian class, he argues, must control these persons with external constraints because they lack any ability to control themselves. These unfortunates are at the beck and call of their desires, he avers.

Modern sophists usually advance their cause under another banner. They prefer to call themselves utilitarians. Among these sophists we may number most prominently Jeremy Bentham and John Stuart Mill. Their motto is the greatest happiness for the greatest number. They would thus appeal to a principle of happiness. But their principle is also a passional happiness. They think human goodness to be desire satisfaction.

I shall focus on utilitarians in their contemporary guise. Philosophers theorizing about politics today may seem to stand in opposition to utilitarianism. John Rawls and Robert Nozick provide conspicuous examples. Rawls and Nozick both protest explicitly against the utilitarian theory. They agree that utilitarianism would in principle permit us to sacrifice the interests of a few persons for the benefit of the many.[3]

But neither Rawls nor Nozick can quite escape utilitarianism and its allure. Though their means differ, their ends are essentially utilitarian. They both agree that our highest good is to fulfill a plan of life. But what is the purpose of a plan of this kind? A plan of life has the purpose of satisfying our desire, they argue. If we have a plan, we can the better satisfy our desires by organizing them and by avoiding conflicts among them.

Rawls and Nozick, in other words, offer similar theories of deferred gratification though they offer dissimilar concepts for deferring gratification. They both agree that our happiness ought not to make others less happy. Rawls argues in effect that those who are more happy ought to benefit from institutions that make more happy those who are less happy. Nozick in effect argues that those who are less happy ought not to benefit from institutions that make less happy those who are more happy.

Whether modern or contemporary, the utilitarians, then, lack a principle of political happiness in the sense of a rational activity of value for its own sake. They advocate happiness only in the sense of satisfying our desire. They would thus subordinate political activity, eudaimonic or not, to personal happiness, and personal happiness they conceive in a passional sense.[4]

My purpose, then, shall be to delineate differences both salient and significant between a eudaimonic philosophy of politics and a sophistic political philosophy. I wish to perform a philosophical experiment, one might say. With the political philosophy of the classical era I shall analyze and critique two contemporary political philosophies of no little import and influence. My focus will be on the overarching theme of eudaimonic politics and not on the minutiae of scholarly commentary.

In my discussion I intend to glean general concepts of importance for my experiment from the Platonic and Aristotelian political philosophies and from their epistemologies and ontologies. I shall take these ancient theories for granted and avoid undue exegetical complications. I do devote some discussion to contemporary commentary. But I limit my discussion to commentary that might help clarify the classical concepts for my reader.

I shall also focus on the commonalities to be found in the Rawlsian liberal theory and the Nozickian libertarian theory. I shall forbear to indulge in an analysis of their more specific differences and of their sectarian controversies. I take the Rawlsian and Nozickian theories for granted as well. I assume for the sake of my critique that their arguments are sufficiently successful, and I critique them as they stand. No doubt their theories do have their imperfections, but my concern is not to improve upon their specifics.[5]

But my reader may wonder, How can we make use of a principle of happiness in a political society? How can we employ a concept of eudaimonic activity to organize a society? I propose to borrow another idea from the ancient Greeks. I wish to suggest that we ought to rest our political philosophy on a concept of polity. We would seem to forgo any consideration of polity today though nearly everyone lives in a polity of a sort. We do so because usually we think a polity to be a democracy or perhaps an oligarchy. Hence, a concept of polity proper remains inarticulate.

I shall take into account polities of two species. These species are what I would call a eudaimonic polity and an expedient polity. I obviously wish to advocate a eudaimonic polity. A polity of this kind is a political society that takes for its end an activity of happiness attainable by most people. This feasible activity I take to be what I shall call artisanal happiness. My assumption is that anyone who is able to engage successfully in an artisanal activity for its own sake is happy.

What is an artisanal activity? An activity of this kind is what one might more commonly call a productive activity. I would suggest that we can be happy when we are making things, in other words. We can recognize that a productive activity itself has value as an end, and we can give priority to its value as an end. I would hardy deny that a productive activity has a value as a means. But I would argue that its intrinsic value ought to be primary and its instrumental value secondary.

The concept of a productive activity as an end starkly contrasts with a concept of production as a means. We can all too easily degrade production and its intrinsic value if we give priority to its instrumental value. The consequence is a productive activity that denies us our humanity for the sake of ever greater output. We can no longer express our rational nature in production. Production, especially on an assembly line, can become banausic in a most pejorative sense.

A polity of expediency is less than eudaimonic. A polity of this kind rests on a mixture of principles. It assumes not a concept of eudaimonic happiness but a concept of hedonic happiness. Its end is none other than the gratification of desire. This polity accordingly rests on ancillary principles needed for our gratification. These principles are concepts of liberty and property.

A polity of this mixed variety is today a utilitarian society. It plainly recognizes that we need both liberty and property to satisfy our desire. A society of this kind thus becomes a compromise between a democratic party, which would take the expression of liberty to its extreme, and an oligarchic party, which would take the possession of property to its extreme.

Any polity, whether eudaimonic or expedient, ought rightly to favor the middle class. That the middle class should be the focus of political theory and practice, is part of contemporary culture though its consideration is falling out of favor. The middle class tends to lend more stability to a political society than either the rich or the poor class do. The rich or the poor too often carry their principles to an extreme, which can occasion conflict. Even in antiquity Aristotle and Plato took note this political fact.

Who are the middle class? A eudaimonic polity would define the middle class to be those who have the ability and the desire to pursue rational happiness. I am advocating an artisanal happiness, which, I would think, most people can attain. But an expedient polity would focus on those who pursue passional happiness. Happiness of this kind one can find in a consumer society. Democrats advocate liberty for consumption, and oligarchs advocate property for production.

My theory, then, constitutes a challenge to ancient political theory. The ancient Greek philosophers in their political theories do not think that productive activities can be eudaimonic. They think that production cannot have intrinsic value, but that it can have only instrumental value. Both Plato and Aristotle explicitly hold that the arts and crafts and their activities are inimical even to virtue and to happiness.

I would argue that the question is one of purpose. Can we not engage in productive activities with the purpose of performing them primary for their own sake? Or must we invariably engage in them solely for the sake of their output alone? Though most do not, some corporations today recognize that even industrial production is a human activity that has both intrinsic and instrumental value. Many cottage industries also exist in which artists and artisans engage in productive activity for its own sake as well as for its results.

My theory is also a challenge to modern political theory. Contemporary philosophers do not appear to advocate eudaimonic happiness of any kind. Rawls and Nozick clearly do not. They prefer happiness of the hedonic variety, and they think that all rational activities are primarily of instrumental value. The upshot is that everyone is an artisan in the banausic sense.

My reader may find that he or she can read this work in more ways than one. Permit me to mention three ways more salient and, I think, more significant. One reading is to take the political philosophy contained herein to be a new theory of democracy. "Democracy" is an ambiguous term. We tend not infrequently to think a contemporary polity to be a democracy. We thus may, with a nod to this usage, take democracy to promote our eudaimonic happiness. This eudaimonic goal I wish to make explicit.

More often we think an expedient polity a democracy, however. We especially do so if a mixed polity claims to give priority to its principle of liberty. But we think a polity of this kind an oligarchy if its principle of property is a priority. My goal is to argue that we ought to make a principle of happiness the end of liberty and of property in our society. We would thus transform into a eudaimonic polity a polity of the mixed variety.

I also wish to extend the franchise, so to speak. Political functions include more than what we today call citizenship. To vote and to hold office are important functions, but they define citizenship only in a rather narrow sense. In a wider sense citizenship would include intellectual activities, martial activities, and artisanal activities. My focus, again, shall be on artisanal activities, and my assumption that most persons can happily pursue these activities, either in industry or in agriculture.

A eudaimonic polity, then, has practical advantages. Eudaimonic happiness defines a finite end for our activity, but hedonic happiness does not. Our pursuit of a profession or an occupation has a limit in its activity, but our desire for wealth or pleasure has an end with no limit. A eudaimonic polity would thus be especially pragmatic in a world of resources decidedly finite. People who are happy do not require excessive liberty or property. But people who are not happy often become licentious or greedy.

I must point out, however, that persons can pursue eudaimonic happiness in more than one specific variety. My purpose is to argue in support of a general principle of happiness and to place this general principle within a theoretical framework. But happiness, including artisanal happiness, can be of different kinds. Different societies may pursue different productive activities, and different persons within a society obviously pursue different activities. The particular species sought vary both by culture and by nature.

Another way to read this work would be to view my thoughts on political philosophy as an analysis of American democracy. The Declaration of Independence explicitly enshrines three inalienable rights to life, liberty, and the pursuit of happiness. Life and liberty political philosophers have surely given due, if at times misguided, attention. But the pursuit of happiness has given them rather scant concern. Yet life and liberty are only ancillary to happiness.

I have in fact often had American democracy in mind as I write. I do so in part because I am not unacquainted with the democracy in which I have resided almost my entire life. I also must perforce write with my own democracy in mind because of considerable ignorance on my part. I simply am neither well informed about nor well acquainted with other democracies that have existed in the past or exist in the present.

I hope that I do not seem jingoistic. In my defense I would say that America is often recognized for being the first democracy in the modern era, and she is, deservedly or not, in the eyes of many taken to a paradigm of democracy. I do not make these assertions because of any arrogance, I assure you. I am well aware of the missteps and shortcomings of my political society. Indeed, my purpose is in part to offer considerations for renovating and reinvigorating the democracy in which I happen to live.

Other philosophers before me have taken American democracy for a modern paradigm. Perhaps Alexis de Tocqueville is the one who did the most to burnish her reputation in the world. Only his insights exceed his praises for this new democracy. He surely recognized that in America democracy was at its foundation a polity though he does not use the term. He sees this democracy as a society in which most persons are of the middle class and enjoy its comforts.

Unfortunately, Tocqueville offers an analysis that would have us believe that American democracy can be a polity not of a eudaimonic variety but only of an expedient sort. But he is well aware of the dangers of hedonic happiness, especially its instability. Persons in the middle class, he argues, have enough to be comfortable but not enough to be content. The wealthy class fear to have fewer comforts, and the poor desire to have more.

Yet I would like to think that, had he but thought of it, Tocqueville would likely approve of my analysis of American democracy. Polity in the true sense is an expression of our better nature. He would hopefully agree that, if we choose act eudaimonically, we can act from what he terms a virtue of beauty and not from a virtue of utility.

One might, finally, read these reflections on polity as presenting a paradigm for what many people proclaim to be a new global society. I shall say nothing of this political phenomenon beyond these few words. My ignorance of global affairs exceeds my ignorance of democracies other than my own.

What little experience I do have yields the impression that those who are today acting on a global scale are those who also concern themselves less with eudaimonic prosperity than with passional and material prosperity. Why should one expect that they would not model their global endeavors on their local ones?

I would aver that we ought to ask, What kind of globalization would we have? Is globalization inevitable? Perhaps. Is globalization inevitably sophistic? Perhaps not. At the very least, we ought to ask the question. Would we prefer to live a global society that is eudaimonic, or would we prefer life a world that is hedonic or pleonectic?

Unfortunately, these broader questions, important though they assuredly are, I had best leave for another occasion. Or for another author.

Our forebears bequeathed to us a political society. They handed down a society of the best kind they no doubt could. But the fact that our society is a gift does not mean that we cannot improve upon it. We especially ought to make changes when society appears less than just. If my arguments do not, perhaps the plain facts of the matter may prove sufficiently persuasive. Can you deny that many persons today live in ignorance, fear, and hunger, not to say degradation?

Too often in our preoccupation with our private lives we forget to ask ourselves, What kind of political society ought we to inhabit? Or even, What kind of political society do we inhabit? We can, if we so wish, create a society of worth for its own sake as an end in itself and not as a mere means for the sake of private interests. But we also can, if we do not so wish, accept by tacit consent the status quo.

I would ask, Ought we not to exercise and to enjoy our rational and political nature? Our humanity is truly a gift god-given to mortals such as we be. And pleasure and property? Are they not but paltry things?

Our humble humanity, then, I shall invoke for my instauration of a new paradigm for political philosophy in our era.

Part One

The Cave: The Turn to the Intelligible

1

Rational Animals

1. Where ought we to begin—we who are audacious enough to believe that our reflections might yield an insight into political society and sanguine enough to imagine that our insight, if any, might have an influence on the course of human events?

Philosophers given to pondering political phenomena exhibit a propensity to begin at the beginning. Modern philosophers are especially prone to begin in this way though the ancients are not entirely disinclined. And rightly so, I think. We surely ought to begin where we have most obviously begun. But we have not, I would submit, begun at the beginning! Where did we begin, then? *In medias res!* Who among us has not been born, willy-nilly, into a political society? Not one of us, I dare say.

I concede that there are feral children, raised without human society by animals in the wild, as were Remus and Romulus of legend. But these poor children are thankfully rare. If not discovered early enough, they must pay most dearly for the errors of those who abandoned them to the beasts of the forest or the desert. They have at best a diminished capacity to philosophize or even to cognize, let alone to socialize, because of those more bestial than the animals that could nourish them but could not nurture them.

The closest we might come to a political beginning would be a state of naïveté. We are initially, and too often subsequently, naïve about our society, into which we are born, and even about our very selves. We are especially naïve about our philosophical and political nature, I shall argue. But our initial naïveté is for us, I admit, a natural state as well. We cannot but be naïve philosophically and politically when we are born even though we are *ab initio* ensconced within a society.

Modern philosophers usually take our political beginning to be found in what they call a state of nature. This natural state most frequently, though not always, constitutes a condition that is rather bleak. Thomas Hobbes, for example, famously declares that we humans initially find ourselves in a natural situation that is a war "of every man against every man." This situation, he famously informs us, entails a life "solitary, poor, nasty, brutish, and short" (*Leviathan* 1. 13. 8–9.).

But we soon discover the disadvantages of war and the advantages of peace, he argues. We learn that there is no justice in an all-out war, and that virtue is nothing but force and fraud (*Leviathan* 1. 13. 13.). We can establish peace if we form a contract with others and grant ourselves only as much liberty against others as we would grant others against ourselves (*Leviathan* 1. 14. 5.). This contract he takes to be the origin of justice (*Leviathan* 1. 15. 1–2.).

Ancient philosophers are not entirely unaware that one might postulate a natural state of this sort. Plato, for example, acknowledges it. In his celebrated dialogue on a just political society, he portrays an interlocutor describing a natural condition strikingly similar in its essentials to a Hobbesian state of nature. Though he does not himself accept it, Glaucon takes the position that by nature to do injustice is good and to suffer it is bad (*Republic* 2. 358e).

People soon discover, Glaucon continues, that the goodness of doing injustice is considerably less than the badness of suffering it. So they readily establish a contract of neither doing nor suffering injustice. Their contract is the origin of justice, he asserts. Justice is a mean between the best, which is to do injustice with impunity, and the worst, which is to suffer injustice without recourse (*Republic* 2. 358e–359a; also see *Gorgias* 483b–483d).

But I find myself obliged to ask, How many of us actually began our political life in a state of nature? Surely, not one of us! How many of us have lived even for a time in a state of nature? Most likely, only those few who have had the terrible misfortune to have been caught up in the clutches of war or poverty in the extreme, I should think. Most people have somehow managed, less through choice than through chance, to escape a fate of this dire sort.

I do not object to the fact that a state of nature is a hypothetical, perhaps mythical, situation. What I suggest is that to begin with a state of nature is to begin with the wrong hypothetical situation. If we wish to begin at the beginning, we surely ought to begin with a consideration of the situation in which we most likely began our political lives. We should do so even though in our reflections we must perforce rely on hypothesis.

My intention, then, is to avoid the presumption of beginning where no one has likely begun. I would venture to assert that any supposed state of nature might itself be an expression of a naïveté at once philosophical and political, and that, if we were to begin unawares in naïveté, we might very well end our philosophical reflections unawares in naïveté. That is to say, if we were to begin with a false presumption about our natural state, we might very likely end with a false assumption about our political state.

What is worse, if we begin with a false assumption, even if we take it for a hypothesis initially, we could all too easily end with the very same mistaken assumption and take it for more than a hypothesis. We might eventually presume to take our initial hypothesis for a non-hypothetical, perhaps god-given, principle of political theory and practice!

But I do not mean to seem so unpolitic. Let us turn to what I take to be our naïve beginning so that I might the better explain myself.

2. A state of naïveté is more germane to our present inquiry than a state of nature not only because it is more proximate in our experience. A state of this kind is germane also because it affords us an opportunity for reflection on our often benighted, if not bewildered, cognizance of our political and philosophical situation and on our capacity, though not unmitigated, for philosophical and political enlightenment.

That any knowledge of our naïveté cannot be other than hypothetical, I readily concede. We shall in fact see that all knowledge allotted to us poor worldlings is and can only be hypothetical. Our knowledge of our very lives, whether political or philosophical, presents no exception. We must employ hypotheses to understand and, presumably, to overcome our initial naïveté about our present endeavors and our past and future endeavors.

The fact that human knowledge is hypothetical does have advantages. We may avail ourselves of various heuristic devices in our pursuit of knowledge, whether political or not. Among these devices, the American pragmatists would remind us, we find experimentation. We shall obviously be concerned in our present inquiry with a philosophical experiment though I would note that our experiments can be either philosophical or political.

But the fact that we only know hypothetically has its disadvantages, too. We poor mortals can, alas, never really and truly know any truth or reality. Our theoretical principles are obviously less than absolute. Even the vaunted postulates of Euclidian geometry, seemingly empyrean, have proved to be less than unexceptional. Not to mention our practical, including political, assumptions and presumptions.

I wish to begin with a philosophical experiment of ancient origin. This particular experiment is no more than a model, and it is, as are all models, a simplification of the facts. But this model I think worthy of our consideration because its simplification, if we take it seriously, can give us a profound insight into our initial state of naïveté, which we may neither remember nor understand as well as we might imagine.

The model in question is actually an allegory. Allegories, I know, are out of fashion today. But an allegory I take to be merely an example albeit an imagined one. We might think of this allegory more fashionably as a hypothetical, contrary-to-fact example. This particular contrary-to-fact example will, I hope, serve to quicken our recollection and make our past, in its essentials at least, clearer to us. Yes, to understand it, we shall have to recollect our past as best we can with an imagined example.

I wish to suggest with this allegory that the philosophical presuppositions of political theories in our day are particularly naïve. These presuppositions for the most part presume political phenomena to be not so much intelligible objects as sensible objects. Philosophers who reflect on politics tend to consider our ideas and impressions themselves not to be objects worthy of our desire. They prefer to take our ideas and impressions to be indicative of other objects, primarily visible and tangible. These other objects, including our material selves and our material resources, they think desirable.

We ought, I would urge, to consider the possibility at least that intelligible objects might themselves be desire-worthy. We might discover that intangible things have not only intellectual value but also practical value. Our intellectual principles, theoretical as well as practical, may prove to have a goodness of their own. If so, these intangibles may prove worthy of our endeavors, perhaps more worthy than tangibles.

Why might this distinction be important? The distinction is important because our philosophical presuppositions inform our political theories, and our political theories in turn inform our political lives. What objects we deem desirable in our theories has consequences for our actions and shapes our actions either felicitously or infelicitously.

The allegory in question I take from Plato. I wish to ponder our political plight with an analysis of his allegory of the cave. Plato himself does not obviously use his allegory to hypothesize a political beginning for us. But with it he surely does portray a naïve mind as well as a mind less naïve. He asserts that the allegory concerns persons both uneducated and educated (*Republic* 7. 514a). He indicates further that the allegory is meant to illustrate a hypothesis about our education. Education, he claims, is a process of turning a soul away from objects of becoming toward objects of being (518b–d).

Plato would thus imply that we might overcome our naïveté if we can turn our attention away from sensible objects to intelligible objects. I am taking objects of becoming and being to be sensible and intelligible entities. Plato is famous for this distinction. The distinction underlies another allegory that serves to introduce the allegory of the cave. He uses what he calls the simile of the sun to distinguish a visible world from an intelligible world and to draw an analogy between the two (*Republic* 6. 507b–509c, esp. 508b–d).

The allegory of the cave, I admit, might seem to be more an introduction to philosophy proper than to political philosophy. Philosophers customarily so take it. But one might surmise that the cave would have some significance for political inquiry. After all, Plato does place his allegory in a dialogue that has the ostensive purpose of setting forth his theory of a just political society.

My purpose, then, shall be to employ what Plato has to say about uneducated and educated persons to show what our political beginning might initially have been and what our beginning might eventually come to be. His hypothesis about human education entails philosophical consequences and political consequences that are hardly insignificant.

Let us ask, How does the allegory of cave illustrate human education? Readers who have any familiarity with it know that this allegory presents a rather unusual scene. We might accordingly refresh our memory. What would we see if we were to enter the cave? We would first discern within the cave a fire burning, and beyond the fire we would make out a path with a low wall constructed along its far side.

If we were to cross the path, we would be able to peer over the wall, and we would discover on the other side, dimly lit to be sure, people held in bondage. Because of their bondage, these unfortunate souls can neither move in place nor even turn their heads. They are constrained to face the far wall of the cave. They are, in a word, pilloried.

But we might have to step aside. Before long we would encounter people coming and going along the path. They walk between the fire and the low wall, and over their heads they hold up objects that are images of natural things, including people, and artificial things. They make use of the fire to cast shadows of these objects on the far wall of the cave. These people sometimes speak, and their words echo off the far wall.

The people holding the objects up would thus appear to be putting on a shadow play of some kind. Indeed, the result of their efforts is what Plato calls an extraordinary show for the prisoners. The flickering shadows on the wall of the cave seem to be animated and even to speak (*Republic* 7. 514a–515a, 515b).

How might this odd scene illustrate an educational hypothesis? Plato states laconically, "Like unto us" the prisoners are (*Republic* 7. 515a). How could the prisoners possibly be like us? He explains only that the prisoners see nothing of themselves except for their shadows on the far wall (515a–b). Remember their constraints. The prisoners might also hear little of their voices except for their echoes off the wall.

The prisoners thus have a rather limited view of their situation. Is this how they are like unto us? Indeed, what they see of their world are merely the shadows of the puppets on the wall of the cave. Plato indicates explicitly that the prisoners take these shadows for the truth (515b–c). They would most likely take their own shadows for the truth, too, I would suppose. After all, they see nothing of themselves except their shadows.

One might say that these prisoners are very much like children attending a puppet theater. The children could easily be captivated by a similar show. But the prisoners are also unlike children at a theater. The children can turn around and see the puppets, and they can stand up and leave the theater if they wish. They might even be invited to come behind the scenes after the show and to see how the performance is done.

The allegory, then, would suggest that a political society might be a theater of some kind. Or, at least, that a society might have a theatrical aspect. The prisoners are in circumstances obviously theatrical and obviously social if not political. They are constrained to look at and to listen to visual and aural images that others create and animate for them.

One can now see how the prisoners are like unto us. We are not literally pilloried in a cave. But we are perforce restricted to a stream of images in our communications with one another, and we can become enthralled with the flow of images. I would think this fact more obvious today than ever given our mass media, including radio, television, and now the internet. But even everyday, face-to-face, communication occurs only with aural and visual imagery.[1]

We can also begin to see how Plato's allegory illustrates his hypothesis about education. Plato already indicates for us that the prisoners are less than well educated. They know little or nothing but the shadows and echoes of their cave because of their constraints. We might say that they are quite taken with shadows playing on the cave wall.

Could the prisoners escape from a more naïve outlook to an outlook less naïve if they were able to turn their heads around and to see the puppets? They would then see the truth of the shadows, which are but images. But could they see the truth itself? They obviously could not. The puppets, too, are images. The prisoners might take for the truth objects that are only artifacts.

But now things become yet curiouser. The prisoners would initially take their own shadows, too, for the truth, would they not? But could they catch a glimpse of themselves, say of a hand or a foot, would they again be taking an image for the truth? After all, the puppets, which cast the shadows, are images. This fact would appear to imply that the prisoners themselves might be images of some sort. They might somehow be puppet-like.

Could one be naïve, then, to take sensible objects for the truth? But are not sensible things really and truly real? you might ask. Plato suggests otherwise. The prisoners and the puppets are sensible objects, but sensible objects appear to be the concern of the naïve. Indeed, he indicates for us that the prisoners would be less than well educated even if they could see the puppets and themselves. Education, recall, requires that we turn from sensible objects to intelligible objects.

Plato does offer an explanation that takes us a little further. When he does, he alludes to another allegory. This allegory appears to have some relevance to his hypothesis about education because it concerns objects of different kinds, and among them are objects of becoming and of being. Or, more explicitly, it concerns sensible as well as intelligible objects.

This other allegory is also well known. It is the figure of the divided line. Plato gives this figure a more literal interpretation. The divided line has four unequal segments. These segments represent both our mental affections and their objects (*Republic* 6. 511d–e). We need concern ourselves at present only with the objects. The line divides into two sections, and each section divides into two segments. The lower section and its segments, he tells us, represent the sensible world, and upper section and its segments the intelligible world (509d).

For the moment we shall focus on the lower section and its two segments. Plato informs us that the sensible world itself contains objects of two kinds. These objects are images of visible things and visible things themselves. Presumably, these visible things are also tangible. The images turn out to be shadows again, as well as reflections, and the visible things are again both natural and artificial objects (509d–510a).

The divided line Plato uses to explain explicitly that the cave with its prison scene represents the visible world, and that its fire represents the sun (*Republic* 7. 517a–b). We might surmise that the shadows on the cave wall and the echoes correspond to the shadows and reflections of the divided line, and that the puppets and the prisoners correspond to the visible objects.[2]

But Plato now redoubles our consternation. We were puzzled by our conjecture that the prisoners in the cave could not escape their naïveté. They are constrained to take images for reality. But, if they could turn their heads, they apparently would see only more images. The artificial objects held overhead by the puppeteers were said explicitly to be images. We surmised that the prisoners themselves might also be images.

Plato confirms our inference. But he goes so far as to state that all visible objects are images! The objects of the visible world are images of the intelligible world. Or, more literally, opinable objects resemble knowable objects (*Republic* 6. 510a–b). All visible objects are akin to the objects held overhead by the puppeteers, in other words. One might say that these visible objects, either natural or artificial, including ourselves, are merely shadow puppets.

We thus find ourselves, or at least our allegorical selves, in a rather odd situation. We are apparently naïve and uneducated if we not only take shadows and reflections of sensible things for reality but also take sensible things themselves for reality. How might we overcome our naïveté? We clearly are naïve to take images, such as shadows or reflections, for truth, but how are we naïve to take visible and tangible objects, which cast shadows and cause reflections, for truth?

Plato would, in more contemporary terms, assert not only that our media for communication are images, but also that the objects of these media are images. One could easily concede that the flickerings of electrons across a television screen or a computer screen are mere images. But could a televised scene or an uploaded scene be an image? If it were a stage setting, the scene would obviously be an image. But, even if it were not staged, the scene would, Plato claims, also be an image.

We appear, then, to have an incredible credulity, and our credulity appears to be incurable. Plato tells us with his allegory that we are naïve to take images for truth.

But we apparently cannot not do so. We see that the prisoners do indeed appear to be "like unto us." We are apparently in bondage of some epistemological or ontological sort if we take seriously the images surrounding us. Our bonds would appear to be our senses, especially our eyes and ears.

What can we learn from our shadowy allegory, then? Obviously, the cave does concern a naïveté of some sort. The allegory implies that we might mistake images, which are objects, for truth, and that we might somehow mistake for truth objects, which are images. But are not sensible objects as real as real can be? How can we be naïve to take empirical objects for reality? How can the objects of our everyday experience be false?

The allegory implies rather clearly that education might possibly be a turning of the soul from sensible things to intelligible things. That is, we might somehow become less naïve if we could turn away from sensible images toward intelligible realities.

3. Plato would suggest that we are naïvely born into a theatrocracy. The allegory of the cave, at least, would imply that we are. That we are born into a society, one could not deny. But no one could deny, either, that a society has its theatrical element. Today it especially does. I need not remind you again of our mass media, both aural and visual, with their images and their machinations all but ubiquitous.

One can surely say that the images in our mass media are by and large images of sensible objects. But could one also say that not only these images but also their objects both are images? Of what would they be shadows and reflections? Might we ourselves be images? Of what would we be shadows and reflections? And if we are but images, would we not be but puppets? If so, who would be our puppeteers? Could they in their turn be images, too?

To seek answers to these questions, we must return to our allegorical cave and complete our survey of this curious cavern. If we now linger in our observations, we shall see an incident that might confirm our speculation about education. A prisoner is somehow set free from his bondage. The prisoner is compelled, Plato tells us, to stand up and to turn his gaze around toward the fire (*Republic* 7. 515c–e). He is then, apparently without ceremony, forced over the wall, conducted past the fire, and ushered out of the cave (515e–516a).

One would imagine that, when he is forcibly turned around within the cave, the prisoner who is released would be able to see the puppets. I would think that, when he is forced over the wall, he might very likely have a better look, though apparently rushed, at the apparatus for the puppet show in its entirety, seeing both the puppets and the puppeteers.

Plato indicates explicitly that the prisoner initially cannot, because of the light from the fire, see the objects casting the shadows on the cave wall. But he implies that the prisoner eventually can, after his eyes adjust presumably, make out these objects. One would be able to show them to him, he states, and to ask him questions about them. But he would not yet be able to answer the questions (515c–d).

If we were to follow him out of the cave, we would observe our prisoner encountering the sunlit world and the sun itself. When he is outside, he needs time for his eyes to adjust, but before long he is able to make out many sensible things. At first he can see only shadows and reflections in water. But soon he can see men and other things, which are the sources of these images. Then he is able at night to see the light of the moon and stars. Eventually, he can see the sun and its bright light (516a–b).

What might be the meaning of this release? Though he does not explicitly do so, Plato would likely assert, I think, that the prisoner who is freed remains "like unto us." He would appear to be using this prisoner and his release to illustrate his educational hypothesis. The prisoner is obviously turning his attention from objects of one kind to those of another. Inside the cave the prisoner turns his attention from the shadows to the puppets. He then turns from the puppets to their originals, one would think, when he sees objects outside the cave.

What are the objects inside and outside the cave, then? Are they sensible and intelligible objects? Are the objects inside images of the objects outside? Plato does explain for us what all these objects are. To do so, he again has recourse to his figure of the divided line. The divided line, recall, has two sections, and each section has two segments (*Republic* 6. 509d). We ought now to turn our attention to the objects of the upper section.

The upper section concerns things in the intelligible world. The intelligible world, as does the visible world, contains objects of two kinds. These objects are those of reasoning and understanding (511d–e). Objects of both kinds we know by hypothesis, Plato explains (510b). An object of reasoning is a conclusion that follows from a hypothesis. We assume a hypothesis to be true, and from it we deduce our conclusion. Geometers, for example, use a hypothesis in this way. They assume the definition of a triangle, say, and from their assumption they draw conclusions about this figure (510c–d).

The object of understanding is a first principle that arises from a hypothesis. We again assume a hypothesis to be true, but now from our hypothesis and, presumably, other hypotheses we induce a first principle. Plato declares this first principle to be non-hypothetical (511b–c). But we mortals, I should think, had best take this principle merely for a higher hypothesis. Mathematical logicians would use hypotheses to understand in this manner. They, for example, might take the hypotheses of Euclidian, Lobachevskian, and Riemannian geometries and on their basis infer a principle that would account for these hypotheses.[3]

Does this figure explain how the prisoners might become more educated when they turn away from the shadows toward the objects inside and then outside the cave? Does it explain why the prisoners and the puppeteers might be images, if they are? Plato clearly implies that the prisoner who is set free turns from sensible things to intelligible things. He tells us that the objects inside the cave represent things in the visible world, and the objects outside the cave represent things in the intelligible world (*Republic* 7. 517a–b).

He also argues that visible objects are merely images of intelligible objects (*Republic* 6. 510a–b). He offers support for this assertion by explaining how the geometers make use of their diagrams. When they reason with their hypothesis, geometers obviously do not reason about the figures that they draw and to which they refer. They rather reason about the concepts that the figures represent. That is, they do not reason about this particular triangle drawn on paper. They reason about the idea of the triangle represented by the figure drawn. Their visible diagram they take for an image only (510d–511a).[4]

Education, then, does appear to be a turning from objects of becoming to objects of being. It clearly would be in an epistemological sense. We are surely less naïve if we are able to see in a visible and tangible object an image of a hypothesis. We are hardly naïve at all if we are able to see in a hypothesis itself an image of a higher hypothesis. Not only would we be able to reason from a hypothesis about an idea, shall we say, reflected in a sensible object, but we would also be able to understand more than one hypothesis about an idea seen in its reflection.[5]

In an ontological sense, too, visible things are images of intelligible things. Objects of becoming appear to find their origin in objects of being. With his cave allegory Plato goes on to imply that visible objects have their origin in the intelligible world. The prisoner, after his eyes adjust to objects outside the cave, soon discovers that the sun is the source of the seasons and the years. This heavenly body causes and governs everything in the visible world (*Republic* 7. 516b–c).

This discovery carries with it the implication that what Plato calls the good is the cause of the visible world and its seasons and years. Socrates does tell us that the good is the cause of the sun. Or, rather, that the sun is "the child and offspring of the good" (*Republic* 6. 507a). The implication is that the good through the sun would cause and govern the visible world. He implies more explicitly that the good with its idea engenders light and its sovereign in the visible world (*Republic* 7 517a–c).[6]

I would conclude, then, that the visible world in its entirety is an image of the intelligible world. The puppets are most obviously images of intelligible entities. They are images of ideas, though hypothetical, that their makers or manipulators hold. But the prisoners and puppeteers would also be images of intelligible entities. These intelligible entities we attempt to divine with our hypotheses if we are given to reflection. We can so do either by reasoning with them or by understanding with them.

Perhaps you do not deign to acknowledge a creation for our sensible selves and our sensible world? Perhaps you do not care to believe that we ourselves and our surroundings, political or no, are artifacts of a creator? If so, I ask only that you grant the implication that ideas, forms, patterns, laws—call them what you will—are the basis for empirical objects. The sensible world with its objects we perceive to be an approximation of our theories, which, we presume, account for our world and all within.

Or, if these metaphysical considerations are still too trying, I would ask only that you think of politics and its arena, which is our proximate subject. Practically speaking, our political world is an image of our political ideas. We use hypotheses, inarticulate or articulate, to reason about and to understand ideas implicit in our political predicament. What is more, we can choose to act on these hypotheses. We then create a political world for ourselves.

The implication, if initially disconcerting, is obvious enough. Assume that political philosophy constitutes knowledge. One might even say that philosophy of this kind constitutes self-knowledge. What Plato is suggesting with his geometric figure of the divided line is that our political reasoning and understanding have an object that cannot be a visible object, not even our dear selves. Rather, any reasoning or understanding takes for its object an idea reflected in a visible object, which now appears to be less a real object than we may have thought.

A political society, then, is an idea embodied in sensible objects, such as our character and our conduct. Or, rather, a society is an idea that we choose to embody in these objects. We can, of course, embody different ideas in our habits and actions. We might, for example, choose to act on an idea that defines an action of value for its own sake, or we might choose an idea defining an action of value for something other than itself. This distinction is an ancient one, one that Plato and Aristotle were not unaware of, and one that we moderns ought not to be unfamiliar with. I shall have more to say of it before long.[7]

But our very idea of human goodness, whether political or not, would be merely hypothetical. Our idea of a political society is hypothetical. After all, our awareness of all our ideas is and can be only by hypothesis. This concept can be a challenge for us because we usually do not see political principles as mere hypotheses. We tend to see them as eternal truths that are decidedly non-hypothetical. But there are not likely many eternal truths truly known to us, not even moral or political ones.

Our ideas, indeed, are hypothetical both when we understand and when we reason about our character and conduct. We may assume our hypothesis to be true, if we are reasoning, for the sake of what might follow from it. We may reflect on or act on a hypothesis and examine its consequences in our reflection or in our action. We may also assume our hypothesis to be true, if we are understanding, for the sake of determining what higher hypothesis might be implicit in the hypotheses that we employ in reflection and action.

The allegory of the cave does, then, illustrate the hypothesis that education is a turning from objects of becoming to objects of being. Education cannot be to turn from one image in the visible world to another visible image. Education is to turn from the visible world itself to the intelligible world. That is to say, we can escape from our naïveté by turning to a hypothesis that we can use to grasp intellectually what we can but grab physically.

But Plato wishes to take us a step further. He wants us to turn from a hypothesis merely assumed to be true to a higher hypothesis or, preferably, to a non-hypothetical first principle, which would be absolutely true. We may assume hypotheses to be true, if we are attempting to understand, for the sake of discovering a more general hypothesis or even an ultimate, non-hypothetical, first principle. This first principle, he asserts, is a first principle of everything (*Republic* 6. 511b–c).

The implication is that a first principle can govern the intelligible world and is the cause of all intelligible things. That is, a first principle can account for all the lesser hypotheses by which we can discover the principle (511b–c again). A more general theory in this way accounts for theories less general. I am given to understand that set theory, for example, can explain lesser theories of mathematics, including geometry.

What may we conclude from our philosophical spelunking? Plato's allegory of the cave remains a contrary-to-fact, hypothetical, example. We ourselves who naïvely thought that we were empirical objects turn out to be what we might call allegorical objects! We are like the figures geometers use when they make their deductions. Or, perhaps, we resemble more the political caricatures found in newspaper cartoons. Our political society is less our flesh and blood selves than it is the ideas that we choose to dress up with our flesh and blood.

We do, then, resemble, more than we might have imagined, the puppets held above the low wall in the cave. We prove to be figments of a hypothesis about who we are and what we are about. But at times, perhaps, of a hypothesis less than well thought out. Or, worse, we may turn out to be figments of a hypothesis foisted off on us by others, perhaps politicians. We may be puppets manipulated by those who are political puppeteers.

Politicians, too, whether puppeteers or not, would appear to be but puppets. They are apparently images of hypotheses and theories, more or less articulate, either of their own devising or of the devising of others.

A political society would, indeed, appear to be a theatrocracy, and the world a theatrocracy, too! The visible world in its entirety, I mean, is apparently a theater of ideas.

4. We must now ask, How might the allegory of the cave enable us to characterize our entrance onto the political scene? I am assuming that we begin our political life in a state of naïveté. The allegorical cave obviously concerns people who are naïve. They are so credulous as to take a world of empirical objects to be real! The allegory suggests further that through education people can become less naïve and more worldly. They can learn to take a world of conceptual objects to be real. Perhaps they become more unworldly.

Our question, then, is, Does education in this sense better enable us to take cognizance of our political situation? Someone less naïve and more educated does possess knowledge and even self-knowledge. We saw that the allegorical prisoners are initially aware of themselves as no more than flickering images on their cave wall. When released from their unfortunate bondage, the prisoners would, presumably, perceive their sensible selves initially, and eventually they would reason about and understand their intelligible selves.

What, then, might be the consequences of this newfound sophistication for political philosophy and practice? Could an ability to understand ourselves and to reason about ourselves yield any insight into politics? One would think that it very well could. To see that it indeed does, we must now follow Plato further and take into consideration his political theory. But we shall find that we may eventually wish to make a modification to his theory. Or, rather, we shall make a modification in its application to our era.

We have focused on the prisoners. We ought now to direct our attention to the puppeteers. The puppeteers would appear to be somehow in charge of the puppet theater in the cave. If they do not set it up, they do keep up, and perhaps take advantage of, the theatrical apparatus. In any event they manipulate the puppets, and with the puppets they appear to manipulate the prisoners.

Who might the puppeteers be, then? Are they naïve persons? Or are they educated persons? The puppeteers bear an important resemblance to their prisoners. They are not held in bondage, at least not obviously, and they do not, if at all practiced, let their shadows fall on the cave wall. But they are visible objects, presumably, and they do have shadows. So they, too, are visible images of intelligible objects. After all, all sensible objects are.

Can the puppeteers, then, grasp intelligible objects? These intelligible objects they can grasp if they permit themselves to reflect. But they can reflect only with hypotheses, more or less articulate. Their hypotheses, I presume, would be, in part at least, political. Our question would be, then, Do the puppeteers reflect on what they are doing? If they do, how well do they reflect? Do they deploy hypotheses with reasoning or understanding?

I shall argue that the puppeteers are politicians, and that they may or may not be philosophers as well. At their best, the puppeteers would be both politicians and philosophers. My hypothesis, I would think, is, once articulated, rather obvious. Can we not speculate about ourselves with a hypothesis, even if political, and can we not encounter images of our hypothesis in action, even if in a political arena? These images would be none other than our persons and our practices.

I would contend, then, that the puppeteers are images of their hypotheses whatever they might perchance be. Their hypotheses they might themselves devise if they are at all philosophical. Or, if less philosophical and less fortunate, others might devise hypotheses for them.

But we must still ask, What hypotheses, regardless origin, do they employ, and how do they employ them? Do they assume a hypothesis to be true and attempt to discover a higher principle and to account for their hypothesis and for its consequences in practice? Or do they assume a hypothesis to be true and merely follow out its consequences?

That a politician can be a philosopher, Plato himself has no doubt. Indeed, he famously proclaims that a politician ought to be a philosopher. The greatest paradox of this theory, he acknowledges, is that a just political society cannot come to be unless and until a politician becomes a philosopher or a philosopher becomes a politician. No society can be free from evil, he avers, nor can any human being be free from evil, if we permit persons to pursue philosophy and politics separately (*Republic* 5. 473b–e)!

This proclamation does seem a paradox. But a philosopher, recall, is not a specialist in esoteric knowledge, such as contemporary analytic philosophy. A philosopher is simply someone who can understand and reason. But philosophers also love knowledge of all kinds. They especially love knowledge proper, which concerns intelligible things. These intelligible things are ideas or forms, such as those of justice or courage. They also love opinion, which concerns visible and audible things. These things are images of forms or ideas, such as just or courageous things (*Republic* 5. 474b–476c).

Plato accordingly requires that those whom he calls the guardians, who are to rule in his ideal society, have a philosophical education. He especially recommends the quadrivium. Students of the quadrivium, if properly taught, study its subjects not merely as sensible objects but rather as sensible images of intelligible objects. When they study astronomy and harmony, for example, they treat the visible constellations and the audible chords as perceptible paradigms of mathematical formulae (*Republic* 7. 529c–530c, 531b–c).[8]

These studies serve to prepare the guardians for dialectic, which is the crown of their education. Plato explicitly draws an analogy to the prisoner released from the cave. As the eyes of a prisoner are able to see animals, stars, and the sun, so the intellect of a guardian is able to grasp what each thing itself is and eventually what the good itself is (531c–532d). The guardians rise from reasoning, which merely accepts hypotheses, to understanding, which grasps a first principle and from it deduces hypotheses (533b–534d).

But Plato is also famous for denying his guardians a life exclusively philosophical. He does not allow them to spend their days, however enjoyable, in the intelligible world. That they must leave the blesséd isles of the quadrivium and of dialectic and return to the cave, he insists. They have received an education that enables them especially to know the truth about justice. They are thus able to see not only the images in the cave but also the things of which they are the images, Plato states allegorically (520a–d).

But how can intelligible objects have practical, especially political, value? you may wonder. Politics is not a matter of theory but of experience, is it not? I would reply that Plato is quite aware that his political theory, or any theory, can never be fully realized. He obviously requires that politicians have a theory. But he reminds us that a theory is a paradigm, and that a paradigm can never come to be. The most one could expect would be that a political theory would find a close approximation in an actual society (*Republic* 5. 472b–473b).

He recognizes, too, that the guardians must have experience. Philosophers are also those whom he calls philodoxers. They love all knowledge, both that concerned with objects of being or intelligible objects, and that concerned with sensible objects or objects of becoming. But knowledge of becoming is more properly called opinion. He explains, however, that philosophers differ from those who are philodoxers only. Philosophers can distinguish knowledge from opinion, but philodoxers mistake for knowledge what is only opinion (474b–476d).

He implies that his philosophical politicians must acquire their requisite experience at an early age. He argues that, when they are young charges, they especially need experience in warfare. Not that they can participate in war, but that they ought to observe their parents and perhaps assist them in some way. With due precautions taken for their safety (*Republic* 5. 466e–467e). They later gain more experience by assuming a command position in war and by holding other offices (*Republic* 7. 539e–540a).

What knowledge do the guardians require, then? They would obviously require knowledge of a first principle. Otherwise, they could not have a philosophical theory for politics. But what would their first principle be? This problem does not seem to be one easily resolved. Presumably, a first principle would be a non-hypothetical principle. But a principle of this exalted variety would amount to perfect knowledge of what our goodness is. Can we mortals know what anything is perfectly? To have knowledge of this kind would be to know the very idea of goodness itself!

After one paradox we now face another. To know what goodness is appears to be beyond the ken of our humble human minds. Could we ever hope to know its true form? Even Socrates demurs when asked to explain its form to Glaucon and Adeimantus. "God alone knows if it is true," he exclaims. "It is an appearance that thus appears." The idea of the good is the last to be seen, and it is hardly to be seen, he tells us (*Republic* 7. 517a–c).

A non-hypothetical principle is apparently too rich for human blood. Any principle for a mere mortal can be hypothetical only. But can a hypothetical principle enable us to understand our political society? If so, what hypothesis about political society could we turn to and use to construct a theory for politics? I shall assume that we ought to formulate a political hypothesis for ourselves and not let others do so for us!

We can still take our lead from our philosopher. Plato does offer a principle for his theory of an ideal society, and he offers a political principle less than non-hypothetical. But this principle is clearly prior to other candidate principles. He shows implicitly that it encompasses other likely principles. This principle can serve for a general theory of politics, in other words, and the other principles can account only for special cases.

The principle in question is, of course, justice. Plato concedes in effect that justice is hypothetical. He does so when he indicates what his method is. His method itself is hypothetical. In his dialogue Plato portrays Socrates proposing to look first for justice writ large in a society and then for justice writ small in an individual. He does so on the grounds that justice is more obvious in society than in an individual (*Republic* 2. 368c–369a).

Socrates then explains to his interlocutors that they will have discovered what justice is only if they find justice in a society and in an individual to be the same. If they find that justice is different in an individual, they will have to turn back to society and to see if what they have found is there, too (*Republic* 4. 434d–435a). Fortunately, they do find that justice has the same form in a society and in an individual and do not have to go back (442d, 443c, 444a).[9]

What, then, is this hypothetical principle? What is justice? Plato argues that justice is for each part in a political society to fulfill its own function (*Republic* 4. 433a–b). A society contains three general parts, he implies. These parts apparently are a philosophical class, a martial class, and an artisanal and agrarian class (433b–d). These classes delineate the basic structure of his ideal society, and, I should think, they are sufficiently general to delineate the basic structure of any society ancient or contemporary.[10]

What functions do these parts have? The philosophers rule society. They are the guardians of society, and they rule because they are wise. Their knowledge is evident in their good deliberations about their society as whole in both its internal and its external relations (428a–429a). Plato is not more explicit about what the guardians know. But he would appear to imply that this knowledge constitutes an understanding of justice, or at least reasoning about justice, because it concerns domestic and foreign relations.

The martial class defends its society against its enemies. They are the auxiliary guardians. They have courage, and they fight for their society. Their courage rests on an imbued opinion about what things are fearful (429a–c). These fearful things would be the foes of their society, presumably. One would think that its foes would be persons who are unjust. They would be those who do not fulfill a function or who prevent others from fulfilling a function.

The artisan and agrarian class provide for the needs of society. Early in his argument Plato enumerates the many items that they supply. A society would at a minimum need persons to supply the most basic provisions of food, clothing, and shelter, obviously, as well as physicians (*Republic* 2. 369c–e). But it would also need carpenters, blacksmiths, herdsmen, merchants, sailors, shopkeepers, and laborers (370c–371e).

Plato thus argues that justice is for each part of a society to fulfill a function. The philosophers must rule their society. Again, please recall that philosophers are those who possess a general ability to employ hypotheses for reasoning and for understanding. The military class defends their society, and the artisan class provisions it.

But do the guardians in his society understand this principle of justice, or do they merely reason from this principle? We can see, I think, that they have an understanding of justice though perhaps not an absolute understanding. Plato argues that the guardians have knowledge of what is best for their society in its entirety. But rulers in other societies, he argues, have knowledge only of what they think best for their society in part. Not surprisingly, they rule for what seems best for their own part of society!

Plato, indeed, espouses a principle of justice that explains all varieties of constitutions. His principle permits him to account not only for an ideal political society but also for five species of society less than ideal. The less worthy species each present only a limited case of justice because those who rule in them assume principles for their rule that differ in accordance with the part out of which they arise.[11]

An examination of the societies less than just is also important for our present inquiry into justice. Two unjust species are particularly prevalent in our own era. Though commonly lauded, these two species are hardly unproblematic. That these species are so prevalent, and that injustice is so prevalent, would so suggest.

What are the other species, then? In one species the martial class has the rule. This species Plato calls timocracy. In a timocracy the auxiliary guardians do not allow the philosophical class to rule, and they enslave the artisan and agrarian class (*Republic* 8. 547e–548a, 547b–c). They espouse the principles of victory and honor, and they constantly engage in war, presumably against other societies and against those newly enslaved (548c, 547b–c, 547e–548a).

Three species permit the artisan and the agrarian class to rule. One species is oligarchy. In a society of this kind, the martial class devotes itself to acquiring wealth (550d–551a). They soon require a property qualification for office holders (550c–d, 551a–b). They go so far in their pursuit of wealth as to enrich themselves by permitting other people to squander all their property and to become impoverished (552a–b).

A more diverse society would appear to follow. In a democracy the working class rules. They kill or expel the oligarchs (555b–557a). They allow anyone to rule, and they often assign offices by lot (557a). Yet no one is required to rule (557e–558a). What is best for their society, they believe, is freedom and even license. Everyone may do whatever he or she pleases (557a–b).

The final and the worst species is tyranny. I shall say nothing of tyranny except to note that a tyrant seeks to engage in actions most heinous for his profit or pleasure (*Republic* 9. 573c–575a).

These unjust species we can distinguish from one another by the desires that determine their end. Timocrats, Plato explains, seek to gratify what he calls their spirit, which is an aggressive instinct (*Republic* 8. 548c), oligarchs their necessary appetites (554a), democrats their unnecessary appetites (560d–561a), and a tyrant his illicit appetites (*Republic* 9. 571b–572b).

One can now see how the principle of justice accounts for the hypotheses implicit in these constitutions. Plato argues that justice requires each class in a society to fulfill its own function. But in unjust societies no class fulfills its function. The philosophers are excluded from rule, and the other two classes, who ought not to rule, take on the task of ruling. Again, the other classes rule not for the end of their whole society but for the sake of their own part of society.

These societies, then, violate the principle of justice. A society needs not only a knowledgeable class but also a class to defend it and a class to provision it. Each class within society ought to have the end of acting for the sake of the whole society. Fighting wars or making money or pursuing pleasure surely ought not to be the sole end of any society. Or ought it?

Is not the worst thing for a class other than the guardians to rule? Plato asks almost offhandedly. He implies that the answer to his question is, Yes. He offers an explanation, but his explanation is not complete. He argues only that for a carpenter to become a cobbler or a cobbler a carpenter is not nearly as bad as for a carpenter or cobbler to become a guardian (*Republic* 4. 434a–d).

We now see why this class usurpation would be bad. A carpenter or a cobbler would most likely have knowledge not of their society as a whole but rather of their own particular functions (*Republic* 4. 428b–d). They accordingly would not likely rule for other functions and their own function taken together. They would more likely rule solely for their own function.

A true philosophical principle thus degenerates into a pleonectic principle, for example, when an oligarchy comes into power with the purpose of moneymaking. Or this principle can degenerate into a hedonic principle of pleasure-seeking when a democracy takes power.

What is an inferior principle in a just society now becomes a superior principle. A class in a society not just, or a subclass, uses its principle to subject an entire society to itself. Though it has a place in society, the satisfaction of necessary or unnecessary desires surely ought not to be the ruling purpose of society.[12]

We shall soon have occasion to consider two unjust societies more closely. They are oligarchy and democracy. Though no society makes bold to declare itself one, people are not infrequently of the opinion that many contemporary political societies are in fact oligarchies. Indeed, many societies do harbor powerful oligarchic institutions, not excluding multinational corporations. These institutions can exert a considerable influence within society and without. They can be all but veritable puppet masters.

Many people today believe that contemporary political societies are most frequently democracies. Surely, many societies, if not democratic, do have a strong democratic element. These societies extend the voting franchise to include almost anyone of mature years. But, unfortunately, persons in these societies constitute a mass market, both local and global. Contemporary marketing agents can manipulate these markets with what would otherwise be deemed virtuosity.

Timocracy and tyranny are less common today. Some contemporary virtue ethicists may approach timocracy in their theories. Though they seldom examine its political implications, they frequently argue that moral principles are simply those of someone recognized to be honorable. But these principles are hardly ever, if at all, martial.[13]

Tyranny is admittedly not uncommon in our era. But no one attempts to offer any justification for a society of this sort with the rather obvious exception of the tyrant himself.

Remember the puppets and their puppeteers? We may now return to our cave allegory and answer our question, Who are the puppeteers? I submit that a puppeteer, despite the less than complimentary connotations of the word, can represent someone who acts from a principle. In a just society a philosopher become politician would be a puppeteer nonpareil. This person would have an understanding of justice albeit hypothetical. He, or she, would know how the philosophical class ought to function together with the military and the artisan classes.

But an oligarch, for example, or a democrat could become a politician in a city less than just. He would then be a puppeteer, but a puppeteer less than philosophical. His regime likely gives rise to the untoward connotations of the word. He would exercise not an understanding of justice but only reasoning about justice. That is, he would take for a principle a lower hypothesis, and he would attempt to rule with it. He would not know how society ought to work together because he would not know his place in society.

One could say in more everyday terms that Plato sets out for us the principles of partisan politics. Philosophers rule with an understanding of a hypothesis for cooperation. Oligarchs and democrats rule with reasoning from a hypothesis for conflict.

What, then, do we wish to take away from our dear Plato? I think that we have to agree with Plato that human knowledge can be only hypothetical. Who would be so brash as to claim that we mortals might know an absolute truth? Only a god could know such a truth if any there be. To know a non-hypothetical first principle would be beyond our petty powers.

But Plato shows that with our hypothetical knowledge we can arrive at a hypothesis higher than customary, and with it, perhaps, construct a theory. We can do so by understanding and reasoning. We understand when we formulate a higher hypothesis from lower hypotheses. When we use our higher hypothesis deduce our lower hypotheses, and when we draw conclusions from our lower hypotheses, we reason.

We need not, then, accept any old hypothesis about political matters without due consideration. We may, again, attempt to understand a given hypothesis by trying to account for it with a grander hypothesis. Or we may examine a hypothesis by reasoning out its consequences in thought if not in action.

Plato himself does so for us. We see that his hypothesis about justice in an ideal society can account for the hypotheses about justice in societies less than ideal. This principle of justice requires that the philosophical guardians, the martial guardians, and the artisans and agrarians each fulfill their function within the city. These classes taken together make up a whole, and each class separately is a mere part.

Yet I must take issue with Plato. I find myself obliged to object that Plato may be less than just to the artisan and agrarian class, whom we would call the people or the working class. I suspect that he may be unduly pessimistic. Without a doubt the working class was problematic in his day, and in our day is no less problematic.

With industrial production and mass consumption this class is in all likelihood more problematic for us than it was for him.

My hypothesis, however, is that the working class is not itself a problem. But the fact that this class is unvirtuous is a problem. Plato argues that the virtue proper to it would be temperance. But he also implies that this class lacks temperance, strictly speaking. Its temperance, so-called, is to be of the opinion that the philosophers and the military are their rulers, and that they are to be ruled. This class requires external restraint to force it to act in a temperate manner (*Republic* 4. 431b–432b).[14]

But I must ask, Can workers not acquire temperance with an appropriate education so that they no longer require an external restraint? Their education would be a political education resting on a general principle of justice, I submit. The principle of justice need indicate merely that each class has a role to play in society, and that the agrarian and artisanal role is to provide for their society. Its role is not to seek to amass riches or to indulge in pleasures!

When he discusses the origin of political society, Plato begins his construction of an ideal society with what appears to be a temperate working class. The very first society, from which arise all other societies, just and unjust, is of artisans and agrarians. These citizens likely have some rudimentary awareness of justice (*Republic* 2. 371e–372a). Their society, Socrates states, seems to be a healthy one and a true one (372e).

Justice arises in this society, Socrates explains, from the fact that people ought to practice an occupation for which they are best suited, and that they ought to do so for the good of all (*Republic* 4. 432d–433d). He explicitly argues that we originally establish a society because we are severally non-self-sufficient, and that we can best supply our several needs through a division of labor (*Republic* 2. 369b–c, 369e–370c).

We can also see that this society would seem to be temperate. Its citizens fulfill only their most basic functions in a bucolic life (372c). These functions supply their elemental needs for food, clothing, and shelter. They are content to live with neither furniture nor flatware, and they take delight only in singing hymns and in drinking wine (372a–d)!

But one might object, Does not this pastoral society soon become an urban society of luxury? The healthy society does become fevered, Plato argues. Before long the citizens no longer aim simply to fulfill their basic functions, but they fulfill their functions for the sake of attaining wealth and pleasure (372d–373d).

I must concede your objection. But I would argue that the objection proves my point. The pastoral city has citizens who are naïve and not truly temperate. Their functions they take to be not for the sake of intelligible objects but for the sake of sensible objects. They do not have an articulate understanding of justice to guide them and to define their roles.

Perhaps they do so well initially because at their founding they are inarticulately aware that they are not severally sufficient and that they must divide their labor among them. But without an education they can soon forget these most basic principles.

What, then, shall we conclude? We may conclude, I think, that we are both sensible and intelligible entities, and that our sensible selves are merely an image, and that our intelligible selves are a reality. We are indeed naïve, then, to take our visible and tangible selves for reality. To take for reality our reasonable and understandable selves, shall we say, is to be less naïve and more philosophical. And more politic perhaps.

5. We may make bold to assert, I think, that we are rational animals (λογιστικόν ζῷον) or, better yet, philosophical animals (φιλοσοφικόν ζῷον). At least, we can become philosophical if we are fortunate enough to find a release from our empirical naïveté and its bondage. We are then able to take cognizance not of becoming only but also of being. We are able to reason and to understand with hypotheses not about sensible but about intelligible things.

That we are able to reason and to understand, means that we can use hypotheses to discover our goodness, including our political goodness. Justice for us lies in the invisible and intangible objects of these intellectual endeavors. We can together with our fellows discover political functions of value for our society in its entirety. Justice concerns not merely the tangible and visible objects too often the sole concern of political endeavors. These objects are only means, I would submit.

Plato argues that in a just society philosophers must return to their allegorical cave. They have an obligation to rule because their society educated them for this function. He concedes that philosophers in other societies need feel no obligation to return. They spring up by themselves (*Republic* 7. 519c–520c). Perhaps they do not have an obligation. Even so, these philosophers, I would think, could not but return to their society. Who among us, if enlightened, would be able to stand by for long without taking part in society?

He also tells us that the philosophers who return to the cave can see better within the cave than those who do not leave. At least, they can after their eyes adjust to the darkness. He compares philosophers to persons who are awake and those who never leave to persons who are asleep (520c–d).

We can now see why. Philosophers who are truly philosophers, we must not forget, love knowledge in its entirety, including both knowledge proper and opinion. These philosophers are both philosophers and philodoxers. They know things intelligible as well as sensible things, and they can see intelligible things reflected in sensible things (*Republic* 7. 520c). They are like geometers who see ideas reflected in diagrams (*Republic* 6. 510d–511a).

But, alas, not all philosophers are free from their naïveté and its curious bondage. We might say that they are philodoxers only. Those who never leave the allegorical cave shadowbox with one another and form factions over ruling, Plato explains (*Republic* 7. 520c–d). They would appear to concern themselves only with sights and sounds, which make up things sensible. They are especially enamored of what he calls Dionysian festivals (*Republic* 5. 475d–e).

One could say, and Plato would no doubt agree, that these persons take their hypotheses to be not about intelligible objects but about sensible objects. They are bound by their senses to rather limited hypotheses. They resemble naïve geometers who would use a ruler or a protractor in an attempt to reason about and to understand not the ideas represented in their diagrams but the diagrams themselves (see *Republic* 7. 528e–529c or 530d–531c).

We can now see what naïveté those have who begin their political theories with a state of nature. Not only do they not rise to a first principle, they do not even rise to a principle! Their hypothesis, if they articulate one, does not concern intelligible entities but sensible entities. They remain on the level of opinion. Their hypotheses very likely concern not society in its entirety but in part only. They preoccupy themselves with a single function.

A philosopher, then, who begins with a naïve hypothesis might very well end with a naïve hypothesis. Those who begin with a hypothesis only about sensible objects might well end with a hypothesis about sensible objects only. They remain but philodoxers. They believe that their hypothesis is about true objects, and that true objects are those visible and tangible. Not to mention shadows and reflections of sundry sorts.

These poor souls begin with an unjust origin for a society, and they end with an unjust society. Does not a corrupt political society, I ask, resemble a Dionysian festival? Is not an oligarchy or a democracy a festival of artisans and agrarians indulging in the acquisition of property or in the pursuit of pleasure? They are not unlike farmers and potters who spend their days feasting and drinking (see *Republic* 4. 420d–421a).

That Hobbes and many modern philosophers fall in among the philodoxers, is by now clear, I hope. They advocate theories that they take to be philosophical, but their theories cannot provide a true foundation for a political society. Their positions frequently underwrite political contracts that constitute little more than nonaggression pacts. They merely place limits on how much people can despoil one another.

One can easily see why the moderns take this position. They rely exclusively on the assumption that sensible entities are good. Hobbes argues that our natural state is a war of all against all. Why? We each have a natural right both to everybody and to everything (*Leviathan* 1. 14. 4). Glaucon offers an explanation for a theory of this kind, and his explanation goes more deeply. By nature to act unjustly seems to be good. Why? We may succumb to greed (πλεονεξία), which we take to be good (*Republic* 2. 359c).

Plato would say that Hobbes and his ilk naïvely turn their attention in the wrong direction. Less than virtuous persons have a keen intellect, he grants, but they direct their intellect to becoming and not to being. They are weighed down and attached to becoming as if by leaden weights. These weights, he tells us, are gluttony and pleasure (*Republic* 7. 519a–b).[15]

Yet we cannot forget, I would remind you, that philosophers are those who know that they know by hypotheses only! We would be naïve in another, higher, sense if we were to take our hypotheses for reality. Our humble hypotheses are only images of an absolute truth—if an absolute truth there be. No one can really and truly be a philosopher any more than one can be really and truly just (see *Republic* 5. 472b–c).

But philosophize we must (*Republic* 6. 497c–d). We must exit the allegorical cave and attempt to glimpse the allegorical sun and stars above. We can surely become more knowledgeable and more just if we lift up our heads and try to live by what we strain to our utmost to know to be good. We would surely live a better life than we would if we were to keep our heads down and to live merely for what we let ourselves crave and covet as if it were good.

2

Political Animals

1. I am endeavoring to begin our reflections on political society at the very beginning. I am hardly alone in this endeavor. But I am arguing that we find a beginning for political philosophy in a state of naïveté rather than in a state of nature. We are born ineluctably into a political society amidst a myriad of sensible images and objects, and we cannot but initially take these objects and images for reality.

We can find an escape from our unfortunate predicament though our escape is not entirely unmitigated. The ancient allegory of the cave illustrates how we can free ourselves and find refuge in philosophy. But philosophy contains illusions of its own. We can turn from sensible images and objects to intelligible images and objects. But we can endeavor to effect this revolution in our perspective only by means of hypotheses. What we take for truths are but tentative tenets. Our refuge is but a respite.

I wish now to argue that our original naïveté is not merely a mental affliction but a moral affliction, too. The allegorical cave dwellers would appear to live in a society of some kind. They fall into two obvious groups. There are prisoners, who are an audience held in bondage, and puppeteers, who are putting on a shadow show. Most philosophers, ourselves included, direct their attention initially, if not primarily and perhaps exclusively, to the prisoners. They are of obvious interest for us because they represent souls originally unphilosophical but eventually philosophical.

But to see its moral dimension, we would do well to direct our attention less to the prisoners in the allegory and more to the puppeteers. The puppeteers impose constraints of some sort on the prisoners. They may not be responsible for them being placed in bondage, but with their performance they appear to be responsible for them being held in bondage. The prisoners and the puppeteers would thus appear to constitute a rudimentary political society. The puppeteers somehow rule the prisoners with their theatrical effects.

The puppeteers might very likely, then, have political motives for presenting the prisoners with their theatrics. Their motives in turn are apt at least in part to reflect political principles. But their principles, which may not be fully articulate, need not be entirely true. Indeed, no human principle can ever be entirely true. All human principles are only hypotheses, more or less remote from a non-hypothetical first principle, which would be perfectly true.

But our political hypotheses, tentative though they are, have political consequences. They do concern our goodness, after all. These consequences, if our hypotheses are less than perfectly true, would be less than completely desirable. We shall in fact see that with their show the puppeteers can either help or hinder the prisoners in their plight. If educated, they are more likely to be helpful to them. If uneducated, they are likely to be a hindrance.

Does this analysis seem far-fetched? Not for us mortals, I should think. No philosophy, however sophisticated, could deny the undeniable fact that we philosophize within a political society. We who indulge in intellectual pursuits may for a time cloister ourselves within an ivory tower above and away from political life and its rough and tumble. But inevitably we find that we cannot but think of our fellows, and that we cannot but interact with them.

We soon discover, too, that our fellow citizens inundate us with images. We have been born, by chance admittedly, into a modern, some would say postmodern, society. We find ourselves, we must surely admit, habitués of a society with omnipresent, almost omnipotent, though hardly omniscient, mass media. We are daily subject to a clamorous and all but incessant flood of images, both visual and aural.

But perhaps we made our entrance at an inopportune moment, you may be thinking, and we merely happened to miss out on an idyllic life free from illusion. I submit that we would be hard pressed to show how we could not have been born into a society with its illusions. Our birth by its very nature implies two minimal societies, each of at least two persons. The one, though perhaps no more than passing, is between male and female, and the other, more obvious and enduring, is between mother and child or, more generally, between parents and child.

Even a minimal society of parents and child entails illusions of various sorts. Human beings, as do many other species, mammalian especially, not only nourish but also nurture their young in at least a rudimentary fashion. We humans must perforce learn a language from our progenitors. With our language comes a full complement of images, more or less general. You who read these words and I who write them are even now pondering verbal images.

We find, then, that philosophy is more likely than not to be ever so slightly compromised not merely ontologically and epistemologically but also morally and politically. Perhaps the ancient allegory of the cave can, if our current political predicament does not, persuade us of this inglorious fact. Perhaps the ancient allegory can also, if we examine it once more, give us a further insight into our inexorable political naïveté and its inadequate philosophical remedy.

2. What, then, are we to make of our moral and political naïveté? What philosophical remedy, though admittedly less than adequate, might we hope to find for it? After we come to grips with our naïveté, I also wish to ask, Do we have political bonds with one another in accordance with a political nature? Or do we have political liaisons in spite of a nature less than political?

I am asking, in other words, May we hypothesize that we are rational animals not only in theory but also in practice? Or must we assume that we are passional animals when we act? That we are, or can be, rational animals both in reflection and in action, shall be my contention. Our rationality can prompt us to act with a rational desire. A desire of this kind originates within our intellect, and it is, paradoxically perhaps, for an intelligible object.

Our passions can prod us to think sensible objects desirable. But must we use this presupposition for constituting a political society? On this supposition we would be essentially passional animals in matters practical. Our rationality would have, to paraphrase a modern philosopher, only the functions of ascertaining more clearly an object of our desire and of determining the means to our desired object. Our intellect would be of means and ends only, in other words.

How, then, might we be animals rational in action generally and in political action specifically? I would now draw your attention to the fact that in a naïve state, as well as in a state less naïve, we face images and objects affecting us in more ways than one. These images and objects can and do occasion within us either cognition or conation. We may simply think about them or we may act on them. If we act, we may seek them or flee them.

Philosophers not infrequently argue that our thoughts and actions differ in their origins. Our ideas and impressions appear to rise from an external sensibility, which consists of our five senses. These mental entities have their most obvious sources in sight and touch. Our knowledge, putatively true, can concern our ideas and impressions or their purported objects. That is, our cognition can concern ideas and impressions themselves taken to be objects or objects presumed to be other than our ideas and impressions.

Desires would appear to arise from what philosophers are not unaccustomed to denominate an internal sensibility. This sensibility we more commonly think of as an ability to feel various emotions or passions. These passions or emotions especially include our aggressive instincts, such as fear or anger, and our appetitive instincts, such as thirst, hunger, or sex. Perhaps worthy of particular mention in the present undertaking would be our decidedly distinct inclination for acquisition.

I wish to argue that we can also know these internal sensations of aggression or appetition to be themselves objects of cognition, or we can take these sensations to concern objects presumed to occasion them. That is, we can know our feelings for what they themselves purport to be or for what they purport to tell us about their objects. They appear, that is to say, to be at once affections of our own nature and affections of a nature other than our own.

With this distinction I intend to show that we can act from our intellect on our knowledge of our passions and emotions, and that we need not act from our emotions and passions themselves. When we act, we can, in other words, take cognizance both of our external impressions and of our internal impressions. Our actions indeed ought, I shall urge, to rest on an awareness of these sensations, both cognitive and conative.

What, then, are we to make of our desires and of their objects? I am about to argue that with our intellect we can find an intelligible object to be desirable. An odd suggestion, I know. But can we not act for the sake of a political society itself or for the sake of a function within society? I shall contend that we can. But is not a political society or a political function an intelligible entity? How might we see or touch a society? I would ask. Or a function within society?

We shall see that we can also take sensible objects of various and sundry sorts also to be desirable. A quaint notion, to be sure. Both our necessary and our unnecessary appetites, for example, respond to objects of this sort. We can take their sensible images to be desirable, too. Are we not often attracted, or at least distracted, by images of food or drink, not to mention sexual images?

Plato clearly recognizes these intelligible and sensible objects of desire. We can in fact better ponder our affections and their objects by returning to his allegory of the cave. Recall again the prisoners and their situation within the cave. They are held in bondage of a sort that does not permit them to move themselves or even to turn their heads. They are constrained to watch the shadows of puppets on the far wall of their cave (*Republic* 7. 514a–515c).

You also may recall that an allegorical prisoner makes an escape from this bondage. A prisoner is, not without difficulty, compelled to stand up, to turn around, and to exit the cave (515c–516c). I would now draw your attention to an overlooked fact about this escape. A person may escape along on more than one route. We can wend our way out on at least two different but not entirely dissimilar paths. Indeed, we may very likely traverse both paths more than once, many times actually, though I shall not insist on this curious fact.

What is this alternative escape route, then? With his allegory Plato indicates that the prisoners inside the cave, before they are forced outside, encounter both images and objects of a sensible kind. The images are the puppet shadows on the cave wall, and the objects are the puppets held overhead by the puppeteers. The prisoners see the puppets after they are released and forced to turn around (*Republic* 7. 515c–d). The images also include the shadows of the prisoners (515a–b). And the objects likely include the prisoners, too.

I would now ask, Can the prisoners feel desire for the puppet shadows and for the puppets? One would think that they would feel some affection for a puppet show and its puppets. Who does not enjoy a theatrical performance? We might also ask, Can the prisoners feel desire for their shadows and for themselves? That they would feel affection for themselves appears quite likely. But how much affection would they feel for their shadows?

I wish to show that we can and do feel desires both for our shadows and for ourselves as well as for the puppets and their shadows. To show that we can, I would remind you what the shadows and the puppets represent in our allegory. Plato, you may also recall, uses the figure of the divided line to explain that the images and their objects within the cave represent the shadows and reflections in the visible world and their objects (*Republic* 7. 517a–b; see *Republic* 6. 509d–510a).

We shall begin with the puppet shadows. The shadows on the cave wall are clearly allegorical. They represent shadows and reflections of visible objects, Plato explicitly states. But the allegory, taken thus literally, would seem to be of rather limited application. People can become infatuated with a reflection of themselves or of others, say, in a mirror or in a photograph. But we are not very likely to become enamored of a mere shadow of ourselves or of others.

Perhaps we ought to take the allegory less literally. Though he does not explicitly so state, Plato apparently includes among these shadows and reflections the imitations of the fine arts. Do not forget that the cave is a theater. But consider, too, what Plato states about poetry. He almost offhandedly indicates that Homer and Hesiod represent the gods and heroes with images (*Republic* 2. 377c–e; but see *Republic* 10. 598d–601b).

One can easily see that they do. When he imitates them in his poems, Homer makes the ancient gods and heroes into verbal images of sensible things. Indeed, he all but brings them to life.

Can we feel affection for these verbal images, then? We surely can. Plato is not unaware of this psychological fact. Young children are especially enamored of these images, he argues. The stories told to them represent types, and these types can be impressed upon them. At an early age children are malleable, and they take their beliefs about these images into their souls, he tells us (*Republic* 2. 377a–b). He appears to suggest that they are apt to believe these types to be good, and that they might desire to act on them.

Because of this fascination, Plato takes very seriously the education of the guardians for his society, critiquing even their nursery rhymes. He clearly implies that nursery stories ought to teach them to be just. These stories, he argues, must be appropriate for their later life (377b–c). That is why he infamously censors Homer for representing the gods and heroes badly. The young guardians must learn that hatred for family or friends is shameful and impious. They are not to hear what Chronos did to Ouranos or what Zeus did to Chronos, for example (377c–378e).

These children, he continues explicitly, will also need to be courageous. The young guardians should not be allowed to listen to stories that might make them fear death. They ought not to be told that Hades is a terrible place, for example. They should not hear what Hades himself has to say about the underworld or what Odysseus or Achilles say about it (*Republic* 3. 386a–387b). Nor should they hear how Achilles lamented for his lost comrade, or how Thetis did for her mortal son (387c–388e).

We thus find that our shadows and reflections can be desirable—if we take them in a broad sense to include the various objects of the imitative arts. We can surely see ourselves not only in the imitations of the Homeric epics but also in those of the ancient tragedies. I need say nothing of our own imitative arts and of our popular media. We may take advertisements, for example, political or commercial, to heart as well. These, too, present shadowy images of ourselves.[1]

I would now turn to the puppets. Recall that a prisoner is somehow forced to turn around from the puppet shadows to the puppets themselves (*Republic* 7. 515c–d). Could he or she feel affection for the puppets? Plato implies that he could. The puppets represent sensible objects in the allegory. That we can desire a sensible object is, I think, a proposition obvious enough. We do feel affection for other persons and for ourselves as well as desire for food or drink.

Our Homeric images could again serve us for proof of this proposition if proof were needed. Plato wishes the young guardians to be temperate, for example. If they were not, they would be able neither to obey their rulers nor to rule their pleasures (*Republic* 3. 389d–e). They would not likely obey their commanders if they were to hear what insults Achilles heaps on Agamemnon, for example, or what he would do, if he could, to Apollo (389e–390a, 391a).

Nor would they likely be able to restrain their desires if they were to hear what inordinate importance Odysseus and Eurylochus claim to attach to food and drink or what Zeus says about his desire for Hera or what passion Ares and Aphrodite have for each other (390a–c). Plato explicitly mentions our desire for money. The guardians ought to hear neither that gods are susceptible to brides or sacrifices, nor that Priam and Achilles could be bribed with gifts (390d–391a).

He also offers the dietary strictures for their training. The young guardians are not permitted to overindulge in drink, nor are they permitted to enjoy gourmet foods, especially pastries and sweets. And they may not cavort with courtesans, either (*Republic* 3. 403c–404e).

We might now perchance wonder, Could a political principle possibly assume that these sensible images or objects are desirable? It surely could. Consider the citizens of the two more common constitutions in ancient times and in our times. In both oligarchies and democracies, Plato argues, the people of the artisan and agrarian class turn toward their appetites, and they seek objects for their satisfaction. These objects are none other than sensible things.

Citizens of an oligarchy, for example, desire useful objects. They wish to satisfy appetites that are necessary (*Republic* 8. 554a; see 558d–559c). Because they give priority to these appetites, oligarchs devote themselves to making money (553b–c). An oligarch shows no interest in education, Plato tells us (554b). He enslaves his intellect together with his aggressive instinct, and he employs them solely to scheme about making more money (553c–d).

Citizens of a democracy desire pleasurable objects. Plato implies that they particularly seek to satisfy unnecessary appetites (558d–559c, 561a). They consider themselves free, and they take their freedom to be a license to do as they please (557b). A democrat eschews truth and even the very distinction between good and bad pleasures, and his appetites he satisfies at whim when they importune him (561b–562a).

I am obliged to point out, however, that a political principle, if it presupposes that sensible objects are desirable, can have untoward consequences. Our desires for sensible objects, necessary or unnecessary, can corrupt a society. The artisanal and agrarian class at the behest of their appetites for wealth or pleasure can become emboldened to usurp political office. If they do, they would most likely employ their newly acquired office not for the impartial benefit of their entire society but for the partisan benefit of their own class (see *Republic* 7. 519b–520a).

Political principles of this sort are less than auspicious in other ways, too, we might note. Besides corrupting society, these principles can have consequences that prove to be destructive of our resources. Our desires for tangible and visible objects have a tendency to extend themselves without limit. But our natural resources are clearly, if not obviously, limited, both locally and globally.

Plato himself reminds us that a naïve wish for comforts and luxuries can lead to conflict over resources. Land is surely a resource of importance in ancient times and in our day. Societies enamored of luxuries, he argues, soon find themselves living beyond their means. They then seek to possess neighboring lands, and their neighbors may seek their lands, Socrates explains to Glaucon and Adeimantus. Their desire for luxuries is the source not of war only but of all human evils, he avers (*Republic* 2. 373d–373e).

These excessive desires can give rise also to what we would call today a dual society. Citizens within a society, Plato implies, can come into conflict with one another over sensible objects. Their society can cease to have any unity and come to be in effect two societies. A society of this kind divides itself into the rich and the poor (*Republic* 4. 422d–423b).

Plato reminds us, too, that by itself excessive wealth or excessive poverty can corrupt the citizens individually. Artisans, for example, can come to neglect their functions. A potter who has become wealthy is likely to be idle or careless with his potting. But a potter who has become poor is unlikely to have the tools or materials for potting (*Republic* 4. 421c–e).[2]

But Plato is not alone. Modern political philosophers provide a veritable tragic chorus for his theory, especially the moderns who philosophize in English. They agree that we humans, when we desire tangible and visible objects, are destined for conflict and war. The moderns find themselves bound to acknowledge these consequences even though they more often than not assume that our natural resources are unlimited.

Hobbes presents a conspicuous specimen. Human beings are for him essentially desirous creatures, and our desires, he assumes, are for objects of a visible and tangible sort. These desired objects, he actually claims, are what is good for us (*Leviathan* 1. 6. 2–7.). He goes so far as to argue that a wish to satisfy even our basic needs can lead us into war. What he deems a natural equality arising from our roughly equal powers of mind and body can embolden some "to come prepared with forces united" and "to dispossess and to deprive" another "not only of the fruit of his labor, but also of his life or liberty" (*Leviathan* 1. 13. 1–9.).

I conclude, then, that politicians and philosophers ancient and modern frequently postulate that we are passional animals, and that we are impelled to political action by our desires. And that our concern for our desires and their sensible objects leads us, inevitably if Hobbes is right, into conflict and war over resources, especially territory.

We shall see that contemporary philosophers, too, often prefer to rest their theories on the fact that we can act on our desires, and that our desires have objects that are sensible things. But these philosophers can too often be blissfully unaware of, or at least they do not take into consideration, the nature of these desires or of their consequences. They do not always take cognizance of the fact that conflict and war can frequently ensue.

What they fail to recognize as well is that, even when open conflict does not, extreme maldistributions of resources and incredible privations and deprivations are likely to result. The upshot in our era is that some persons are possessed of property in an amount inordinate by the most extravagant standards, if we may call them standards, and some persons are dispossessed of property to the extent that they cannot fulfill their most rudimentary needs.[3]

I am about to urge that we might better create a political society, and that we might better serve our wants and needs, if only we would take for the primary objects of our desire objects that are intelligible. But what might these intelligible and desirable objects be—if any there be? Can these objects enable us to forsake our desires for sensible images and objects and to wend our way out of the allegorical cave?

3. I would now ask, Can our desires, including our political desires, be rational rather than passional? Can our rationality, in other words, have a desire of its own, and can a desire of this kind, if any, be political? One might also wonder, What would a desired object of this rational and political kind be? That our passions take sensible

objects to be desirable, and that these objects can be thought political is by now more than obvious, I should think.

These questions, we shall see, are tantamount to asking, Can we be cognizant of our external impressions and of our internal impressions in the same way? That is, can we view our affections, both our sensations and our passions, as themselves objects as well as affections of objects other than themselves? Or must we take these affections to be concerned only with objects presumed to be external to us and felt to be more or less desirable?

To answer these questions, we shall return to the allegory of the cave for another philosophical foray. We ought now to consider not the scene within the cave but the scene without. Let us continue to observe the prisoner who is freed from his, or her, bondage and forced to turn toward the puppets and the fire. Recall that the prisoner is forced past the apparatus of the puppet theater and is shown the way out of the shadowy world inside the cave to the world outside with its bright sunlight (*Republic* 7. 515c–516a).

Recall, too, how the prisoner, once outside, has to let his eyes adjust to his new surroundings. He at first looks only at shadows and reflections of sensible things, Plato tells us. He then looks at sensible things themselves, including people and other objects. He continues his exploration of this new world by looking at the stars and the moon by night. Eventually he is able to look at the sun itself and to see its nature. He discovers that the sun is the cause of the seasons and the years and of all things visible (516a–516c).

What does this portion of the allegory mean? Plato interprets it for us. He uses the figure of the divided line to explain that sensible objects outside the cave represent things that are intelligible objects (*Republic* 7. 517a–b). An intelligible object he identifies with an idea of the good. An idea of this kind, he further informs us, engenders both light and the sun in the visible world and also truth and understanding in the intelligible world. This idea, he adds almost incidentally, one must have who is to act intelligently in public or in private (517b–c).

But an idea of the good we poor souls can know only hypothetically. With a hypothesis we can, you may recall, attempt to reason or to understand. We may take a hypothesis for an assumption about an idea, and from it we can deduce a conclusion. Or we may again take a hypothesis about an idea for an assumption but induce from it a higher hypothesis—a first principle should we be so fortunate (*Republic* 6. 510b). A hypothesis mathematicians use to draw conclusions and dialecticians to arrive at a higher principle (510b–d, 511a–d).

One can now espy, I think, an escape from our cave and from our naïve desires for sensible things. We can do so if we focus on hypotheses for the moment. Plato explicitly argues that the proper objects of our hypotheses are intelligible things rather than sensible things. Geometers, he argues, reason about the ideas represented by the figures of their diagrams and not about the figures themselves. A diagram of a triangle, for example, is for them but an image of an idea of a triangle (*Republic* 6. 510d–511a).

Consider again the puppets. What does this philosophical fact tell us about them? Our hypotheses, if Plato is right, are about ideas in the intelligible world, and these ideas have reflections in the sensible world. The puppets are things in the sensible world, are they not? And so they would be images of our hypothesized ideas. People surely have in mind an idea for a puppet when they make or manipulate one, and their idea finds an image in their puppet and its antics.

But the puppets are not unlike unto us. We are obviously things in the sensible world, too, are we not? So we, too, are images of ideas in the intelligible world. Or, rather, we are images of our hypotheses about ideas. I would ask, When we act, do we not have an idea of who we are and of what we are about? Or, rather, ought we not to have ideas of these kinds? Our ideas find their images in our character and conduct.

We can now see how we may desire objects other than sensible things seemingly so attractive. I assume that we can use a hypothesis to guide our conduct. Indeed, on occasion at least we do. If so, I would ask, Can a hypothesis define an object of desire for us? We may answer this question if we ask a more obvious question, Can a hypothesis define an intelligible object? And then a question less obvious, Can an object of the intelligible kind be political?

My hypothesis is that an intelligible object can be political. A political object of this kind is a rational action! Is an action not an intelligible thing? Can we see an action? Or do we see images of it? But can an action, at least on occasion, not be political? And can we not choose to perform an action of this kind primarily for the sake of itself and not for the sake of its consequences?

An action of this kind, then, is eudaimonic. A eudaimonic activity we can perform entirely for its own sake. Philosophy is an activity of this kind. With Plato I take philosophy in its broadest sense. In this sense, philosophy is understanding and reasoning with hypotheses not merely about more esoteric academic topics, though it can concern those, but also about more exoteric topics, such as those in the moral or natural sciences or even those in everyday life.

But a eudaimonic activity we can also perform both for its own sake and for the sake of something else. Actions of this kind are rational, and they are primarily ends in themselves and secondarily means to other ends. Practical activity, either political or personal, can be of this kind. Productive activity, of both the beautiful and the useful arts, can be, too.

Plato himself confirms our inference about these rational and political activities. That justice is a eudaimonic activity, he clearly implies. Indeed, it constitutes our political happiness. But justice is an intelligible entity. It is an idea, and an idea that can serve to guide our action. It defines a rational action of value primarily for its own sake but also of value for the sake of its consequences. Or ought we to perform a just action merely for the sake of its consequences, supposedly its benefits for us?

Plato makes this concept of justice the very heart of his political theory. Glaucon challenges Socrates to show that we ought to act justly for its own sake not merely for the sake of its consequences (*Republic* 2. 357a-358b). To fulfill this challenge, Socrates takes for his very purpose in his discussion with Glaucon and Adeimantus (367e-368b). He undertakes to argue that justice does have value for itself. That it also has value for its consequences, is not at issue. They agree that it does.

How does Plato define justice, then? He begins by showing that we have a tripartite soul. With the principle of contradiction, he argues that our soul has a rational part and an irrational part, and that our irrational part has an aggressive and an appetitive part. He cites Homer, for example, to show that our rationality must be distinct from our spirit or what we would call our aggressive instinct. When he returns home, Odysseus uses his intellect to calm his seething spirit, which is incensed with the suitors and their unseemly conduct (*Republic* 4. 435e–441c).

These three parts of the soul each have a function of its own, he continues. The rational part has the function of ruling our soul. This part ought to rule because it alone is wise and has forethought for the whole soul (441e). The aggressive part of our soul has the job of defending us. It does so by preserving the assertions of reason about what is to be feared and what not (442b–c). And, presumably, acting on these assertions.

The rational part, in fact, finds an ally in the aggressive part. These two parts learn to work together through their education in music and gymnastics, both taken in the ancient sense (441e–442a). Together the rational and spirited parts rule the appetitive part. The appetitive part, Plato argues, requires their rule because it is most insatiable in its pursuit of material things (442a–b).

Justice, Plato concludes, is that the rational and the irrational parts of our soul all work together. Justice of this kind he calls justice writ small. Each part does its own work, and no part does the work of another (441d–e). A just activity is an inner harmony between the rational and irrational parts of the soul. This harmony he compares to the harmony of a musical scale of high, low, and middle tones (443c–444a).

We can see, if we accept this concept, that justice for Plato can also constitute our happiness. Life would not be worth living if one were not just, Glaucon declares to Socrates. Presumably, a life not worth living would be a life less than happy. A life without justice would not be worth living, he adds, even if one were to pursue all the power, property, and pleasure in the world. Our very soul would become corrupted (*Republic* 4. 444e–445b; also see *Republic* 1. 353d–354a).

Glaucon implies, therefore, that a just activity is primarily to act for the sake of a rational activity itself. A just action is of higher value for its own sake than actions of value for the sake of other things. A further implication would be that a life is not worth living if one were to pursue justice only for its consequences. The pursuit of an ulterior end—power, property, or pleasure—would make life less than happy, in other words.

My reader may hesitate. If so, consider Plato's example of justice, which might initially seem less than likely. His example is the auxiliary guardians. They have the function of defending society. One might well think that these guardians would not likely engage in a rational activity. They have qualifications that would render them fit for an aggressive life of war and conquest. Psychologically they are spirited, and physically they are strong (*Republic* 2. 374e–375b).

The guardians, indeed, develop the very qualities that can make them a threat to any society. They are a military force trained and equipped to prevent their enemies from attacking and sacking their society. Not only are they the most spirited and the most fit, they also develop the best fighting tactics, and they train with the most diligence (374d–e). Why, asks Socrates, might they not be tempted to anticipate their enemies and to plunder their society themselves (375b–c)?

But this group, though the most able to destroy it, turn out to be the ones who preserve their society. The guardians must become philosophical, Plato famously argues. The very best qualified study philosophy in its entirety (*Republic* 7. 535a–540c). But those less qualified, through their education, become habituated to opinion about what is courageous for them to do (*Republic* 4. 429a–430c; *Republic* 7. 522a–b). With its deliberations their intellect is thus able to rule their spirit, with which they are able to fight well (*Republic* 4. 442b).

The auxiliaries clearly desire a rational object. They desire to fulfill their function, which is to defend society. This function is rational because it reflects their belief about what is courageous. Indeed, they appear to perform a courageous action primarily for its own sake. They seek felicity, Plato argues, and not festivity (*Republic* 4. 419a–421c). That is why they are content to receive only room and board for their pay (*Republic* 3. 415d–417b).

Socrates concludes almost with astonishment that through education their political society has managed to purge itself of any excess. At least, it has done so in the persons of its guardians, who would in their turn, presumably, purify the other parts of society (see *Republic* 3. 399e). But notice that the guardians purge their society more by force of intellect than by force of arms. They make peace with themselves more than with their fellows. That is, their intellect is at peace with their aggressive and appetitive impulses.[4]

Yet one might still wonder, Is the political hypothesis that the guardians use for ruling their soul truly a first principle? Could the guardians actually attain knowledge of a non-hypothetical principle? They very likely could not if they are merely human. But could they perhaps grasp a more general political hypothesis that might include more specific hypotheses as special cases? They very likely could, I would suggest.

Their political principle is obviously justice. Plato calls justice in political society justice writ large. It mirrors justice in an individual. Each part of a society ought to do its own job. The philosophical guardians with their knowledge ought to rule their city, the auxiliary guardians with their courage ought to defend the city, and the artisans and agrarians ought to be sufficiently tractable to provision it (*Republic* 4. 433a–e).

Consider the auxiliaries again. Plato grants them not knowledge but right opinion. But with their opinion they are aware of their virtue and their function. They have the virtue of courage and the function of defense. This function, recall, turns on recognizing the friends of their society and its foes (*Republic* 2. 375c–376c). How are they to recognize who is who? An opinion about justice would enable them to do so. A friend of the city would be someone who fulfills a function, and a foe someone who does not.

We can see more clearly that justice can serve for a first principle if we look more closely at its underlying psychology. Though we cannot know if it is absolutely first, or, rather, though we know that it is not absolutely first, we know that this principle is prior to hypotheses employed by persons in societies less than just. This principle permits Plato to account for the principles, so-called, of persons who live in unjust societies. The persons in these societies act for the sake not of intelligible but of sensible objects!

The philosophical guardians of a just society ought to rule because they primarily exercise their cognitive faculties and possess knowledge especially of what is desirable for all parts in their society. The guardians, if we may so call them, of other societies primarily exercise faculties other than cognitive, and they deem desirable for their society what seems desirable for their part of society only.

Consider, for example, the two political societies not uncommon in our own day. Both oligarchs and democrats wish to satisfy desires, and they seek the objects of their desires as their ends. Persons of both these kinds rise from the artisan and agrarian class. The oligarchs take for their principle the acquisition of wealth, and the democrats take for their principle the enjoyment of wealth. The one seeks to satisfy their necessary desires, and the other their unnecessary desires (*Republic* 8. 553a–555b; 558c–562a).

But society itself can be its own end! A society can itself have a value for its own sake! What would be the end of society? What would be its value? The end of society is the fulfillment of its political functions taken together. Its functions have an intrinsic value of their own though they also have value for their consequences. Their harmonious organization itself has its own value as well as valuable consequences.

A society does not have the end of satisfying necessary or unnecessary desire. Or ought a society to exist for the sake of an end other than itself? If so, its value would be secondary to an ulterior end, usually private profit or pleasure. But I would not deny that these desires, even if they are not the primary, do require satisfaction.

We can now see how justice rests on knowledge of our internal sensations and not on a desire for their purported objects. Consider our aggressive instinct, for example. Its end our rationality sets for us. It has its purpose in a political function. What Plato calls our spirit the better enables the auxiliary guardians to defend their society (*Republic* 2. 375a–b). Appetitive instincts, too, have a rational function. They have an end in provisioning society.

Justice, then, requires that persons have knowledge of their passions and their proper role in their society. We can know our affections themselves as objects. We might say that we can become free from an emotional bondage. Why? We need not permit our instinctual urges and cravings to define for us what might seem to be a moral or political purpose.

Can we not agree with Plato that we have a rational political function valuable in itself, and that our rational function is prior to any irrational function? Indeed, our rational function provides us with a purpose for the satisfaction of our desire. We ought to satisfy desire so that we are able lead a rational life. Besides, satisfaction requires so little.[5]

Let us now return to the allegorical puppets and the puppeteers. The puppets are images obviously. But of what would they be images? They are most likely images of a political principle held by the puppeteers. Of what political principle would they be images? Their principle can obviously be a concept of an intelligible object or a concept of a sensible object. The principle can be one of justice or another principle less just.

The puppeteers are images of political principles, too. After all, the puppets embody the principles of their puppeteers and their desires. With their puppets the puppeteers can imitate an action performed for the sake of a rational activity itself or an action done for the sake of an emotional passivity or, rather, for the sake of its object. Their principles can be for the sake of political functions or for the sake of private interests. They can be correct or corrupt, in other words.

Plato argues, in sum, that we can engage not merely in a rational activity that is theoretical, but we can also engage in a rational activity that is practical. Our theoretical activity of reasoning and understanding can determine for us what the nature of our practical activity might be. But a concept of ourselves as a passional animal can also serve for a theoretical hypothesis though not a cogent one.

We are, then, animals with a nature at once rational and political. Our rational nature can inform a rational desire, and our rational desire can be for a political object. Our intellect can take cognizance of a political principle, and our political principle enables us to fulfill a function with a political content. And our political function we can fulfill for its own sake.

Our political happiness is quite natural, then. Indeed, a just man is naturally happy! Even a political society can be naturally happy! A political society can be a symphony, as it were, of political functions fulfilled by us for their own sake. A society need not be a cacophony of functions foisted on us by aggression and appetite.

I would also conclude that intelligible objects are more desirable than sensible objects. But I could not deny that sensible things are desirable. My assumption is solely that rational activity desirable for its own sake has greater value than irrational passivity of value for its consequences.

Plato would surely agree. Our higher desires show that our lower desires are not paramount. But our higher desires do not deny our lower ones. The sun and the constellations are more worthy of our affection, but the puppets and their shadows retain their allure.[6]

4. We might now remind ourselves, if we could have forgotten, that we are born into a political world as well as into a natural world. We cannot change our political world more than superficially any more than we can change our natural world more than superficially. Yet we do face a fundamental political choice about what kind of society we might wish to inhabit. After all, only for our ends and only by our efforts does a society exist.

This fundamental choice our very nature delineates for us. When we reflect on our nature, we cannot but discover that we face a twofold option for our political action. The one option, which I advocate, rests on the hypothesis that we are rational animals, that we have rational desires, and that our rational desires are, in part at least, political. If I am right, we can through our intellect itself engage in an action, at once rational and political, for its own sake.

The other option, which I reject, relies on the hypothesis, more common in our era, that we are passional animals, that our desires are and can only be irrational, and that irrational desires are ultimately not political but personal. But we need not assume, I contend unabashedly, that our rationality is subservient to a desire for an ulterior end, which not infrequently occasions excessive efforts for objects deemed useful or pleasurable.

What is at stake, then, is our political life itself. That our political life can be eudaimonic, I would aver. A political society can be primarily a common activity that is in itself an end of value for its own sake. What ought a political society to be if not a community of intrinsic value, pray tell? Or ought we to live together in a society merely to exploit one another for the sake of attempting to satisfy insatiable appetites?

But we now face an obstacle seemingly insurmountable. A eudaimonic society would surely appear to be eminently desirable, you may agree. But how feasible would a society of this sort be? you may ask. Could we possibly establish a society for the sake of our happiness? In other words, Is Plato's principle of justice anything other than an impractical ideal—doubtless fine enough in theory but in practice at best dubious?

I am obliged to concede that Plato offers a principle of justice that is not entirely feasible. Indeed, Plato himself indicates that it is not. But I shall argue that we may, nonetheless, make use of his principle. We can accept his general idea of justice, that a political society consists of different parts, and that these parts together find their ends in their functions. But we must make an adjustment to his idea in its implementation. We must revise its application to the artisans and agrarians.

The question of feasibility comes to the fore when one asks what kind of happiness ought to be the end of political society. Happiness in its highest form is the activity of philosophy. But can a political society actually exist for the sake of philosophizing even in a general sense, gleaned from Plato, of understanding and reasoning about ideas? Can a society exist solely for the sake of theoretical science, to put the matter in contemporary terms?

We must admit that philosophical happiness cannot be political happiness in its most practical form. Plato agrees that philosophy, though the eudaimonic activity most desirable, is not the form most practicable for politics. But, we must ask, if not in theoretical activity, in what form might happiness be feasible? Though Plato does not, Aristotle thinks that practical action is better for most societies. But I wish to argue that a still better activity, for our era at least, would be production.

That productive activity might practicable, is hardly a uncontroversial proposition, however. That this activity might be eudaimonic, probably appears as paradoxical to the modern ear as it would to the ancient. Production, especially of the modern industrial variety, seems most times to be considerably less than a moral activity. This activity would seem to be at once pleonectic and hedonic. In our mass markets it seems pleonectic on the side of production, and on the side of consumption it seems hedonic.

But I would ask, Cannot our production and consumption be rational activities with an intrinsic value of their own? Or need we make our productive and consumptive activities subservient to our appetites? I would also ask, Can we not moderate our production and consumption? Or must we take these activities to their extremes?

I must again acknowledge that happiness is of two kinds. Happiness in its primary form has intrinsic value solely, but in a secondary form happiness has both intrinsic and instrumental value. In other words, philosophy taken to be concerned with the absolute truth, or its human approximation, is its own end. Knowledge of this kind is knowledge for the sake of knowledge. Any theoretical science can be philosophical in this sense.

But practical action and production can also be felicitous. They are of value both for their own sake and for the sake of something else. Justice for Plato is an end of value for itself and for its consequences, I would remind you (*Republic* 2. 357b–358a). Both production and consumption can be of value for their sakes and for their consequences, too. Farming or gardening, for example, can be its own end, but these activities also produce foodstuffs. Dining can be itself an end, but it also nourishes us.

Now one might well expect that Plato would strongly advocate a political society for the sake of philosophical activity. He clearly argues in favor of an ideal society in which philosophers rule. Philosophers should rule because they have knowledge of what is good for their whole society (*Republic* 4. 428a–429a, 441e). He argues also that philosophers ought to rule because they are able to grasp that which always is the same. They have in their soul a paradigm for governance (*Republic* 6. 484b–d).

But Plato apparently thinks that philosophers are so rare that they could rule, if rule they could, only in a monarchy or aristocracy (*Republic* 4. 445c–e). He anticipates that few people would qualify for enrollment in philosophical studies. They would have to have an extraordinary combination of intellectual abilities (*Republic* 6. 485a–487a; *Republic* 7. 535a–536b). These few would also have to pass rather difficult tests not entirely academic (*Republic* 3. 412d–414b; *Republic* 7. 539e–540a).[7]

He recognizes, too, that a society cannot subsist on theory alone. He argues that those who study philosophy cannot linger in their studies but are obliged to fulfill a political role in society. Their class is no different than any other class of citizens, he explains. Each class has a benefit to provide for society. With their knowledge they can best provide the benefit of ruling (519c–521b).

Nor is he sufficiently sanguine to think that these philosophers will always attain rule. Upon their return to the cave they are likely to encounter a reception less than heartfelt. A philosopher would initially cut a ridiculous figure because his eyes would not be adjusted to the dim light. The cave dwellers would think that he had ruined his sight. Nor would they be averse to executing him if he attempted to enlighten them (*Republic* 7. 516e–517a).

Plato concludes, reluctantly perhaps, that his ideal society is "not impossible." He actually leaves the matter up to divine intervention or to good fortune. Only if, he plainly states, a god might inspire a ruler to devote himself to philosophy, or if a fortunate circumstance might compel a philosopher to rule, could his ideal political society come to be (*Republic* 6. 499a–499d, 502a–c; *Republic* 7. 540d–e).

What alternative to monarchy or aristocracy does Plato have to offer? None, unfortunately. Monarchy and aristocracy, on his account, are rational and other constitutions are passional. Timocracy, for example, seeks to appease our aggressive instincts. Oligarchy and democracy are little better. An oligarch seeks to satisfy necessary appetites, which are primarily for property, and a democrat satisfies unnecessary appetites, which are for all manner of frivolities.[8]

I suggest that we turn to the Stagirite. Aristotle agrees with Plato that a philosophical society has the best end (*Politics* 7. 1–3. esp. 1325b14–32). He also agrees, albeit in passing, that a society of this kind would be a monarchy or an aristocracy (*Politics* 3. 15. 1286b3–7). But he, too, argues that a society of either kind would not be the most feasible. Monarchy and aristocracy rest on cultural and natural assumptions "not easy to accept." These constitutions, he implies, would require that those who rule differ from those who are ruled as gods and heroes do from humans (*Politics* 7. 14. 1332b16–27).

Admittedly, Aristotle does not argue explicitly that a monarchy aims at philosophical happiness. But he does argue that this constitution has a ruler who is distinguished in virtue, and who stands head and shoulders above all others. A monarch in his sense would appear to possess philosophical virtue among other virtues because he has in their entirety the virtues that others have separately (*Politics* 3. 17. 1288a15–29). But a monarchy would most likely occur within a society only early in its development (*Politics* 3. 15. 1286b8–11). And it would likely be merely a transitional constitution (*Politics* 3. 15. 1286a9–28; 1286b11–22).

An aristocracy more clearly has for its aim a philosophical life. Those who rule in it are the best absolutely, Aristotle states (*Politics* 3. 4. 1279a33–37; 4. 7. 1293b1–5). They ought in fact to rule only in the prime of their intellectual life (*Politics* 7. 9. 1329a2–17). But he again implies that this constitution assumes a standard of virtue unattainable by most people. Echoing his teacher, he states that an aristocracy requires an education in need of a fortunate nature and resources, and that it "rests on prayer" (*Politics* 4. 11. 1295a25–31).[9]

Yet Aristotle does take us a step closer to a eudaimonic society of a more practicable sort. We find in his theory an alternative to the highly estimable but hardly feasible constitutions of monarchy and aristocracy. This alternative points the way toward yet another option that is more practicable for our era. Or so I shall argue. Happiness in these alternative constitutions takes the form of a rational activity with value both for itself and for its consequences.

Aristotle advocates happiness in the form of a practical activity. The practical activity that he commends for most societies might strike us today as somewhat odd. It is martial activity. Martial activity, he indicates, can have value both for itself and for its consequences. He might thus seem to argue in favor of conquest and empire. But he clearly does not. He explicitly argues, on the contrary, against endeavors of this sort.[10]

This more practicable constitution Aristotle calls polity. A polity aims at a eudaimonic activity of a kind attainable by the people, he argues. Only one person or a few persons can distinguish themselves in all virtue, including, presumably, philosophical virtue. But the people are able to attain martial virtue, he explains. He refers to those who have the means to acquire heavy armor (*Politics* 3. 7. 1279a37–1279b4). They would be none other than the ancient hoplites.

What is martial happiness, then? Happiness of this kind would be courageous activity, which can have both intrinsic and instrumental value. What is its intrinsic value? A person acting courageously, Aristotle argues, is someone who acts steadfastly in the face of the most fearful object of all. This object is death. Death is most fearful because it is the end. A courageous person, he concludes, is without fear of death, especially in battle (*Ethics* 3. 6. 1115a24–35).

But courageous action has an obvious instrumental value. This value is the defense of society. Aristotle cautions, however, that courage ought not to take on the instrumental value of conquest and despotism. These ends, he argues, are unlawful because a lawgiver or a citizen ought not to do to others what he would think unjust if done to himself. They are also absurd because one ought to be a master not over all persons but only over those who by nature require a master (*Politics* 7. 2. 1324b22–41; see also *Politics* 7. 14. 1333a30–1334a10 or *Ethics* 10. 7. 1177b8–12).[11]

Aristotle, then, breaks with Plato. Though he does not explicitly do so, he could no doubt distinguish a polity from a timocracy. At least, he could distinguish an

Aristotelian polity from a Platonic timocracy. A polity takes for its goodness happiness of a kind found in martial activity, but a timocracy seeks to satisfy our aggressive instinct. Timocrats, as their name suggests, seek the ulterior ends of defending their honor and of seeking victory over others (*Republic* 8. 548c).[12]

We see, then, that Aristotle finds a practical constitution in polity. But how desirable is polity and how practical is it? In our era the military class is a rather small part of society. This part today hardly constitutes a "martial people" (*Politics* 3. 17. 1288a12–15). Perhaps modern societies might have had more numerous soldier-citizens in an earlier era. A modern counterpart of the hoplite in ancient Greece would likely be the minuteman of colonial America, for example.

Can happiness take another form more practical than martial happiness? I am proposing that it can. What I shall call an artisanal happiness is more appropriate for a contemporary society. Happiness of this kind I take to be a eudaimonic activity found primarily in production. This activity would include not only the activities of the fine arts with their beautiful products but, more importantly, the activities of the industrial and agricultural arts with their useful products.

One might call artisanal happiness artistic happiness. This activity arises from the virtue of production, and this virtue in the classical sense is, strictly speaking, art. But the term "art" in the contemporary sense suggests rather narrowly fine art. That we have a tendency to identify art in general with fine art would suggest in fact how far the other arts have been demeaned and degraded.

So I have employed the term "artisanal" instead. I admit that this term, too, carries a risk of misunderstanding. It is apt to suggest to a modern ear only what are called the useful or necessary arts. But the term is less misleading for our purpose. Fewer people can practice the fine arts, and more people the necessary or mechanical arts. Arts of this kind are surely more prevalent within society today or within any society.

Who are the artisans, then? I take what we commonly think to be the oligarchs and the democrats both to be of the artisanal class. These two groups constitute what we often call the people or the working class. After considerable thought I classify them in this way because oligarchs and democrats seek the same general end. They both wish to appease their appetites and most frequently in ways less than virtuous.

But oligarchs and democrats differ specifically about the appetites that they want to satisfy. That oligarchs seek to satisfy their necessary desires, and democrats their unnecessary desires, I shall assume with Plato. An oligarch is in fact generally a producer, who supplies products to others for the sake of turning a profit. A democrat is generally a consumer, who demands products for the sake of attaining a pleasure.

One might be tempted to identify the industrial class with the oligarchs and the agricultural class with the democrats. I trust that my readers would agree that the industrial class is oligarchic. The agricultural class might seem democratic because in the not so distant past they were less wealthy and more numerous. But today they no longer are. To see that they are not, one need only reflect on present-day farming operations with their industrial machinery and huge landholdings.

Of course, I shall also include within the artisan class a group most often thought to be democratic. This class would be those whom we commonly recognize to be the workers in society. Whether in the factories or in the fields, workers today do not often find their goodness in their function. They seek goodness outside of their function on weekends in the pleasure of using and consuming industrial and agricultural products.

We now face our fundamental political choice. We are obliged to decide whether we ought to pursue oligarchic and democratic functions as eudaimonic or as pleonectic and hedonic. I am arguing that, whether industrial or agricultural, our productive activities do possess intrinsic value as well as instrumental value. When we engage in these activities, we can constitute a society for the sake of these activities themselves. We can find in them a common ground for a community.

Artisanal activity that is eudaimonic would have many advantages for our era. An important advantage would be simply the good of participating in a community for its own sake. I submit that most political societies today suffer from a common malaise in the loss of community. Too frequently our societies subordinate political activities to their consequences. These consequences result in little more than a less-than-subtle exploitation of each other for private gain.

Artisanal activity has other advantages as well. An activity of this kind can moderate our production and our consumption. To become happy and to be happy, we need only produce goods in moderate quantity for consumption. Why? Our products are obviously instruments, and our instruments find their end in our activities themselves, not only in philosophy and other sciences but also in our practical action. We need not endeavor to produce or to consume as much as possible.

If we were to value our productive activities for their own sake, we would, I should think, have less need to acquire and to accumulate material resources. How much do we need to be happy in an ancient eudaimonic sense? With less acquisition and accumulation we would very likely come to have less disparity of income and wealth. Perhaps more persons could in turn live their life well and not struggle merely to live.

I probably ought to leave further speculations on these benefits to others more versed in the empirical sciences. But I cannot forbear to assert that another benefit would also appear to follow. Would we not have fewer conflicts over our social and natural resources? We might well find these conflicts reduced not only within societies but also between them.

I do not deny its due to philosophical happiness, though not in itself practical. Nor do I deny martial happiness its due. There surely are roles in any political society for philosophy and theoretical activity as well as for the military and defense activity. But I would assert that a contemporary polity cannot rest on philosophical or martial happiness primarily. The theoretical and martial classes are simply too small.

I would ask, If a practical activity can, why cannot a productive activity have both intrinsic and instrumental value? How different are practical and productive activities? Not very different, I should think. They differ not in their intrinsic value but in their instrumental value. Practical actions have instrumental value in that we engage in them to fulfill our needs. But productive actions have instrumental value in that we engage in them to create the material means by which we fulfill our needs (see *Ethics* 6. 5. 1140b6–7).

Does my proposal have any precedent? I am now obliged to tread lightly because I am not an expert in political policy or practice. But even an inexpert cannot fail to notice that we find precedent in political policies and practices designed to favor philosophical and martial activities. Many modern societies obviously provide opportunities and resources for scientific research, and all societies provide for a defense force.

Nor is political support for the arts unknown. Both the fine arts and the useful arts enjoy government subsidies. The fine arts have long been recipients of governmental sponsorship for performances in drama, dance, and music, and for exhibitions of the visual arts. Support for the useful arts is not less frequent. Governments frequently provide incentives and subsidies for manufacturing and farming enterprises.

We might also note that public education is today all but universal except in the most impoverished countries. Federal governments and provincial governments fund educational institutions from preschool to postdoctoral.

A word of caution, however. The purpose of governmental practices and policies at present tends to be less than eudaimonic. Scientific research frequently, though not always, benefits corporate interests defined by larger profits. I need but mention the military–industrial complex. Agricultural supports usually favor corporate farming and larger profits. And public education too often reduces to vocational training even in higher education.

Even more precedent we can find, unlikely though it may seem, in private enterprise. There clearly are what we might call artisanal corporations. Expert or no, one cannot fail to see that some corporations, even major corporations, look upon productive activities as valuable in themselves and do not see production as valuable solely for its output. Viewed in this way, corporate production can and often do, paradoxically perhaps, yield a superior product.

There also are businesses explicitly artisanal. Cinema production companies and musical ensembles, for example, have established themselves independently of colossal corporations in their fields. Artisanal bakeries and breweries are also flourishing. Not to mention a long tradition of artisanal distillers. Single malt distilleries go back centuries, though some now suffer from corporate interference. Nor could one fail to note the organic food movement, the slow food movement, and the established and emerging farmers markets.

I am, then, proposing a political theory that would seem to depart from the ancient tradition. Plato and Aristotle would very likely take exception to my concept of artisanal happiness. They both imply that the artisans and agrarians cannot attain happiness because they are unable to attain virtue. The ancient philosophers would in effect relegate these persons to an unfortunate status reminiscent of the prisoners in the allegorical cave.

Plato argues that temperance in a political sense is that the few who are better control the worse who are many. The few have measured desires, which follow from understanding and right opinion, and the many, said to be free, have desires and pleasures that are "many and strange" (*Republic* 4. 431b–432b). But temperance of this kind cannot be virtue. This temperance is merely restraint and restraint from an external not an internal source.

Aristotle implies rather clearly that the artisans and agrarians cannot be part of a eudaimonic society though they are necessary to society. A political society that aims at a eudaimonic activity requires virtue in its citizens. After all, happiness is an activity in accordance with virtue. But artisans and businessmen, he informs us, lead a life contrary to virtue, and farmers, because they lack leisure, are incapable of virtue (*Politics* 7. 9. 1328b33–1329a2).

Indeed, when he considers what aim a political society ought to have, he reminds us that happiness is the human good but takes into consideration only philosophical and martial happiness. He does not trouble himself with even a mention of productive activity (see *Politics* 7. 1–3.). He implicitly classifies the artisans with slaves, who are merely living property (*Politics* 7. 8. 1328a21–37).

Nevertheless, I would like to think that I remain within the tradition. I can, indeed, claim support for artisanal happiness and its practicality from both Plato and Aristotle. Do not forget that only the guardians who rule are full-fledged philosophers. Only they receive an education in the quadrivium and in dialectic. The auxiliary guardians receive an education in right opinion. But right opinion is sufficient for their function, Plato argues. With it they can tell what is fearful for their society and what is not (*Republic* 4. 429a–430c).

The artisans, I would argue, need not have a full-fledged philosophical education, either. They would likely find that right opinion would suffice for their function as well, I should think. Their function is not to defend their society but to provision it. But would not right opinion be sufficient to tell them what production they ought to engage in and what production they ought not?[13]

Aristotle, too, could lend us support. He is a proponent of good laws supportive of public education. Arguments can by themselves lead only the few who are well-born and love what is noble to act well, he argues. The many, who live by passion, need good laws and punishments to force them into acting well (*Ethics* 10. 9. 1179b4–20). But good laws habituate people and prepare them for education and instruction, he continues (1179b20–1180a24). The laws, he explicitly states, ought also to provide for education (1180a34–1180b13).[14]

In sum, I would conclude that the eudaimonic constitution most practicable for our era would be a polity for the sake of artisanal happiness. Happiness in an artisanal sense is an activity of production valued primary for its own sake and not merely for its consequences. Because it takes for its end an activity, happiness of this kind requires only modest production and consumption. It would avoid the extremes that often lead us into conflict and into war (see *Ethics* 10. 8. 1179a1–17).[15]

I recommend, then, for our era a eudaimonocracy—for readers who might share a penchant for neologisms, especially those of ancient Greek origin. I recommend a eudaimonocracy primarily for the sake of what I call artisanal activities. The alternatives, all too familiar perhaps, are a plutocracy or a hedonocracy, usually in a combination of one sort or another.

5. I would conclude that we ought, at our very best, to be what we might deem philosopher artisans—if to be a philosopher is to act on understanding and reasoning and if to be an artisan is to perform a productive activity for its own sake and for its consequences. I again take philosophy in a wide sense, which includes both knowledge and opinion, and I take artisan in a wide sense, which includes both the fine and the quotidian arts.

My conclusion has an important corollary, that all persons ought to have some grasp of our rational and political nature. Philosophers proper, who devote themselves to the study of theory, I do not deny a place in a political society. But those ought also to engage philosophy who perform an artisanal function in a society. At least, in a modicum. They surely ought to know what an impartial principle of justice is, and how it differs from a partisan principle, if one may use the term.

We are, then, a political animal (πολιτικόν ζῷον). Our political nature is the very foundation of our political society. I accept with Plato the modest assumptions that we form a society because we are separately non-self-sufficient, and that we can best approximate self-sufficiency with a division of labor (*Republic* 2. 369b–c, 369e–370c). But a political society once formed can constitute a eudaimonic activity and need not consist of a pleonectic or a hedonic passivity.

The conclusion that we are philosopher artisans, is not at all unplatonic, I would ask you to note. Plato in effect admits of a philosopher artisan when he compares a guardian to an artist. The guardians, as do painters, work with a paradigm to which they refer when creating a society, he explains. They look to the ideas of justice, courage, and temperance and sketch out the virtues in human beings. They create image of the virtues in their souls (*Republic* 6. 500b–502a).

But the guardians, Plato cautions, cannot sketch out virtues in society as perfect as those in the paradigm. They can only create an approximation. They again resemble painters, whose portraits are more perfect than any living person could ever be (*Republic* 5. 472b–473b).[16]

Without a paradigm the guardians, so called, would be unable to establish justice within a political society or to preserve its justice, he argues. They would likely lose themselves among the many sensible objects and images. They would be as if blind (*Republic* 6. 484b–d).[17]

Plato reminds us, then, that we ought to live out our lives, even our political lives, in concert with our nature. With our reasoning and understanding we must work to discover a general hypothesis about justice, and we ought to use our hypothesis to form and to rule a political society.

Those philosophers who would have us start our philosophizing about politics with a state of nature have an insight, I must admit. We cannot deny that we have a nature, or that our nature is the foundation for a political society. When we escape our political naïveté, we, indeed, discover that we possess a nature at once rational and political. We are then able to act in accordance with a principle also rational and political.

But, if we remain naïve, we remain mistaken about our nature. We might think that all our desires are only passional and private. We might return, perhaps unwittingly, to the hypothesis that Glaucon presents to Socrates, or to one similar, that we are by nature greedy animals. Glaucon, of course, though he expounds it, does not accept a hypothesis of this unsavory sort.

Modern philosophers recognize that political society rests on our nature, but they are those most often mistaken about it. Hobbes, to recur to a conspicuous example, rightly reminds us that we can never escape from our nature, and he shows that it underlies not only political society but all society. But he does not allow that we have a nature rational and political, or that we can enjoy a rational and political activity for its own sake.

He naïvely assumes that we are but passional animals. We naturally are, he argues, in a perpetual state of war because of our desires for gain, safety, and glory (*Leviathan* 1. 13. 3–9). To show that we are, he instances the fact that we lock the doors to our homes and even the chests within our homes (*Leviathan* 1. 13. 10; also 1. 13. 11–12). He finds himself obliged to argue in effect that a political society rests on nothing more than external restraint. He argues that political sovereignty possess a power that is, though conventional, absolute (*Leviathan* 2. 17. 13–15; see, too, 2. 18. 1–15).

A caveat is now in order. Plato warns us that those who are philosopher guardians—and no doubt those who are philosopher artisans—can become easily compromised. He offers two causes to explain why societies tend to be inimical to philosophy. These causes plainly rest on the mistaken notion that we are but passional creatures, and that we ought to pursue sensible goods.

What are the two causes? Those who are philosophers appear to many persons to be worthless or worse, Plato argues. Philosophers would appear worthless because other persons do not understand their principle. Plato offers an image of a ship and its crew. A true helmsman of a ship seems to be a useless stargazer to a mutinous crew. A crew of this scurvy sort wants to sail the ship themselves even though they are ignorant of navigation (*Republic* 6. 487e–489c).

The analogy would suggest that philosophers seem useless to persons in other classes who want to rule society. A philosopher knows what justice is, and he wishes to rule for the sake of society in its entirety. But oligarchs or democrats, for example, do not know what justice is, and they want to rule for their own class separately. They would rule society not for the sake of all classes performing their functions together but solely for the sake of their own class performing the function of making money or of pursuing pleasure.

But philosophers can also become vicious. A person with a philosophical soul has extraordinary abilities, and with these abilities he or she can become exceptionally good or bad. Without an education a person with a philosophical soul can fall prey to a monstrous and mighty beast, Plato argues. This beast is the assembled many. At its various public gatherings sophists arise, and they all too eager and willing to tutor a budding philosopher in its opinions. These opinions one can easily take for wisdom itself (491a–493e).

The image of a monstrous beast would appear to rest on the same assumption as the nautical image. One would think that the assembled many might well have the goal of acquiring property or of pursuing pleasure. These ends, if they are uneducated, they would be apt to take for their political principles. They would, in other words, very likely neglect the interest of their whole society and act on interests of their own.

Plato warns us, then, that a political society can be just only when those least eager to rule undertake to rule. Rulers of this kind are rich in goodness and not in gold. They obviously seek an intelligible good. But when those hungry for gold endeavor to rule, a political society can only be unjust. These rulers seek a visible and tangible good. Rulers of this ilk corrupt their society and draw it into internecine warfare (*Republic* 7. 520e–521b).[18]

We can now see why an unjust society, besides its other infelicities, can only be of a short, nasty, and brutish duration. An unjust society is cancerous, we might say. One part within it corrupts the whole in the pursuit of its own partial interest. Because it becomes inordinate, the one part hinders the other parts from fulfilling their functions. But no part separately can ever be self-sufficient. All parts, if Plato is right, must work together within a division of labor.[19]

Part Two

A Eudaimonic Polity:
An Opportunity Overlooked
in Contemporary Political Thought

3

Liberty and Slavery

1. One might wonder whether anyone in our era could possibly possess liberty of the political variety. The predominant political societies today are either oligarchic or democratic. But neither an oligarchic nor a democratic society espouses a political liberty worthy of the name. These societies do advocate and advance liberty, but their liberty is primarily of a private sort. Oligarchs seek freedom to acquire property for themselves, and democrats seek freedom to indulge in their pleasures.

But one might wonder as well whether anyone in any era could enjoy political liberty. We are born into and live out our lives within a society not of our choosing. Our political society and our political selves are thrust upon us. If we were somehow to escape from these ineluctable circumstances, we would still have cause to ask whether any supposed freedom could truly be freedom. We perforce begin our lives, you may recall, in a state of naïveté, and our naïveté, we find, we cannot entirely overcome.

We must, indeed, begin our analysis of liberty *in medias res*. There is nowhere else we could begin. I propose that we who feel an obligation to philosophize about political matters today would do well to undertake an analysis of political philosophy today. I shall presume that our philosophy can be of some consequence for our practice, and that our practice can be of some consequence for our philosophy. Our political speculations and actions, I should think, are not entirely incongruent.

For our present inquiry I wish to take into consideration two contemporary philosophers whom I shall take to be paradigmatic. These two philosophers are John Rawls and Robert Nozick. I choose Rawls and Nozick in part because they have undeniably contributed to current political theory and practice, as you are doubtlessly aware, and in part because they plainly expound perennial perspectives on political thought and action, as I shall presently show.

Rawls and Nozick offer philosophies of a political society that we ought, strictly speaking, to denominate a polity, though they tend, as do most people, to think it a democracy. But a polity can promote either of two ends. It can be for the sake of a rational activity prized for its intrinsic value, which would be our happiness, or for the sake of a rational activity performed for its instrumental value, which ultimately would issue in desire satisfaction. A polity can, in other words, be for the sake of a eudaimonic activity or a hedonic passivity.

A polity for the sake of a eudaimonic activity is a polity proper, but a polity for the sake of a hedonic passivity is a mixture of other constitutions. A polity of either kind has in common two similar principles though they utilize them for dissimilar ends. These principles I shall denominate an oligarchic and a democratic principle. A democratic principle determines what freedom a political society respects, and an oligarchic principle determines what property distribution a political society protects.

A polity of the eudaimonic kind rests its foundation on a principle of happiness in the sense of a rational activity with intrinsic value. To its eudaimonic principle it subordinates its democratic and oligarchic principles. A polity of the mixed kind is without a principle truly eudaimonic. It is most often a compromise of expediency between its democratic and its oligarchic principles, neither of which by itself is apt to promote happiness in any rational sense.

Both Rawls and Nozick theorize about an expedient polity of the mixed variety. In their analyses they do not take into account in an essential way a principle of an action with intrinsic value. They in general mix political principles that are democratic and oligarchic though their oligarchic and democratic principles differ in specifics. We tend to think their constitutions democratic because they devote not inconsiderable attention to their concepts of liberty.

They also attempt to combine more than one democratic principle in their polity. The democratic element of their constitutions is itself a mixture of two principles, in other words. They both recognize that a society ought to guarantee political liberty for its members though their concepts of this liberty differ. They also argue that a society ought to provide its members with personal liberty. On this concept they agree.

The ancient Greek philosophers, too, recognize both a polity proper and a mixed polity, and they recognize subspecies of the mixed variety. These subspecies depend upon the particular mixture of their democratic and oligarchic principles. A constitution of this mixed kind they call a democracy if it leans toward its democratic principle, and they call a constitution of this kind an oligarchy if it leans toward its oligarchic principle.

But the ancients did not recognize that one might combine two democratic principles in a single constitution. They thought that these principles define democracies of different kinds. Aristotle, for example, recognizes both principles (*Politics* 6. 2. 1317a40–1317b17). The one principle, he explains, defines liberty under law, but the other he thought tantamount to license. He argues that democracies degenerate from the one to the other (*Politics* 4. 6. 1292b25–1293a12; *Politics* 6. 4.).

My hypothesis shall be that any principle of political liberty ought to promote our political happiness. Our political freedom ought to be, in a word, eudaimonic. I hope that this proposition does not prove unduly controversial. To be free, ought we not to have the ability to pursue our goodness, and is not our goodness our happiness? We ought, I shall argue, to be able to pursue a properly human purpose, and we ought not to acquiesce in a purpose less than human.

I shall show that Rawls and Nozick offer us principles of political liberty less than eudaimonic. They advance democratic principles that have an end in an action that does not have intrinsic value but merely instrumental value. Though they do recognize political freedom, they ultimately subordinate their political freedom to private freedom that permits one to do as one pleases. They defend a society that offers freedom merely in a hedonic sense.

Alexis de Tocqueville, I would note, saw that American society embodies these two democratic principles. He argues that we seek freedom both in big things and in little things. Freedom in big things is our political sovereignty, which enables us to elect a powerful and protective government. Freedom in little things is individual freedom, with which we manage our private affairs (see *Democracy* 2. 4. 6. 806–808).

But he sees in these principles of liberty a danger of oppression. His fear is that taken together they could result in a new despotism. A democracy, he explains, with "an immense and protective power" might well safeguard the enjoyments of its citizens and watch over their destiny. But it might also keep its citizens with their enjoyments "in perpetual childhood" (805–806).

I shall focus my analysis in this chapter on these democratic political principles. I propose to distinguish political liberty and private liberty and to argue in favor of the liberty of the political kind. I shall obviously be going against the prevailing philosophical trend. Modern and contemporary political philosophers by and large reduce political liberty to the personal kind. Rawls and Nozick present no exception.

My intention, then, is to define and to defend political liberty proper and to redress the grievous wrong done to her and to address its potential danger.

2. What is political liberty? I wish to argue that liberty of the political kind, if truly liberty, is a capacity to strive for human goodness of a political variety. But human goodness is happiness. Political liberty, then, is an ability to pursue happiness in a political sense or, at least, to seek an approximate happiness in this sense. In other words, to have political liberty is to be able to participate in a political community for the sake of the community itself.

I shall argue further that this eudaimonic capacity consists of two primary facets. We must have a concept of our political happiness, and our concept must serve for a principle of political action. If we are to pursue it, we must obviously know what constitutes our happiness, even our political happiness, and we must choose to act on our concept of happiness. That is, we must through our own knowledge and through our own efforts engage in an action worthy of choice for its own sake.

I would urge that our political theories and practices ought to have the purpose of assuring that we can pursue happiness of the political kind. I take this proposition to be nothing less than self-evident though we do evidently lose sight of it. Why else, pray tell, would we attempt to theorize about the various political societies within which we find ourselves if not to discover how we might seek human goodness together with our fellows? Why else might we attempt to put our theories into practice if not to pursue our happiness together with others?

I would underscore that our happiness, even our political happiness, is itself a rational activity not an emotional passivity. To be happy, we must not only possess knowledge of what we are doing and choose to act on our knowledge, but we must also act for the sake of our very action itself. Our eudaimonic action is and can only be its own end.

I would make explicit two qualifications, which I shall assume without argument. Our rational activity, to be eudaimonic, we must perform in accordance with a mean. This doctrine is simply that we ought to act with moderation, and that we ought not to overdo or to underdo an action. We must also act from mental and moral habits if we are truly to engage in a felicitous activity. We ought in a political arena through our action and its repetition to develop habits that in turn facilitate our action (see *Ethics* 2. 1–6.).

This concept of liberty I take to be an ancient one, and we shall grasp it more clearly with a glance at its origins. One can easily espy its rudiments in Plato, for example. But, unfortunately, Plato and the ancient Greek philosophers generally do not much discuss freedom in an honorific sense. They apparently saw freedom most often in its abuse. They are willing to devote some discussion to our human capabilities, however, especially our political ability. I shall assume that our political ability is our political liberty.

Plato presents an example of political liberty in the persons of those whom he calls the guardians in his ideal society. He argues that the guardians ought to have political knowledge and to hold political office. These guardians are at once philosophers and politicians. Until philosophers become kings or kings become philosophers, political society and humanity will have no respite from evil, he declares (*Republic* 5. 473c-e). The very phrase "philosopher king" implies a unity of knowledge and action.

What knowledge do these philosopher guardians have? They have knowledge in a general, even liberal, sense. They would hardly be content with knowledge in the narrow academic sense so common among contemporary philosophers. Plato argues that they love knowledge of all kinds (*Republic* 5. 474c-475c). A guardian has not only knowledge about what form a thing can take, but he also has opinion about what form a thing does take (475e-476d). His opinion includes experience in both political and military matters (see *Republic* 7. 539e-540a; also *Republic* 5. 466d-467e).

The philosophical guardians know, more specifically, what is good for their society in its entirety and not in part only (*Republic* 4. 428a-429a). Their knowledge includes the principle of justice. This principle, Plato concludes after a lengthy argument, is that every person ought to fulfill a political function for which they are best suited (432b-434d). The principle, he argues explicitly, requires that the philosophers rule. Only they have knowledge about justice itself and have true opinion about its images in political affairs (*Republic* 7. 519b-520e).

Plato rather clearly implies that these guardians can initiate action with their intellect and their knowledge of society. The guardians would most likely rule society with their reason because they have knowledge about and deliberate well about political matters (*Republic* 4. 428a-429a). But he argues quite clearly that they rule themselves with their intellect. The rational part of their soul ought to rule precisely because it has knowledge. Their reason rules their aggressive instinct, and with their aggressive instinct it rules their appetitive instincts (*Republic* 4. 441e-442b).[1]

He argues further that the guardians act for the sake of their actions themselves. They can attain their happiness solely through performing well their function in society. They do not attain happiness through feasting and drinking (*Republic* 4. 420b-421c). Indeed, they lead a rather lean life. They can possess neither houses nor land (419-420a). Their only property is what is necessary for their function, presumably their armor and weapons, and for their services they receive only room and board. They are forbidden so much as to touch gold or silver (*Republic* 3. 416c-417b).

We find in Plato, then, a source for our hypothesis that political freedom is to have knowledge of political happiness and to act on our knowledge. The philosopher guardians exemplify political liberty of this kind. They possess a principle of political happiness, and they choose to act in accordance with their principle. They know their political function, they choose to fulfill their function, and they fulfill their function for its own sake.[2]

A liberty similar to this kind we also find in the auxiliary guardians, who provide defense for their society. The auxiliaries possess knowledge of a sort, and they possess the power that goes with arms. They do not possess philosophical knowledge concerning their society, but they do possess opinion about what is fearful for their society and what is not. This opinion provides their spirit with the courage needed to fulfill the function of defending their society against its enemies. This courage, Plato explicitly remarks, is political courage (*Republic* 4. 429a–430c).

Unfortunately, we find no liberty among the artisans. Plato implies that the guardians and the auxiliaries must subject the artisans to external constraints. The artisans have knowledge, or more properly opinion, about their crafts and skills (428b–c, e.g.). But their opinion about these abilities does not appear sufficient even for a temperate life. The artisans and their appetites the guardians and auxiliaries must restrain (430c–432a). They apparently lack not only moral virtue but even self-restraint.[3]

Aristotle offers an analysis more explicit and more exacting. But he does not explicitly consider liberty or freedom, either. He does discuss voluntary actions, however, and I shall assume that a voluntary action is a free action. To be sure, he offers a discussion that is not without controversy. His discussion probably occasions controversy because it focuses on nonvoluntary and involuntary actions. Perhaps actions of these sorts he considers more obvious. But his discussion is sufficiently clear for our purpose.

One can say, I think, that Aristotle finds two prerequisites necessary for voluntary action. If we act voluntarily, we must act with knowledge, and we must act from an internal cause, to use his term. We must especially know the principle of our action, he implies. At least, one who acts nonvoluntarily does not have knowledge of what he must do and must not do (*Ethics* 3. 1. 1110b28–30). His choice would appear to be mistaken because he is ignorant of a universal (1110b31–33).[4]

Aristotle also argues that an action can be voluntary only if its cause lies within ourselves (1110a15–18). We must act from an internal cause, in other words. We act under compulsion if our action is the result of an external cause. We hardly act voluntarily, he explains, if we are carried away by kidnappers or by winds (1110a1–4). Indeed, one might wonder whether we would be truly agents, who could be said to act.

This internal cause of voluntary action, I would venture, is our very nature. A nature for Aristotle is precisely an internal cause of motion and rest (*Physics* 2. 1. 192b13–23). That we have a nature, I hope is not a controversial proposition. But our nature can be only our rationality. Our rationality is what distinguishes us from other animals and from plants. Other animals possess a nature of perception and passion, and plants have a nature of nutrition and growth (*Ethics* 1. 7. 1097b33–1098a7).[5]

We can see, too, that our rationality is the source of our happiness. Our rational activity is our function, and within our function resides our goodness, Aristotle argues (*Ethics* 1. 7. 1097b22–33). But our goodness is our happiness. We attain our goodness, he explains, when we perform our function well, and we perform our function well when we engage in an activity in accordance with virtue (1098a7–18). That our happiness is of value for its own sake, he also argues (1097a15–1097b6).

Aristotle leaves little doubt that a citizen can act for the sake of happiness, and by implication that a citizen, if happy, would engage in rational activity. Even an ordinary person, he argues, would agree that a person who is happy must have virtue and engage in virtuous activity (*Politics* 7. 1. 1323a21–1323b29). He continues that a political society, too, is happy when it engages in virtuous activity (1323b29–36a). The only question for him is whether philosophical activity or practical activity is best for a society (*Politics* 7. 3. 1325a16–21). He does not consider productive activity a candidate for political life.

He prefers philosophy, arguing essentially that a philosophical life, which would be a life of theoretical activity, would be best because it is the most final and independent (*Politics* 7. 2. 1325a21–1325b32). But he argues that for most people a practical life would be best. He would appear especially to favor the military activity of the ancient hoplite (*Politics* 3. 7. 1279a39–1279b4). An artisanal life he finds decidedly unvirtuous (*Politics* 7. 9. 1328b39–1329a2).

Aristotle, then, implies that liberty, including political liberty, requires both knowledge and practical ability. We must know what our happiness is, and we must act on our knowledge from an internal cause. A philosopher does when engaged in politics, and a hoplite does when engaged in defense. But an artisan, he thinks, does not.[6]

From these ancient sources we can now see, if we had any doubt, how our liberty depends doubly on our rationality. To be free, we must act in accordance with our rationality, and we must act from our rationality. We also ought to act for the sake of our rationality itself—if we wish to be happy. That is, we ought to use our reason for the sake of its own activity. Our happiness is of reason, by reason, and for reason, we might say, echoing a famous formulation.

This concept of rational freedom, you may have already surmised, we encounter not only in the ancients but also in the moderns. Perhaps a brief reflection on a conspicuous example might be helpful. Immanuel Kant offers a rather similar concept of our goodness. He argues that our will, when it is good, finds its end in its own activity (*Grounding* 1. 394, 396). But our will is nothing other than practical reason, he informs us (*Grounding* 2. 412–413).

Kant argues explicitly and famously that we are free, and that our freedom lies within our rationality. How is our rationality free? He explains that with our reason we can choose to act on a concept of goodness recognized by reason itself (*Grounding* 2. 412–413). This concept is for him the moral law. This law finds expression in its three well-known formulae (421, 429, 430–431).

He also argues that our choice arises from a pure spontaneity. At least one thing in itself is an independent cause, and this one thing is our will, he explains (*Grounding* 3. 452–453). Our reason can be the sole cause of our action without any dependence on an alien cause. Other things are subject to alien causes (446).[7]

The example of Kant, however, might give a philosophical reader pause. Kant thinks that our morality is other than our happiness. He, unfortunately, accepts the view that human happiness is not rational but passional. He thinks that our happiness lies merely in desire and its satisfaction, and he argues that reason is ill-suited for this purpose (*Grounding* 1. 395-396, e.g.).

This difference between the Kantian concept of happiness and the ancient Greek concept I take to be verbal. His concept of a rational activity of value for itself is in its essentials the ancient concept of happiness. The ancient concept of a rational activity the Greeks also distinguish from mere desire satisfaction. Both Plato and Aristotle surely do.

But does not Kant also hold that our moral principle is of a transcendental sort? one might object. That we are aware of the moral law through our reason alone, he insists (*Grounding* 2. 406-412). He famously holds, too, that our spontaneity exists in an intelligible world and not in a sensible world. Only a cause of this eminent kind can operate independently of other causes, he claims (*Grounding* 3. 452-453).

I would argue that we do not need a transcendental principle. An approximation will do. We can employ a moral principle that is hypothetical, and we can act from reason on a hypothetical principle. I would also argue that we can act well without a transcendental spontaneity. We need only distinguish within ourselves a cause internal to us from a cause external to us. We need have only a nature, in a word.

My hypothesis, then? Political liberty is of our reason, by our reason, and for our reason. My assumption? Each of us can be a rational cause of a rational action that is itself an end. I postulate, in other words, that within a political world we can move ourselves, and that we can move ourselves for its own sake. Otherwise, we could not attain any political happiness.

That we can move ourselves, gives us, I might note, a general resemblance to other animals and plants. Aristotle states simply that entities of this kind are myriad (*Physics* 2. 1. 193a3-4). But we can act on knowledge, and other animals and plants cannot. I defer to Kant. We can move ourselves in accordance with a concept of a law, but they move themselves only in accordance with a law (*Grounding* 2. 412-413).

Slavery of the political variety, then, would be ignorance of the requisite knowledge for free action or an inability to act from an internal cause of action. That is to say, political slavery can be nonvoluntary if we act from a false principle or without a principle. Our nonvoluntary action of this kind can arise from a false political theory, I would ask you to note.

Our political slavery can also be involuntary if we are subject to external constraints. These constraints are those external to our reason, and they can lie in our own emotions or in our circumstances. Would it be too much to say that political circumstances can constrain and constrict our liberty both emotionally and materially?

Alexis de Tocqueville takes care to warn us about what he calls an "organized, gentle, and peaceful enslavement" in modern political society (*Democracy* 2. 4. 6. 806). His fear is that people, especially those in a democracy, would give up any bother of thinking about political matters and permit their sphere of free choice to become restricted. They could easily, he argues, become reliant on a government, which by working for their happiness, taken in the hedonic sense, would gradually deprive them of their autonomy (805–806).

Why this fear of despotism? He argues that the people in the modern era do not seek political happiness in any sense, but that they pursue only a private hedonic happiness. They turn in on themselves "in a restless search" for "petty, vulgar, pleasures with which they fill their souls." Each lives solely "in himself and for himself." They too easily lose sight of their political society though they keep their family and friends in sight (805).

We can now see how to allay this fear. People would do well to pursue political happiness in a eudaimonic sense rather than to subordinate political to personal happiness, especially in a passive sense. To know a principle of political happiness and to act on a principle of this kind is not only to participate in a political life with our fellows. A principle of political happiness also enables us to act in concert with our rational and political nature and to insure for ourselves autonomy within a political arena.

Tocqueville himself endorses citizen participation in politics and in social and economic institutions. To curtail government, he advocates the election of regional assemblies, the formation of scientific, political, and commercial associations, and the freedom of the courts and the press (*Democracy* 2. 4. 7. 810–813). He also commends respect for social conventions and for individual rights (813–814).

But, alas, he does not appear to see that these institutions might have a value for their own sake. He finds their origins in our passions. He urges us only to act on a "precautionary fear" rather than to acquiesce in "a feeble and indolent terror." This fear, he explains, those who live in a democratic society would feel because they have a natural "frustration" with regulations and "a natural liking for independence" (818).[8]

I speak of a liberty undoubtedly moral, then. A true political philosophy can only be a moral philosophy. But the moral liberty of which I speak is of a political variety not of a personal sort. The difference between liberties of these kinds lies in what activities we can choose to engage in. We are free politically when we choose actions that are political. That is, when we choose among functions within a society, whether we choose a political function broadly or narrowly conceived.

Personal freedom, by contrast, enables us to choose actions more properly private. These actions are functions within lesser societies, which would include congregations and corporations, fraternities and families, and various other associations and affiliations. They would also include our individual actions.

Human liberty, however, is not absolute, I would remind you. We find ourselves born with a nature not of our choosing into a world not of our making. We are perforce free and yet not free. We can be free because we can have knowledge of our nature and our world and we can be a cause of our actions. But we are not free because we must act under circumstances thrust upon us. We choose neither our nature nor our society. We resemble sailors at sea in a storm, who find themselves obliged to make the best of their plight (see *Ethic* 3. 1. 1110a4–19).

But our liberty, even when political, enables us to perform actions of intrinsic value rather than merely to engage in instrumental actions for the sake of indulging our passions. And with our liberty, mitigated though it is, we can so easily approximate happiness in a political sense!

3. One might think that contemporary philosophers would espouse a similar concept of political liberty. Happiness of the variety that I am advocating would seem to resemble what they often call a meaningful life or, more specifically, a rational plan of life. They would, presumably, advocate liberty of a kind that would enable a person to fulfill a plan of this kind.

We ought to consider, then, how philosophers today define a plan of life, and we ought to compare their concepts with our concept of political happiness garnered from the ancient Greeks. We shall then compare their concepts of liberty with our concept of political liberty gleaned from the Greeks. What we shall find is that their concept of a life plan has consequences for political freedom not unworthy of our attention.

The two philosophers whom I wish to discuss are John Rawls and Robert Nozick. Other contemporary philosophers and also earlier philosophers present theories similar to theirs. But Rawls and Nozick take up positions that are currently very influential inside academia and outside as well. I do not mean to single them out, then. I take them to be paradigmatic both because they present positions influential today, and because they present positions recurrent in theory and practice.

We shall see that both Rawls and Nozick advocate not a eudaimonic polity but an expedient polity. They offer theories of polity that rest not on a principle of happiness but on a democratic principle of liberty and on an oligarchic principle of property. I do not claim that a principle of happiness does not entail principles of liberty and property. It does. But I do contend that a principle of liberty or of property need not entail a principle of happiness. At least, not a eudaimonic principle properly understood.

In the present chapter I wish to consider what democratic principles Rawls and Nozick have to offer. No one could deny that the one philosopher is decidedly liberal, and the other avowedly libertarian. Indeed, one might easily argue that Rawls offers a positive concept of liberty and Nozick a negative concept. Yet we shall soon see that their concepts have much more in common than these common labels might suggest.[9]

We shall begin with John Rawls. Does Rawls espouse a political liberty that we might deem voluntary? Does he advocate liberty of a kind that rests on a knowledge of our rational nature and on a cause internal to our nature? We shall see that he does neither. Liberty on his account assumes that we have knowledge of an activity less than eudaimonic, and that we are prompted to action ultimately by passion. This liberty, so-called, would be both nonvoluntary and involuntary, to use Aristotelian terms.

Rawls does hold the view that human goodness is happiness. But he does not define happiness as a rational activity of intrinsic value. He argues that our good is what "is determined by the most rational long-term plan of life," and that we are happy when we are "more or less successfully in the way of carrying out this plan" (*Theory* 2. 15. 79-80). We can think a person happy, he reiterates, when "in the way of a successful (more or less) execution of a rational plan of life" (*Theory* 7. 63. 359-360).

But a concept of human happiness cannot be a concept of a plan. A concept of happiness resembles that of a plan in one sense. It is a concept of an activity. But in another sense a concept of happiness does not resemble that of a plan. It is a concept of an activity that has an intrinsic value, and that we fulfill for its own sake. A concept of this kind would be of a political function in a large sense. It would include not only what we customarily take to be a political function, such as voting or holding office, but also engaging in a profession or an occupation.

A concept of a plan is an action not of intrinsic value but of instrumental value. Any plan is an activity that is a means to an end other than itself. We fulfill a plan, even a plan of life, not primarily for the sake of itself but rather for the sake of something else. This something else is too commonly the acquisition of property or the procurement of pleasure.

We might ask, though, What purpose does a rational plan have? Is its purpose our happiness? Rawls does assert that our good is "the satisfaction of rational desire." But a rational desire, he indicates, does not take for its end a rational activity. A desire of this kind finds its end in satisfaction. A rational desire is simply a rational plan, and a rational plan permits a "harmonious satisfaction" of our "interests." That is, a plan of this sort is merely a way to schedule our activities so that our "various desires can be fulfilled without interference" from one another (*Theory* 2. 15. 79–80; 3. 63. 360–364).

One can see already that Rawls is advocating desire of a kind not essentially rational but merely passional. He implies that what he calls a rational desire has for its purpose not a rational activity but an irrational passivity. He in effect advocates what one might call, paradoxically perhaps, restrained unrestraint. We use our reason to restrain our various passional desires but only so that we may the better satisfy them. We leave our passional desires unrestrained in that they determine our ends.[10]

One might wonder, then, Does the Rawlsian concept of our goodness inform his political theory, specifically his concept of liberty? I must answer that it does. The concept of a rational plan Rawls assumes in what he calls the original position. The original position, my reader may be aware, is a hypothetical situation in which persons choose principles of justice for their society (*Theory* 1. 3. 10). The principles chosen "assign basic rights and duties" and "determine the division of social benefits" (10–11).

The original position relies on assumptions about the persons who select principles of justice. This situation assumes that the persons are free and rational, and that they are concerned only with their own interest (*Theory* 1. 3. 10). Rawls explains that they have the rationality "standard in economic theory." That is, their rationality is of means and ends only. When he states that they are concerned with their own interest, he means that they are "mutually disinterested." They do not take an interest in the interests of each other (*Theory* 1. 3. 12; also 3. 22. 112).

He further explains that the persons in the original position are free because they have "fundamental aims and interests" in designing their society. They have a "highest-order interest" in how their social institutions shape their other interests. They are "beings who can revise and alter their final ends and who give first priority to preserving their liberty in these matters." They do not care to bind themselves to any particular interest, but they do want to be able to advance their interest (*Theory* 1. 26. 131–132; 3. 82. 475–476).

These persons are also behind what Rawls famously calls a veil of ignorance. They do not know what they conceive to be their own particular good, nor do they know their social position or their natural ability. Their ignorance about these matters, he argues, precludes them from seeking principles skewed to their own advantage because of contingencies either social or natural (*Theory* 1. 3. 11; 1. 4. 16–17; and 3. 24.).

But the persons in the original position, though they do not know its details, do know that they have a plan of life. Rawls explicitly states that they have a concept of their good (*Theory* 1. 4. 17). He also explains that their good is a rational long-term plan (*Theory* 3. 22. 111-112). The rationality of their plan entails that they want more rather than fewer of what he calls primary goods. They wish "to protect their liberties, widen their opportunities, and enlarge their means" to promote their plans (*Theory* 3. 25. 123). A plan of this kind enables them to satisfy more desires rather than fewer, he reiterates (123–124).[11]

Rawls, then, rests his theory of justice on assumptions about persons who choose principles of justice. He assumes that the persons in the original position have a rationality of means and ends; they have a rational plan of life but do not know its details; they take no interest in one another; and, more importantly for our purpose, they are free.[12]

I would now ask, How free are the persons in the original position? We are obliged to conclude, I think, that the persons choosing principles of justice cannot be voluntary agents. They act nonvoluntarily because they base their actions on a false conception of our goodness. They are unaware of what eudaimonic happiness is, and they know only a concept of plan of life. Their concept of goodness is not rational, even if they are able to revise it, because their life plan takes primarily for its aim desire satisfaction.

These persons also act involuntary because they do not act on a cause internal to their rational nature. They act on their passion, which is a cause external to their rationality. They obviously do not perform a rational activity that is an end in itself. They instead engage in a rational activity that is a means to other ends. Their proximate end is the possession of primary goods, but their ultimate end the satisfaction of their desires.[13]

But perhaps we should consider the political society that the persons in the original position establish with their principles of justice. Rawls explains that after they select them, these persons use their principles to establish a constitution for their society and to formulate their laws (*Theory* 1. 3. 10, 11–12). We might find that the liberty in the society established with their principles takes for its end a rational activity of intrinsic worth.

What principles of justice, then, do the persons in the original position choose? Rawls argues that they would decide in favor of two principles. The one principle he calls the principle of equal liberty, and the other is what he calls the difference principle. The difference principle is not our present concern. This principle pertains to an unequal distribution of social and economic benefits (*Theory* 1. 3. 13–14).[14]

Our present concern is the principle of equal liberty. This principle states that we ought to have "equality in the assignment of basic rights and duties" (*Theory* 1. 3. 13–14; also 5. 46. 266). Rawls stresses the importance of the principle. Our liberties are "inviolable," he declares (*Theory* 1. 1. 3–4). The principle of liberty also has priority over his difference principle, concerned with social and economic benefits. Equal liberty, he is wont to reiterate, cannot be compromised for any benefits of these other kinds (*Theory* 1. 1. 3–4; 2. 11. 53–54, 55; 3. 26. 132; 4. 39. esp.; and 5. 46. 266).

One might think the equal liberty principle would define political roles. And it would seem to do so. The equal liberty principle defines the liberties of citizenship commonly understood. They include, for example, freedom to participate in political life by voting or by holding office and freedom of speech and of assembly. They also include freedom of conscience and thought, freedom from oppression and assault, freedom to possess property, and freedom from arbitrary detention or forfeiture (*Theory* 2. 11. 53).

Our question becomes, then, Do these liberties enable one to engage in political activities as ends in themselves? That they might do so, is not likely. For what purpose would one exercise a right to vote and to hold office? The principles of justice, Rawls continues, are meant, through basic social institutions, to distribute primary goods, and these goods are of use for advancing a rational plan of life (*Theory* 2. 11. 54–55). The liberties of citizenship would thus serve to secure more rather than fewer primary goods and to procure more rather than less desire satisfaction.

Perhaps liberty of speech and assembly or liberty of conscience and thought might underlie a political role of intrinsic value. Freedoms of these kinds can obviously serve a public function. But these freedoms, too, appear to be essentially for the sake of life plans. Rawls argues, for example, that freedom of conscience includes freedom to pursue religious, philosophical, or moral interests (*Theory* 4. 32. 177–178). But these freedoms guarantee merely matters of personal commitment, he explains (*Theory* 4. 33. 180–183).[15]

I would observe that political liberty in this sense, even if it were properly conceived, would be only one political freedom in a larger sense. Political liberty of this kind is the freedom to vote and to hold public office and the freedom to speak and to assemble. These are important liberties, to be sure. But other political activities are not under consideration. Philosophical freedoms might fall under freedom of speech and assembly, but martial freedoms and artisanal freedoms receive no mention.

We arrive at the same conclusion, then. Rawls offers a concept of political liberty that is nonvoluntary and involuntary. On his theory we exercise of our liberty of citizenship for the sake of our rational plans, which have the aim of satisfying our desire. We thus have no genuine political principle, and we most likely act from a passional cause.[16]

But a reader tutored in political philosophy might object. Does Rawls not contend that he gives priority to the right over the good? He would consequently not seem to commit his theory to any concept of goodness. I admit that he claims to do so. Rawls argues that a theory that gives priority to the good would be teleological. It would define the good independently of what is right, and it would suppose that the right maximizes the good. Rawls explains that his theory is not teleological, and that it defines the right independently of what is good (*Theory* 1. 5. 22).

But if we are to grasp his position, we must not fail to distinguish what is good in a general sense and in a specific sense. In a general sense, our good is a plan of life, and our plan of life has the end of satisfying desire. That is why the persons in the original position prefer more rather than fewer primary goods. In a specific sense, our good would be to satisfy particular desires of our own and our preference would be to garner particular primary goods for ourselves.

Rawls does not give priority to the right over the good in a general sense. He explicitly assumes that those who are in the original position have a plan of life and a preference for more rather than fewer primary goods. He gives priority to the right over the good only in a specific sense. Those in the original position choose the principles of justice to attain eventually whatever particular goods they might seek. These particulars only are subject to the veil of ignorance.[17]

My reader might harbor another objection. Rawls especially defends his concept of liberty by arguing that his concept expresses our nature as both free and rational. He argues that the theory is amenable to a Kantian interpretation. The veil of ignorance assures that persons in the original position act autonomously on the basis of their free and rational nature. They cannot act heteronomously, he argues, because the veil precludes any possibility that they might select principles on the basis of their "social position or natural endowments" (*Theory* 4. 40. 222).

I must answer that the persons in the original position do act heteronomously. The veil of ignorance does not preclude that the persons who decide on principles of justice act out of self-interest, unfortunately. The veil only limits their self-interest to the general knowledge that they seek satisfy their desires. The persons know that they wish to satisfy desire, and they desire primary goods, which are "rational to want whatever else one wants" (222-223). The veil excludes self-interest only about what particular desires they might seek to satisfy.[18]

We can now see that Rawls offers a principle of equal liberty that combines liberty of two kinds. These two kinds Aristotle expounds for us. The hypothesis of a democracy, Aristotle reminds us, is the concept of liberty. Liberty may mean for all to rule and to be ruled in turn. This concept implies that all are equal. Or liberty may mean for each to live as he or she wishes. This concept implies that one ought to be ruled by no one. But to be ruled by no one is hardly possible, and so again all rule by turns (*Politics* 6. 2. 1317a40–1317b17).

The Rawlsian principle of equal liberty entails both these concepts of ancient liberty. This principle clearly implies that all are equal, and it implies that all rule and are ruled, or at least could rule and be ruled, by turns. The principle especially guarantees the equal liberty of voting and of holding office. It also guarantees ancillary liberties, such as those of speech and assembly, which would seem to support egalitarian rule.

But the Rawlsian principle would seem to guarantee these liberties so that people can do as they please. The liberty of citizenship essentially enshrines the concept of living as one might wish. Its ultimate aim is to enable a person to acquire more rather than fewer primary goods, and these goods in turn enable one to have more rather than less desire satisfaction.

Perhaps Aristotle is right to argue that these two principles of liberty define two different constitutions. To subordinate the liberty of citizenship to personal liberty is essentially to advocate a democratic principle to do as you please.

I am advocating a eudaimonic polity in an ancient sense of the word. A polity of this kind constitutes a political society of men and women who engage in political activity for its own sake. They are free and rational because their political activity is a rational activity of value for itself. This polity is a society of persons who have the liberty to aim at political happiness, in a word. Their happiness today, I would argue, ought to be of an artisanal variety.

Rawls argues for polity in an ancient sense, too. But he advocates a polity that cannot be eudaimonic. His polity is an expedient mix of democracy and, we shall see, of oligarchy. The democratic element, we already see, is less than felicitous. His concept of liberty is not for the sake of an activity intrinsically rational but for the sake of an instrumental activity essentially passional.

Liberty for Rawls, then, does not enable one to fulfill a political role in a society for its own sake. Liberty only enables one ultimately to attain desire satisfaction for oneself. Its function is to exploit a political society for the sake of personal pleasure.

4. We shall now turn to Robert Nozick. Nozick, too, might initially seem to advocate a concept of liberty very similar to our own. But Nozick and Rawls will turn out to be philosophical bedfellows. Despite their salient specific differences, they yet share general assumptions about our rational and political selves that are all but the same.

Nozick advocates a concept of polity quite similar to the Rawlsian concept. His polity is not a eudaimonic but a mixed polity, and it also rests on principles of democracy and oligarchy albeit defined differently. I now shall consider what democratic principle Nozick has to offer. We shall see that his principle of liberty is fundamentally the same as that of Rawls though his particular formulation is quite different. What I mean is that his principle aims at the same end though it works through different means.

Nozick might seem to advance a concept of goodness similar to the ancient concept of happiness. He does not assert that we have a rational desire, but he does, as does Rawls, advocate what is rather obviously a plan of life. He argues that we can give our life meaning if we can guide our life "in accordance with some overall concept." We need to formulate long-term plans of life, to make decisions on the basis of abstract concepts, apparently of a life plan, and to limit our behavior accordingly (*Anarchy* 3. 49–50).

The abilities needed for a long-term plan of life would seem to be prerequisites for a happy life. These abilities, Nozick states succinctly, are rationality, free will, and moral agency. Our rationality apparently enables us to formulate a plan, our will to decide on the basis of our plan, and our agency to carry out our plan (48–50). To be happy, we would also need to formulate a concept of happiness, to choose on the basis our concept, and to act upon our concept.

Can we, then, be happy when we have a long-term plan? Human happiness, you may perchance recall, is a rational activity of intrinsic value. This concept of happiness is a concept of an activity, but it is a concept of an activity primarily an end in itself. But a plan is obviously a concept of an activity primarily of instrumental value. A whimsical person, I suppose, might enjoy formulating quirky plans and carrying them out for fun. But for persons with less whimsy a plan does not commonly have an end internal to it but only an external end.[19]

Nor does Nozick specify what the end of a long-term plan for our life might be. Rawls thinks that our end ultimately lies in our satisfaction of desire. A plan of life for Nozick does not appear to have any positive content. He does not care to discuss our nature and its function, either. He does not even indicate that we have a nature, as far as

I am aware. He would almost appear to assume implicitly a Rawlsian veil of ignorance. We are not offered any specifics for a life plan.

Why does Nozick not indicate any content, if only general, for a plan of life? That we have plan is apparently more important for Nozick than what our plan might be. Our plan for him constitutes the very meaning of our life. But its value for political theory has no positive significance. Its significance is only negative. A plan of life merely provides a basis for not being harmed. This consideration is explicitly why Nozick discusses a life plan (*Anarchy* 1. 3. 48, 50–51).

Nozick, then, advances a political theory that does not appear to grant us any surety of political liberty worthy of the name. He does not trouble himself to define a principle for our action. He does not care to take up the concept of what, if any, function we might have. But we can act voluntarily only if we chose to follow a principle. I am arguing that a principle of happiness would serve us well. It defines for us a function at once rational and political.

Nozick might seem to assert that we can act from an internal cause. He clearly asserts that we have free will, and he implies that we can act autonomously. But he explicitly does not care to define what a free will might be or what an autonomous action might be (*Anarchy* 1. 3. 48–49). He is content to argue only that we possess an ability to shape our life and to give it meaning (50–51).

I would wonder, Can we act from an internal cause if we have no definite principle of action? If we act without a principle, are we more likely to act from reason or from passion? I should think that, if we are unprincipled, we would most likely possess a cause of action that is but passional. But a passional cause, if we are essentially rational beings, would be external to our nature.

We ought now to ask whether Nozick allows his nonchalant attitude about principle to inform his political philosophy. Nozick takes his beginning for political theory to be a state of nature. This concept he borrows from John Locke. Quoting Locke, he informs us that in a natural state persons have "perfect freedom to order their actions and dispose of their possessions and persons as they think fit." But this perfect freedom has its bounds, and these bounds a law of nature determines. This law requires that no one "harm another in his life, health, liberty, or property" (*Anarchy* 1. 2. 10).

What is perfect freedom, then? Nozick does not say, nor, apparently, does he care to say. He would appear to think our freedom perfect because, still quoting Locke, one may engage in an activity "without asking leave or dependency upon the will of any other man." He may also deem our freedom perfect because our activity apparently need not conform to a principle of any kind or to a nature of any kind. Individuals may do with their persons and property "as they think fit" (10).

Is perfect freedom voluntary? Do we act with knowledge in a state of nature? The sole principle of action explicitly stated is the law of nature. But this principle is negative. The principle is not one that prescribes any action for oneself. Rather, it proscribes any action harmful to another. The law of nature is less a freedom to act than a freedom not to be acted upon. It requires that no one be harmed in their life, health, liberty, or property, not even ourselves presumably.

Apparently, one could advance a plan of life. But a rational plan of life for Nozick need not entail acting on a principle of action with intrinsic value. A person would thus be free to use this natural freedom for purposes other than happiness in the ancient sense. Without a principle one would more likely than not engage in nonvoluntary action, I would think. Admittedly, one could follow a eudaimonic principle. But a principle of this kind Nozick clearly does not take for the basis of his theory.

Would one act from an internal cause? Nozick does not require that we act from reason, and he would appear to assume that we most likely would not. His concern is primarily not with those who follow reason but with those who follow passion. He observes that persons do not always conform their actions to the law of nature, nor do they enforce the law in an appropriate manner. Their passions can especially carry them away when they punish others (*Anarchy* 1. 2. 10, 11–12).

Nozick, then, offers a concept of liberty that he does not specify to be voluntary. He expounds no principle of action other than an indefinite instrumental one. His concern is rather with nonvoluntary and involuntary actions that might harm one. These actions are those which violate the law of nature in their transgression or in their enforcement.

Perhaps we ought now to consider what Nozick has to say about a political society. Does his concept of liberty in a state of nature inform his concept of political liberty? Or is political liberty of a kind other than the perfect liberty, so-called, in a state of nature? Perhaps liberty within a political state can enable us to pursue political happiness.

How does a political state arise? Persons in a state of nature create a political state, Nozick argues. But they do not simply meet together and decide to form a state. He differs explicitly from Locke on this point. But he does recognize, quoting Locke again, a state arises from the fact that we each "may make satisfaction for the harm" that we suffer from those who violate the law of nature (*Anarchy* 1. 2. 10–11). Those in a state of nature develop a political state through their attempts to rectify violations of the natural law.

In their efforts to take satisfaction, persons in a state of nature soon band together into what Nozick calls a protective association. Those who attempt to enforce the law of nature by themselves are subject to "inconveniences," he argues, agreeing yet again with Locke. These inconveniences are well known. They are that the law of nature does not cover every contingency, that we apply the law more favorably in our own case, and that we may lack the power to enforce the law (11–12).

People join together in a protective association and attempt to overcome these inconveniences by assisting one another with their enforcement activities. The members of a protective association are originally volunteers, and they may have varied motives, from being "public spirited" to acting "in exchange for something," Nozick explains. But these members soon discover that a protective association has inconveniences of its own. They find themselves always on call, and they are at the call of anyone who feels aggrieved (12–13).

The members of an association then decide to hire persons to perform their enforcement functions for them. By so doing they free themselves from always having to be on call for assistance. They also establish procedures to evaluate claims for protective services from people who feel that they have in some way been harmed and, presumably, to determine how to redress bona fide claims of harm (13).

But a protective association cannot long endure. Out of protective association arises what Nozick calls an ultraminimal state. There is another inconvenience apparently. Persons in a state of nature, he argues, are likely to form several protective associations, and these associations are likely to come into conflict. In this conflict one association, or a federation, eventually becomes dominant. The dominant association comes to have a monopoly on the use of force (*Anarchy* 1. 2. 15–17).

An ultraminimal state arises when the dominant association begins to flex its muscle (*Anarchy* 1. 3. 26–27). Persons who are not its members may attempt to defend themselves against its members with unreliable enforcement procedures. These procedures obviously entail risks of harm. With its monopoly on force the dominant association can prevent these persons from defending themselves in a risky manner. And prevent them it does until and unless their procedures are known to be reliable (*Anarchy* 1. 5. 88–89, 101–103, 108–109, 118–119).[20]

But we learn that an ultraminimal state, too, is short-lived. This state finds that it has a moral obligation to protect everyone who interacts with its members even if they do not pay for its services. Because it denies them their right of defending themselves against its members, it has a moral obligation to compensate those who are not members, Nozick argues (*Anarchy* 1. 5. 113–114, 114–115, 119). The least expensive and most convenient compensation, he concludes, is for it to provide for their defense against its members (110–113).[21]

A political state for Nozick becomes, then, a minimal state. This state he identifies with the night-watchman state familiar in modern political philosophy (*Anarchy* 1. 2. 25; 1. 3. 26–27). It has a monopoly on the use of force. Or, at least, it has a practicable approximation to a monopoly. It also provides protection for all persons within its territory. Or, at least, for its members and for all who interact with its members (*Anarchy* 1. 5. 113–118).[22]

An ultraminimal state, too, has a monopoly on the use of force (*Anarchy* 1. 3. 26–27). In this aspect it is similar to a minimal state (see *Anarchy* 1. 2. 23–24). But an ultraminimal state protects only those who pay for its services. It does not protect those who do not pay even if they have a grievance against a paying member (*Anarchy* 1. 3. 26–27). A protective association neither has a monopoly on the use of force, nor does it protect those who do not pay (*Anarchy* 1. 2. 22–25; 1. 3. 51).

We see, then, that a protective association, a dominant protective association, an ultraminimal state, and a minimal state all rest on the law of nature. Nozick bases his political theory on an examination of hypothetical arrangements contrived within a state of nature to enforce its law. These arrangements and their inconveniences are what occasion the development of a protective association into a minimal state, he suggests (*Anarchy* 1. 2. 10–11).[23]

Could one find happiness in a minimal state, then? Perhaps we ought to ask, Who, if anyone, would possess political liberty in a minimal state? Who are, in a word, its citizens? Nozick, curiously, does not discuss any freedom properly political. At least, I cannot see that he does. He apparently does not do so because his minimal state has no citizens. This state comprises only those persons who hire other persons to protect them.[24]

Nor is the function of protection a proper political function. There are no new rights in a political state, Nozick argues. Each person possesses a right of self-defense before any state comes into existence (*Anarchy* 1. 5. 88–90; also 108–109, e.g., or 118). An ultraminimal state is simply the sole entity whose agents have, though delegation, the de facto power to exercise this right even though every one has the right de jure. A minimal state arises from an ultraminimal state only because it is obliged to use its de facto power to protect those who do not pay for its services (118–119).

Could those, then, who exercise the right of self-defense be happy? They quite possibly could. A minimal state has the end of self-defense, and self-defense is an activity that can have value for its own sake. A martial activity can have intrinsic value. Plato recognizes its intrinsic value in his auxiliary guardians, though he does not think it the end of his political society. An activity of this kind Aristotle argues ought to be the end of a polity. He favors the heavy infantry and its defensive activity.

But Nozick does not consider the possibility that one might find happiness in martial activities. The persons who might seem to fulfill a eudaimonic function in his minimal state are the persons who are protective agents. These persons the members of a minimal state hire. But they would appear to have a function without intrinsic value. Their function is primarily to protect those who hire them.

Nozick is concerned only to augment a natural right of self-defense. He does not argue that those who engage in self-defense find that their activity constitutes their meaning of life. Self-defense apparently remains for them an instrumental activity. The protective agents take for their purpose to enforce the law of nature and to protect life, health, liberty, and property. This they do by enforcing restraints and by seeking reparations.

Those who perform this activity would appear to be no more than mercenaries. The protective agents are not likely to pursue their activity as an end in itself because they are mere hirelings, who work for wages. Admittedly, they might possibly pursue their work as an end in itself. But that they might do so Nozick does not take into consideration.

What kind of liberty would one find in a minimal state, then? Unfortunately, we do not find any voluntary action but only nonvoluntary action. The persons in a minimal state possess no concept of happiness. The law of nature does define a natural liberty, but its liberty is not positive but negative. The natural law has the function of ensuring that we do not suffer harm at the hands of others. Is the fulfillment of this function through hirelings happiness? How could it be?

But could natural liberty of this kind have its end in an activity constituting happiness? Unfortunately, this liberty finds its purpose in a liberty to do as one pleases. The law of nature prevents us from being harmed so that we may pursue a plan of life. Though it possibly could, our plan of life need not rest on a concept of happiness. The law of nature requires us only to place a side-constraint on our actions (see *Anarchy* 1. 3. 28–30).

We arrive, again, at a restrained unrestraint. Persons are restrained because they must not harm one another when they devise and implement their plan. They are unrestrained because their life plan most likely has an end determined by their passional desires.

Nor are those living in a minimal state likely to act from an internal cause. They are more likely prompted by an external cause to join a protective association. They are less likely to act from reason than from passion. In particular they would appear to act out of fear. Indeed, Nozick offers an extensive analysis of potential risks and resultant fears to justify a minimal state and its monopoly on force and its use (*Anarchy* 1. 4.).

Freedom from harm is surely necessary for happiness, whether political or personal. But freedom of this kind hardly suffices. The persons who pay for protection have the liberty to pursue happiness. But not all those who are free from harm are happy.

Nozick claims that he is following Immanuel Kant with his theory of political constraint. Kant argues that individuals cannot be used as mere means, he explains. The categorical imperative in its second formulation states that persons are ends and not mere means. We cannot, he concludes, act against an end that they would choose (*Anarchy* 3. 30–32). But political philosophy concerns only "*certain* ways that persons may not use others. Primarily, it concerns physical aggression against them." These constraints against aggression, he continues, are inviolable (32–33, his italics).

Kant would surely object to this interpretation of his categorical imperative. The second formulation concerns our rational nature, he argues, and not merely an end that we might choose. Our rational nature, and presumably its activity, exists as an end in itself (*Grounding* 2. 428–429). We cannot, then, act against the rational nature of another. This prohibition is inviolable. Whether or not a person would choose an end, is not at issue.[25]

Nor are our violations limited to physical coercion. We may violate the rational nature of another with a false promise, for example (429–430). I suspect, too, that we may also violate the rational nature both of ourselves and of others with a false political principle.[26]

We can now see that Nozick, too, offers a mixed polity with two democratic principles. These principles of liberty both have their origin in the state of nature. The state of nature has within it a law of nature. This law is a principle of natural liberty that implies equality and, we may say, rule by turns. It clearly applies equally to everyone, and everyone can in turn enforce it.

But for Nozick the law ultimately provides a foundation for a night-watchman state. Individuals within a society can delegate their right to enforce the law of nature to others. The upshot is a liberty not political, strictly speaking, but a liberty more properly personal and one exercised by proxy.

The state of nature also provides a perfect freedom. The night-watchman state enables us to enjoy an unhindered personal liberty to do as we see fit. When we act, we need not ask leave of anyone. This liberty Nozick elaborates with his concept of a plan of life. We are free to formulate a life plan for ourselves, and we are free to follow our plan. And our plan enables us to do what we please.

Nozick, then, has a theory of polity essentially the same as the Rawlsian. His political society is a polity of expediency. True, Nozick does not offer a positive concept but only a negative concept of political freedom. But much as the principle of equal liberty serves for Rawls as a means to a personal freedom to do as we wish, so the law of nature and its political outgrowths serve for Nozick as a means to a personal freedom to do as we wish.

5. Political liberty is of two kinds. These kinds the ancient philosophers deem to be liberty proper and mere license. Liberty of either kind we can find in a polity. A

eudaimonic polity, I argue, rests on a liberty proper to political society. Its liberty gives us a potential to attain political happiness. We can fulfill this potential if we permit ourselves to act with knowledge of a moral principle, which is a concept of our political role, and if we permit ourselves to act from an internal cause, which is our rationality itself.

A polity of expediency rests on political license. A polity of this kind does not secure any political liberty with a potential for happiness. Its political liberty essentially takes for its end personal liberty. An expedient polity provides persons with a liberty to do what they please. What they please to do is most often to acquire property in a quantity more than sufficient to procure pleasure for themselves in various and sundry forms.

We can now see that Rawls and Nozick, unfortunately, defend a polity of license. Both philosophers advocate liberties of two kinds. They advocate what they take to be a political liberty, and they argue that liberty of this kind is inviolable. Rawls specifically recognizes a liberty of citizenship that includes, among others, the right to vote and to hold office. Nozick recognizes a liberty that is merely a right not to be harmed.

But Rawls and Nozick compromise any possible political happiness for the sake of an unworthy personal liberty. They do not advance a liberty properly political. Their concepts of liberty provide not for voluntary action but only for nonvoluntary action. They do not rest their political theories on a principle truly moral. They do not offer a concept of rational happiness but only a concept of passional happiness.

Nor do Rawls and Nozick see that our action can have an internal cause. They do not argue that we are essentially rational animals, nor do they argue that our rationality has value in itself. They assume that human rationality has value only for the sake of satisfying desire, which for them is passional.

They in effect advocate an akratic polity. Political liberty in their theories is for the sake of personal liberty, but personal liberty is for the sake of desire satisfaction. Their polity in effect enshrines political slavery. Citizens in a polity of the Rawlsian or Nozickian variety are enslaved to ignorance and instinct. They act on false principles at the prompting of passion.

Alexis de Tocqueville, then, would appear to offer an accurate appraisal of American democracy. If we may assume that contemporary political philosophy has a reflection in contemporary political society. A Rawlsian or a Nozickian polity is and can only be a naïve and infantile society. A polity of either kind denies us a political liberty resting on our rational and political nature. It offers instead political liberties essentially democratic in a pejorative sense. Its political liberty is for the sake of a personal liberty to pursue puerile pleasures.[27]

We perforce begin our lives in a political society, and we must initially act both nonvoluntarily and involuntarily. Yet we can develop a capacity to act in a voluntary manner if we are of a mind so to do. Our nature is both rational and political. We can, if we so desire, discover principles both rational and political, and we can, if we so endeavor, engage in action on these principles for its own sake. We can, in a word, strive to attain political happiness.

But we must acknowledge that our nature also keeps us from performing actions absolutely voluntary. We remain, after all is said and done, not divine but human beings. Our knowledge of principles and our ability to guide our actions with principles is decidedly finite. We can possess only a freedom less than absolute, but with a less than absolute freedom we can pursue a happiness less than absolute. We can formulate principles as best we can, and we act on our principles as best we can for the sake of our action itself.

4

Rightness and Fairness

1. We humans have an obvious need for resources if we are to live well. That is, if we are to be happy. Our political life is no exception. To live a political life well, we must also have the requisite means to perform the activities appropriate to our place within a society. A philosopher must have books and leisure at least, if not pen and paper or perhaps a computer; a general needs troops and matériel; a baker or brewer needs kettles, utensils, and ingredients.

We must, indeed, have resources if we are simply to live within a political society. The prerequisites for mere life are obviously food, clothing, and shelter. Without these bare essentials, or with them in short supply, we can merely eke out a life that is at best little more than nasty, brutish, and short, to paraphrase a modern political thinker.

These felicitous or necessitous resources, when possessed by ourselves or others, we more commonly take to be property. The question we now face is, How ought we to distribute property within a political society? What property ought people to have? The answer is obvious, I should think. At least, in its general formulation it is. A person ought to have property of appropriate quality and quantity to enable him or her to pursue happiness.

Again, I am limiting my inquiry to happiness in a political sense only. Our present concern is to determine what resources one might require to fulfill a function within society. What property one ought to have to attain personal happiness is a worthy but distinct question.

Any question about property is bound to hearken back to an ancient conversation. This conversation presents a fundamental distinction pertaining to property and its distribution. Plato portrays the conversation in a short dialogue between Socrates and Gorgias. In the dialogue Gorgias appears with two followers, who serve him for impromptu seconds. Our present interest concerns Callicles, who is the more experienced and more practiced follower.

Readers familiar with the dialogue will no doubt recall that Callicles recognizes justice of two kinds. Justice, he implies, is either natural or contractual, and these kinds are opposed to one another (*Gorgias* 482e). Justice by nature is that those who are more capable ought to rule those less capable, and that the more capable ought to have more than the less capable. This fact is abundantly clear, he informs us. The ancient Persian kings Darius and Xerxes present obvious examples (483c–e).

By contract justice is that those who are less capable ought to rule those more capable, and that the less capable ought to have, if not more, then at least an equal share of property. Those with less ability, Callicles argues, establish laws for the sake of themselves and their interests. But because they are inferior, the less able do not demand a larger share but allow themselves to be content with an equal share (483b–c).

I would point out that Callicles recognizes essentially one political function though he implicitly divides it into two kinds. The difference between these kinds is one not of quality but of quantity. The function is acquisition, and it differs with regard to how much one can acquire. Natural justice allows those who are more able to have more property, and those less able less property. But contractual justice requires the more and the less able to have an equal amount.

The positions outlined by Callicles we can easily espy in political philosophy today though the incidentals have changed. I intend to show that John Rawls and Robert Nozick take positions strikingly similar to those set forth by Callicles though neither philosopher mentions this ancient sophist. Rawls and Nozick do, I am obliged to note, present philosophies more refined and sophisticated than does Callicles. As Plato portrays him, Callicles appears to be a rather harsh character, almost a caricature.

Nozick surely favors justice by nature. He begins with a state of nature and its law of nature. The law of nature, I grant, does not explicitly assert that those who are more capable ought to acquire more property than those less capable. But this law does not prohibit those more capable from acquiring more than the less capable. The law permits a person to acquire as much property as he or she is able, and it prohibits one only from taking property already acquired by another.

Rawls clearly advocates a theory of contractual justice. But his contractual theory is more compromising and less radical than that which Callicles offers. He considers the possibility that property ought to be divided equally. But he argues in favor of dividing property unequally. His distributive principle permits those more able to have more than an equal share though less than they might have had, and it gives those less able a share less than equal though more than they might have had.

What are we to make of this sophistical strain in contemporary political thought? I shall respond again by availing myself of resources bequeathed to us by the ancient philosophers. I turn once more to Plato and Aristotle. Socrates himself replies to Callicles with a lengthy argument. But his argument in its details need not concern us. He concludes that natural law, despite objections from Callicles, provides a foundation for justice and happiness, and that justice and other virtues enable us to be happy (*Gorgias* 506c–508a).

I shall accept the Socratic position that justice ought to enable us to attain happiness. But I shall differ from both Plato and Aristotle in advocating not a philosophical or a martial happiness of the political variety. I am advocating instead an artisanal happiness. Fewer people can attain philosophical or martial happiness than the artisanal variety, and yet artisanal happiness retains the advantages of the philosophical or the martial.

I would observe, though, that the controversy between natural and contractual justice has its origin in our concept of human nature. If we hold, rightly I think, that our nature is rational, we need find no opposition between natural and conventional law. Natural law for us can only be rational, and rational law can provide a basis for cooperation with one another.

But we find an opposition between natural and conventional law if we think our nature passional. Our nature would require us to satisfy our passions, and the more the better. But their satisfaction can quickly lead us into conflict with each other. And so one must then invoke conventional law to restrain natural law, so-called, and to limit our conflict.

2. I would now draw your attention to a paradox too often overlooked in contemporary political philosophy and implicit in the ancient discussion between Socrates and Callicles. The paradox is that an action need not be right and yet it can be fair. Put more pointedly, the paradox would be that an action can be wrong and yet be fair!

This paradox, as do all, turns on the ambiguity of a word. The ambiguity in question, now for the most part forgotten, lies in the word "justice." "Justice" can mean both what is right as well as what is fair. What is right and what is fair can be in accord with each other, but they can also be in conflict with each other. I wish to suggest that rightness and fairness come into conflict when rightness is forgotten and its prerogatives neglected. Fairness then becomes usurpacious.

Justice, I shall presume, ought to aim at what is right. What is right, I would argue, ought to aim at our happiness. My argument for this proposition need not detain us long. What is right ought to promote our goodness, and our goodness is our happiness. We have by now established that it is, I hope. I would conclude, therefore, that rightness ought to aim at human happiness. What, then, is our happiness? Happiness, you may perchance recall, is a rational activity of worth primarily for its own sake even if the activity is political.

What is fair concerns the distribution of things deemed to be good and the rectification of their maldistributions. But what goods can we distribute? Can our happiness be distributed? Not likely if happiness is an activity. Our happiness consists solely in actions that we must ourselves choose to perform and choose to perform for their own sake. What we can distribute are goods of the body, such as health, and material goods, such as wealth. These goods are the means to our happiness. Or, rather, they ought to be but are not always taken to be.

One can see already how rightness and fairness can be either in concord or in discord. We can, indeed we ought to, distribute goods, such as health and wealth, in a manner that promotes our happiness. We ought to do so both to those who are able to be happy and to those who have a potential to be able, so to speak. To those who are able we can allocate employment and appointments. To those with a potential we can allot education and training.

But we can also distribute these goods in a way that does not promote our happiness. Distributions of this infelicitous sort can even hamper and hinder happiness. What is right and what is fair then clash. We neglect happiness and allow political principles, so-called, other than happiness to come to the fore. The usual usurpacious principles are those of an often less than refined pursuit of property or pleasure.

With this conflict arises our present paradox that justice can be wrong and yet fair. We may find our very nature denied and denigrated if we are subject to covenants or contracts contrary to it. I assume that human happiness is the fulfillment of our rational function, and that our rational function we by nature possess. We are rational animals, in other words. But human contract and convention can fulfill functions less than rational when they provide primarily for the production of wealth or for its consumption.

The distinction between rightness and fairness I have acquired from the ancient Greek philosophers. Plato deployed this distinction without using these precise terms, and after him Aristotle took up the distinction and used terms more similar to our own. Yet neither Plato nor Aristotle offers an analysis as complete and as explicit as one might wish. But their analyses do complement one another, and, taken together, they allow us to discern more clearly the distinction as well as its consequences.

This distinction underlies the difference between polities of a eudaimonic kind and of an expedient kind. A eudaimonic polity is obviously a right constitution in the ancient sense. It rests on a principle of happiness. But a polity of the expedient variety is merely a fair constitution. It rests on a mixture of democratic principles of liberty and oligarchic principles of property. Its oligarchic principles are our present concern.[1]

Let us begin with Plato. Plato offers a resolution for our paradox that consists in nothing less than the main argument of the *Republic*. But we need not rehearse his argument in all its complexity. He does not address our paradox explicitly in terms of rightness and fairness. But he does take up a philosophical problem occasioned by the distinction between action intrinsically valuable and action valuable instrumentally.

In the dialogue Plato depicts Glaucon presenting a position with which we are already familiar. The position is essentially the one that Callicles advances. Though he does not accept it, Glaucon expounds the view that justice can be natural or contractual. By nature to do injustice is, supposedly, good and to suffer it is bad. But the goodness of doing injustice is considerably less than the badness of suffering it. Justice by contract, consequently, is neither to do nor to suffer injustice and to avoid their extremes (*Republic* 2. 358e–359a).

This position, Glaucon implies, rests on a prior distinction. The prior distinction concerns what value justice has. Glaucon asks simply, Is justice valuable for its own sake or valuable for its consequences (357b–d)? He thinks that justice has value for itself, but many people think that justice has value only for its consequences (358a–d). The implication is that justice thought to be valuable only for its consequences is the basis for the distinction between natural and conventional justice, he points out (358e–359b).

This distinction between justice valuable intrinsically and valuable instrumentally gives rise to our distinction between rightness and fairness. Justice is rightness if it is a rational activity with value as an end in itself. After all, happiness is a rational activity of intrinsic value. But justice is only fairness if it is an activity of value as a means only. Fairness is an activity of instrumental value for obtaining material things. This concept of justice, Glaucon explains, arises out of greed (πλεονεξία) (359b–c).

Socrates proclaims in response to Glaucon that justice is among the highest goods. These goods are of value both for themselves and for their consequences (*Republic* 2. 358a). Justice resembles health, which we also enjoy for itself and for its consequences (357b–358d). He focuses the subsequent argument on what value justice has for itself, however. He no doubt does so because this value is what is in question. Its value for its consequences is not at issue.

We shall presently see that justice has for Plato primarily intrinsic value and secondarily instrumental value. We might conjecture that, because it is an activity of intrinsic value, Plato would find justice itself to be happiness. Justice would be political happiness, I should think. After all, political happiness is to fulfill a function within a political society for its own sake. But let us see if our conjecture proves correct.

To show what value justice has, Plato introduces his famous analogy between justice writ large and justice writ small. Justice writ large is justice within a society, and justice within an individual is justice writ small (*Republic* 2. 368c–369a). Justice within a society is that each part of society fulfills its own function (*Republic* 4. 433a–b). Justice, he reminds us, we usually think to be that each person has what properly belongs to him. But what most of all belongs to a person is his proper function (433e–434d).

Plato argues that a society has three parts with different functions. These parts are a philosophical, a martial, and an artisanal and agrarian class. The philosophical class, when properly educated, rules with its knowledge of society as a whole (*Republic* 4. 428a–429a). The martial class defends society against its enemies with right opinion, received through education (429a–430c). The philosophical and the martial classes control the artisanal and agrarian class, which provides, presumably, goods and services for society (431b–432b).

These parts, when they are just, have a felicitous interaction with one another, Plato explains. Their interaction is the happiness of a whole political society. Each part performs its proper function, and no part interferes with the function of another. That the happiness in society is the happiness of the whole and not of any one part, he reiterates (*Republic* 4. 419a–421c).

Justice writ small is idiosyncratic to the argument. Justice of this kind is that each part of an individual soul fulfills its own function (*Republic* 4. 441c–e). Our reason, if properly educated, knows what is best for our soul as a whole and rules with its knowledge. Our aggressive part, when educated, defends our soul with its opinion. The appetitive part, which the cognitive part together with the combative part rule, nourishes the soul, presumably (441e–442d).

Justice in our soul is also a harmonious interaction between its parts. A person who is just has an ordered soul, Plato argues. A just person has a soul in which each part performs its own function, and in which no part attempts to assume the function of another. This internal interaction Plato memorably likens to the harmony of a musical scale composed of three tones—a high, a low, and a middle. Together these tones make up one harmony (443c–443e).

A just person, Plato concludes, aims to preserve this harmony within his soul whether he acts in politics or in private or tends to his body or acquires wealth (443e–444a). He offers what he calls commonplace tests in place of an argument to show that someone who is just would not engage in an activity that is not his, and that he would not seek to acquire property that is not his. Would a just man neglect the gods, disrespect his parents, or commit adultery? he asks. Would he break contracts, embezzle money, or rob temples (442d–443b)?

Justice writ large, then, is for each part of a society to fulfill its political function, and justice writ small is for each part of a soul to fulfill its function. One might think that persons must have a just soul if they are to act justly within a political society. The philosophical guardians, for example, have a just soul and they act justly. They have knowledge of what is good for their society and their soul, and with their knowledge they harmonize both their soul and their society.

But not all person are just who do what is just. The auxiliary guardians cannot be just in a strict sense. They do not have knowledge but only opinion. They do have a just soul albeit in a subordinate sense. The justice in their soul rests on their opinion about who is a friend of their society and who is a foe (*Republic* 4. 429b–c). With this opinion they can organize their soul, and they can defend their society.

The artisans, unfortunately, have a soul not at all just. They have a rather limited opinion about society. Their opinion is that the guardians, philosophical and martial, are to rule, and that they are to be ruled (431c–e). They cannot be just but they do what is just. They exhibit restraint merely.[2]

Socrates is about to conclude, then, that justice in this sense is intrinsically valuable. That is, that justice is primarily of value for its own sake. But Glaucon anticipates his conclusion with an analogy to health. Life is not worth living, he argues, when our soul is ruined any more than it is when our health is ruined even if we can do whatever we might wish (*Republic* 4. 444e–445b).[3]

One might surmise, similarly, that life is not worth living if our political society is ruined and everyone can do whatever they might wish. No part of society would be doing its own job. Plato explicitly reminds us that in a just society a cobbler ought to cobble and to do nothing else, and a carpenter ought to carpenter and to do nothing else (443c). A carpenter and a cobbler ought not to indulge themselves (420d–421a).

What can we learn from Plato? What I call rightness Plato delineates with his discussion of justice and its value. He shows that justice ought to aim at an action of intrinsic value, and that an intrinsically valuable action is of more worth than an action of mere instrumental value. An intrinsically valuable action of this kind I would take to be our political happiness in a broad, ancient, sense.

Indeed, a harmonious life lived with others within a society would surely have an intrinsic value greater than a life lived with instrumental value in pursuit of material goods within a society. Is not a community of activities valuable for itself plainly of greater worth than an association of activities valuable for its consequences of inconsequential baubles?

Aristotle has the honor of making the distinction between rightness and fairness explicit though he uses slightly different terms. He points out that "justice" has an ambiguity, and that we do not find its ambiguity obvious because its meanings are so close (*Ethics* 5. 1. 1129a26–31). He uses primarily the terms "lawfulness" and "fairness" to distinguish its senses. He also uses two other, more esoteric, terms "wholeness" and "partialness."

Term "lawfulness" is an unfortunate one because it has an ambiguity of its own. This term is a homonymic genus. That is, it designates both a genus and a species within its genus. The lawful as a genus includes as its species the lawful and the fair. Lawfulness and fairness thus differ as whole to part though they also differ as part to part (*Ethics* 5.

2 1130b10–16). Hence, arises a paradox, similar to our initial paradox, that an action need not be lawful, but it can be fair.[4]

That lawfulness in its specific sense aims to produce and to preserve happiness in a political society, Aristotle argues rather explicitly. How does it do so? Simply through what the law requires. He states that law ought to aim at the common advantage, and he implies that the common advantage is our happiness though he allows for other ends less felicitous. He explains explicitly that the law requires eudaimonic activities. It requires that we perform actions of courage and temperance, for example. One ought not to desert in battle, nor ought one to indulge in adultery (*Ethics* 5. 1. 1129b14–25).

He argues further that a political society has a happiness proper to it. When he takes up what is good for a society, he explains at length that a happy life is the most choice-worthy (*Politics* 7. 1. 1323a19–1323b26). He then continues to argue that a society is happy when it acts rightly, and that it acts rightly when it acts from justice, wisdom, and courage, for example (1323b29–36a). His conclusion is that the best life both for individuals and for societies is a virtuous life (1323b40–1234a2).

Fairness, too, ought to aim at our happiness. Justice of this kind concerns the distribution of external goods, such as honor or property as well as the rectification of their maldistributions (*Ethics* 5. 2. 1130b30–1131a9). These goods, Aristotle explains, are not good for us in an unqualified sense though one might think that they are (*Ethics* 5. 1. 1129b1–6). What is unqualifiedly good for us is our happiness, of course (*Politics* 7. 13. 1332a7–18). External goods are good only in a qualified sense. They are good for our happiness or, rather, they ought to be (see *Ethics* 5. 3. 1131a24–29).

Aristotle reminds us, then, that rightness rests on our human nature. Rightness concerns our happiness, and our happiness is an activity of our rationality (see *Ethics* 1. 7. 1097b22–1078a18). But fairness rests not so much on our nature as on our fortune. At least, in large part it does. Though we can distribute them, external goods are not entirely within our purview (see *Politics* 7. 1. 1323b27–29). Wars and other calamities vividly illustrate this fact.[5]

Justice, then, in the sense of what I call rightness takes for its goal the happiness of a political society. Both Plato and Aristotle offer cogent arguments to show that it does. Even to this day most political societies still have laws on the books that require of us virtuous activity, such as courageous and temperate activity.

I would argue for a polity resting on justice in the sense of rightness rather than fairness. Rightness constitutes for us a good life rather than merely a life. Those who without thought of rightness would advocate a principle of fairness aim not at a good life but at a life merely. They would pursue not happiness but only wealth or pleasure.

I concede that the ancient ideal of a philosophical life would promote happiness in a form best of all. But a philosophical life, if taken as a principle of rightness, would not be attainable by most people. Nor would a martial life. A polity resting on a principle of happiness for an artisanal life would appear more practicable in our era. A life of this kind most people today would likely be able to attain.

Contemporary philosophers more often than not advocate a polity resting on principles of fairness. They are, unfortunately, the oligarchic and the democratic theorists among us. For them an artisanal life is not a happy one. A life of this kind is one lived under empire and exploitation. It is a banausic life in a most pejorative sense.[6]

We also see, curiously, that Callicles offers a formula for justice that is literally correct. Justice on our analysis turns out to be that the more capable ought to have more. But we now see an ambiguity in his formula. Who is the more capable? Are they those more able to engage in action of intrinsic value or those more able to engage in instrumental action? Are they eudaimonically or pleonectically more capable?

I take the more capable in a eudaimonic sense to mean a greater ability to participate in political happiness. Callicles takes the phrase in a pleonectic sense to mean more able to amass and to consume resources. But those who are more able to carry out a political function surely ought to receive more resources than those who are simply greedy, I should think.

3. Today political philosophers tend to overlook rightness in the ancient or in any sense, and they attempt to rest their theoretical endeavors on fairness only. In their efforts to establish a foundation for political society, they generally ignore human activities of intrinsic value, and they turn instead to activities of instrumental value. They accordingly conceive of fairness not as providing the means for political participation but as imposing restraints on private pursuits.

Though they appear to oppose one another, John Rawls and Robert Nozick share the same purpose of using fairness to develop their political philosophies. Neither philosopher devotes much attention to our happiness though they do give it mention. They are content to leave any question of our goodness to personal preference. Both philosophers direct their attention only to obtaining what would be the means requisite for happiness. Nor do they think that obtaining these means has a limit in happiness though they claim that it has a limit.

Rawls and Nozick do offer different concepts of fairness. Rawls draws our attention to the distribution of property. He argues that we acquire property through social cooperation, but that we disagree about how to share the property so acquired. He is concerned that persons who are more capable might gain more than they ought, and that persons who are less capable gain less than they ought. To avoid these consequences, he invokes what he calls the difference principle and the maximin rule.

Nozick draws our attention to the acquisition of property and the rectification of improper acquisitions. He is especially concerned to curtail and to correct any improper acquisitions. He argues that we acquire property through our own efforts, and his concern is that these efforts might leave either those more capable or those less capable with less than they ought to have. To prevent these consequences, he deploys what he calls entitlement principles and the Lockean proviso.[7]

We shall begin with Robert Nozick. Nozick is well known for offering a contemporary theory of a state of nature. From this state he derives what I am calling a concept of fairness. The state of nature, he tells us, is a state of perfect freedom bounded only by the law of nature. Persons may engage in their actions and make use of their possessions as they see fit, provided only that they do not harm others in their life, health, liberty, or possessions. This concept of a state of nature he takes explicitly from John Locke (*Anarchy* 1. 2. 10).

Notice that persons in a state of nature are presumed to be propertied. They have not only life, health, and liberty, but they somehow have possessions as well. How they might have come to have their possessions in the state of nature, Nozick does not indicate. Perhaps they acquire property through the exercise of their perfect freedom. But he does not specify what they do with their freedom. He indicates only that with their freedom they may do as they wish with the possessions that they have.[8]

Notice, too, that persons in a state of nature would have for their sole concern in their use of their property that they not harm others. They would appear to exhibit little or no concern to help others. That persons do not take possessions away from others, Nozick finds to be of particular interest. That persons do not take away possessions from us, would also very likely be of interest, I would imagine.

Perhaps because of this presumption of property, Nozick attempts to answer the question of how one can acquire property. He does so when he develops a theory of distributive justice. But his theory, he informs us, is less a theory of justice in distribution and more one of justice in holdings (*Anarchy* 2. 7. 149–150). He calls it the entitlement theory (150). When he expounds it, he devotes his attention to the acquisition of property and to the limits of its acquisition.

He adumbrates three general principles that an entitlement theory ought to have without offering much by way of a defense for them. The first is the principle of justice in acquisition. This principle would indicate how an unheld thing comes to be held originally. The second principle is the principle of justice in transfer. It would indicate how one person acquires a thing already held by another through purchase or gift, for example. A third principle is simply to reiterate the first two (150–151, 153).

He also makes explicit mention of rectificative justice. Not everyone respects the three entitlement principles, he acknowledges. People steal from one another, for example, or even enslave one another. A principle of rectification would explain how one corrects unjust holdings of these sorts (152–153).

Nozick continues with an attempt to explain how persons can come to acquire property in accordance with his theory. His explanation focuses on the principle of justice in acquisition. He apparently does so because everyone who justly holds property must come to possess their property either directly or indirectly through a just acquisition. After all, no one can justly possess property other than through original acquisition or through transfer.

What theory of just acquisition does he have, then? He indorses a mixed-labor theory. This theory he also claims to take from John Locke. According to the theory, we can become owners of an unowned object if we mix our labor with the object (*Anarchy* 2. 7. 174). We might, for example, clear a plot of virgin land and thereby become its owners. Or we might simply pick an apple off a tree or pick up an acorn from the forest floor.

Nozick candidly admits that his theory of mixed labor appears to be at best suspect. He worries, among other things, about how much of an unowned object we might claim if we mix our labor with it. If we clear a plot of land, why could we not claim an entire continent or a whole planet? He also wonders why mixing our labor with an object would make it ours. Could not mixing our labor be a way of losing it (174–175)?

He has no theory to answer these questions. He declares explicitly that no one has yet devised a mixed-labor theory that is "workable or coherent" (174–175)! Nor would his theory, if he had one, address essential moral questions. People do have possessions, and people ought to have them. But ought they to have the possessions that they have? What property should people have, in other words? And, How much property should they have?

Nozick offers an entitlement theory, then, that takes him back to where he started out. His theory keeps us essentially in a state of nature subject only to the law of nature. He assumes that we somehow come to have property, and that we ought to hold on to the property that we have acquired. But, again, his theory does not offer us a concept of just acquisition. The theory cannot show how we come to possess justly the property that we possess.[9]

Nozick does point out, however, that the acquisition of property has its limits. Any acquisition is subject to a condition. This condition he claims once again to take from Locke, and he calls it the Lockean proviso. This proviso appears to follow from the law of nature not to harm another. An appropriation of an object must insure that there remain, in Locke's words, "enough and as good left in common for others." The proviso, he states, has the purpose of preventing an appropriation from worsening the situation of others (*Anarchy* 2. 7. 175–176).

How are we to interpret this proviso? Nozick asks. He finds that there are a stringent and a weaker interpretation. Either interpretation rests on the assumption that resources are limited. The stringent interpretation would mean that an acquisition of an object is not permissible if other persons cannot make any appropriation. The weaker interpretation would mean that an acquisition is not permissible if others can no longer make use of objects left unappropriated (175–176).

He argues with a reductio that the stringent interpretation would rule out any appropriation. The argument is a clever regress. It is that some ultimate person, given limited resources, would not be able to appropriate an object and leave enough and as good for others. But the penultimate person would not be able to appropriate and leave as much and as good either. Otherwise, the ultimate person would be still able to appropriate. And so on for each previous person (175–176).

The weaker interpretation, he argues, prevents the regress. A person can appropriate an object if there remains enough and as good for others to use "without appropriation." Those who are not able to appropriate, would apparently be able to use the remaining, unappropriated, objects in common. He concedes, though, that the use of these objects could be subject to inconveniences, such as crowding, unless appropriation stops soon enough (176).[10]

Nozick argues, then, that those who cannot appropriate property would not have less. He actually goes so far as to claim that those who cannot appropriate would likely have more. Private property increases the social product, he explains. He lists "various familiar social conditions" to show that it does. The conditions are increased efficiency, encouraged experimentation, and specialized risk taking as well as better resource conservation and alternative sources of employment (177).[11]

That we provide a social product for others, the law of nature does not require, however. Any social product is apparently a fortuitous side benefit of private property. Nozick returns to what the law does require. The law of nature demands only that we do not make others worse off. To satisfy the law, he argues, we can establish an economic baseline for comparison. This baseline we may determine, if I read him correctly, by comparing percentages of income and wealth on developed and undeveloped resources (177).[12]

With these arguments Nozick concludes that the appropriation of property "satisfies the intent" behind the Lockean proviso (177). The weaker interpretation shows that we can acquire private property without harm to others. If they are not better-off because they have the advantages of increased social product, others are not worse-off because they do not fall below a baseline of income and wealth.

We see, too, that he takes for his primary concern rectificative justice. I so assert because his concern is to prevent violations of the law of nature. His purpose to define what the limits of acquisition are and what would not violate the natural law. His Lockean proviso is meant to insure that no private appropriation prevents others from utilizing resources left behind for them to use in common.

I must now ask, Is the entitlement theory of property right? What foundation ought a political society to have for the acquisition of its property? Nozick finds a limit for acquisition in natural law. But he has, I would argue, an impoverished conception of natural law. I agree with him that the acquisition of property has a natural limit. But this limit lies in our nature and its functions. It does not lie in not depriving others.

I would suggest that a theory of property ought to rest on the fact that we are by nature rational animals, and that we can perform a rational activity for its own sake. Even if we were in a state of nature, we would remain eudaimonic creatures or creatures potentially eudaimonic. If we are to be happy, we must, then, perform rational activities, and if we are to perform rational activities, we must have the necessary means. Unless we have property, we cannot engage in a rational, or, indeed, any activity.[13]

I, too, can take inspiration from John Locke. Though he appropriates it, Nozick neglects to take up the Lockean concept of acquisition in its essentials. Locke does have a defensible theory of acquisition though I shall modify it. He does not argue that property originates in our rational nature. But he surely argues that property originates in our animal nature. Simply put, we need property to live. He rests his concept of acquisition on the brute fact that we can sustain ourselves only if we can obtain "meat and drink, and such other things as nature affords" (*Treatise* 5. 25.).

The mixed-labor theory, Locke argues, arises from the fact that we have property in our person and in our activities. Our labor and work, for example, are ours. We have property, too, in that with which we mix our labor (27.). Why? That our activities are our property, no one can deny. Nourishment, for example, is ours. But when do acorns or apples, if we nourish ourselves with them, become ours? When we digest them? Or when we eat them? When we prepare them? Or when we bring them home? he asks. These foods become ours when we gather them up. If gathering them up did not, nothing else could make them ours (28.).[14]

Notice that Locke does not interpret his proviso to mean that we ought to leave enough and as good for others to use without appropriation. The proviso would appear to mean that we ought to leave enough and as good for others to appropriate. How could you or I consume an apple or an acorn without appropriation? Indeed, Locke explicitly assets that what is left in common is of no use without a taking and a removing of it, and that a taking and a removing is a beginning of property (28.).[15]

Yet Locke does not go far enough, I would argue, when he rests his theory of property on our life functions. We ought to have resources sufficient to enable us to function as rational beings as well as animal beings. Do we not have property in our rational nature as well as our animal nature? Do we not have property in our rational activities as well as our animal activities? If so, ought we not to have property in that with which we mix our rational activities. We ought, I dare say, to be able to acquire resources for a good life as well as for a life.[16]

With Nozick I can assume that people are possessed of property. To make this assumption, however, we need not imagine that we are in a state of nature. People in a political state have property. A property distribution is for us a given. The question is, How is property distributed? Do we want simply to accept the distribution that we have inherited? Or do we want rather to ask, What distribution ought we to have in our society?[17]

I must also ask, Ought we not to distribute resources for the purpose of our political society itself? I mean for a political society in which our activities have value for their own sake. Should our distributions not enable us to realize our political nature and to enable our fellows to realize their political nature? Or should a distribution enable us only to acquire private wealth for our private pleasure?

I could argue, then, in favor of a Lockean theory of acquisition. We ought to be able to acquire what resources we need for our happiness. Again, I speak of political happiness and not of personal happiness, and I speak of political happiness in a broad sense. Should not we and our fellows be able to avail ourselves of the resources needed for our participation in society? To deny ourselves and others these resources is to deny us any function in society. That is, to deny us not only our rational but also our political nature.

The distribution of property ought to be, in a word, eudaimonic. Any distribution ought to have the purpose of granting those with the ability and the desire an opportunity to participate in a political activity of value for itself. We ought to provision our fellows and ourselves with what we and they need to develop and to exercise our and their eudaimonic capabilities in a political arena. By so doing we can create of political community of value in and for itself.

But how ought we to acquire the means to our political happiness? A mixed-labor theory cannot likely enable us to acquire property though an original acquisition. There is, practically speaking, precious little left in common. I answer that we ought to place things in common so that worthy persons can avail themselves of them. These persons must exhibit an actual ability to fulfill a political function or a potential more likely than not to acquire an ability to fulfill a function.[18]

Nozick would no doubt object. He argues that we cannot use moral merit for a principle of property distribution. He apparently agrees with F. A. Hayek that we cannot distribute property by merit because we ought not to impose a pattern of property distribution on society, and because we cannot know who is meritorious and who is not (*Anarchy* 2. 7. 158–159).[19]

I would answer that we need not impose a pattern on society. Nozick himself admits that we establish patterns in society with individual transfers of property. We do so simply because we have reasons for our transfers. He even asserts that we may transfer property because we wish to serve a cause or to help attain a goal. But he also states that we often make a transfer because we perceive another to be of benefit us (158–159).

We can, I would also argue, perceive others to have moral worth in a broad political sense. We do in fact distribute property so as to enable persons to participate in political society, and we make our distributions with an understanding of who is worthy and who is not. We do so through both public and private institutions. There is little controversy, though some, about the idea that government ought to provide for education and to protect against unemployment, for example. There is, oddly, more controversy about providing for health care and for subsistence.

But our governmental institutions actually undertake more than these basic provisions though we tend to forget that they do. Many national and local governments, for example, provide support for the natural sciences, the fine arts, and the medical arts, for martial activities, and for artisanal and agrarian activities. A government usually supports these activities with its tax laws and with various grants and loans.

Private corporations do the same. Businesses invest in research and development on a regular basis. When they hand out bonuses and raises, employers surely take into account how well their employees perform at their jobs. Or, at least, they ought to do so. They also provide training programs for employees whom they think have an ability to learn new skills. Not to mention the fact that they offer employment to persons deemed promising.

I must concede, however, that these institutions, public and private, need not have a eudaimonic motivation. Indeed, today they most probably do not. That they do not is a failure of contemporary political theory, I think. But my present point is that we commonly believe that our public and private institutions ought to take into account the abilities and accomplishments of the persons to whom they disburse property.

Nozick would likely offer a rejoinder with what is probably his most famous counterexample to a pattern theory. His imaginary counterexample is a professional basketball player. Wilt Chamberlain, he argues, could upset a perfectly patterned distribution of property by imposing an admissions surcharge on those who want to see him play. To maintain the pattern, say of equality, would require continuous interference (*Anarchy* 2. 7. 160–164).

But I would respond, What pattern do we wish to maintain? This counterexample would in fact reinforce and enhance a pattern of distribution based on merit, would it not? The basketball fans are willing to pay an extra charge because they recognize that Chamberlain is an extra-talented player who merits a surcharge. If he were not worth it, they would not pay it. This pattern would be self-maintaining.[20]

I would conclude with the observation that Nozick develops a political philosophy with a glaring blind spot. His theory does not take into account persons for whom his Lockean proviso has little or no application. One billion people, at least one billion, live in contemporary political societies and needlessly suffer from the most extreme poverty. I repeat, one billion people, approximately one person in seven, suffer from abject poverty every single day. Not to take from them is not enough. Indeed, they have little or nothing to take![21]

Why does he offer a philosophy so fundamentally flawed? He does not possess a principle of rightness but only principles of fairness. Consider his principle of justice in acquisition. That his principle of acquisition is inadequate, he himself candidly admits. He cannot explain why mixing our labor with an object would make it ours. But Locke can explain why. We must make a thing ours with our labor because we must nourish ourselves. Locke shows that we need property if we are to sustain our life.

Nozick offers no principle by which to define harm, then, except not to take property from another. His interpretation of the law of nature does not take into account other prohibited harms. The Lockean statement of the law of nature clearly asserts that we may not harm another neither in their life or their health or their liberty nor in their possessions. He himself quotes this statement explicitly and in its entirety.

He also fails to take into account the harms that we may cause another by leaving them with little or no property. The Lockean concept of our animal life not only provides a basis for a mixed-labor theory of property, but this concept also would be adequate to address the life needs of those in extreme poverty though not their needs for a good life. They ought surely to have at least sufficient property to live if not to live well.

Nozick, then, develops a theory that falls short of Locke's theory because he neglects the concept of animal life. His theory cannot provision people with sufficient property to sustain their life. It overlooks present distributions clearly unfair by a Lockean or, indeed, any decent standard. Who could deny that some persons have no property to speak of and few prospects of attaining any. Do they possess enough to sustain their life? Far too many do not. Not to mention their health or their liberty.

What I am suggesting is that Locke himself applies the principle of animal life to the proviso. What does he mean when he asserts that we ought to leave enough and as good in common for others? How do we know whether we have left enough for others or as good for them? I would take him to mean that we must leave enough and as good for others to live! We must leave sufficient resources for appropriation by others to sustain their life and to enjoy their health and their liberty.

I would urge against Locke, however, that human beings surely ought to live a good life and not merely a life. We are rational animals, after all. We ourselves must choose to live a good life, and no one else can choose for us. But can we have an opportunity to choose a good life if appropriate resources are not available to us? We ought, if we are to fulfill a Lockean proviso, to leave enough and as good to enable others to live a life well. We ought not to harm them by taking away resources, such as an education and employment, needed for their happiness.

In sum, Nozick offers a theory of distributive justice that is neither right nor fair. He neglects rightness, and he attempts to offer a theory that is fair. But only what is right can determine what is fair. Consequently, his theory is both wrong and unfair. This philosophical fact finds confirmation in its political consequences for political society today. A few people have all but a monopoly on property, and many people live in abject poverty.

Fairness alone not enough! With his Lockean proviso Nozick would seem to protect both the better-off and the worse-off. But he is in effect gives a free rein to the better-off. Many persons have no property worthy of a rational being or even of an animal being. They have little or nothing to take from them. Some persons can hardly scrape together enough to stay alive. Some cannot stay alive. Need I quote statistics? All you have to do, should you have any doubt, is to turn on your television set and watch the evening news.

Only a principle of rightness, I would reiterate, can provide a criterion for a concept of fairness. Rightness ought to define a purpose for fairness, and this purpose ought to be human happiness. Our happiness determines how property should be distributed. Fairness cannot be a first principle of political philosophy.

I would advocate, again, that we distribute property with the intention of promoting artisanal and agrarian happiness. Productive activities we can perform as ends in themselves, and these activities most people can perform.

Why do we have property, then? So that we may engage felicitous activities with our fellows. How much property do we need? Enough for our and their felicity, I dare say.

4. John Rawls offers a political philosophy similar in its general outlook to the philosophy that Robert Nozick offers. He, too, rests his theory of justice not on a concept of rightness but on a concept of fairness. He actually calls his theory with its original position of equality "justice as fairness" (*Theory* 1. 3. 10, e.g.)! But Rawls offers a political theory dissimilar to the theory of Nozick in significant specifics. His theory of fairness focuses on justice in a distributive sense rather than in a rectificative sense.

If we are to grasp his concept of fairness, we must turn to what Rawls calls the original position and see what its basic assumptions are. The original position resembles a state of nature in the contractarian tradition, Rawls tells us (*Theory* 1. 3. 11). This position, you may perchance recall, is a hypothetical situation in which persons choose principles of justice for their society (10). The principles chosen determine basic equalities of rights and duties and the acceptable inequalities of social and economic benefits, he explains (10–11, 13–14).

Who, then, are the persons choosing principles of justice in the original position? Rawls assumes that they are free and rational, and that they are concerned only with their own interest (*Theory* 1. 3. 10). They are free, he states, because they can "revise and alter their final ends" (*Theory* 1. 26. 131–32; 3. 82. 475–476). They have the rationality of economic theory. That is, their rationality is of means and ends only. And they take no interest in the interests of others. They are "mutually disinterested" (*Theory* 1. 3. 12).

These persons are also situated behind what he calls a veil of ignorance. They know neither their own good nor their social position nor their natural ability. Their ignorance about these matters, he argues, prevents them from selecting principles biased in their favor because of any social or natural contingencies (*Theory* 1. 3. 11; 1. 4. 16–17).

Rawls, then, rests his theory of justice on assumptions about persons who choose principles of justice. These persons, he assumes, do not know what they take to be their good, they can revise their ends, they have a rationality only of means and ends, and they do not take an interest in each other.

We might suspect already that Rawls does not consider a concept of rightness in developing his theory. The persons in the original position have a rationality that would appear to preclude happiness in any sense resembling the ancient sense. Their rational activity is not one of intrinsic worth, but it is one of instrumental worth only.

We might also harbor a suspicion that justice as well would very likely have little worth, if any, for its own sake. One would think that, because their rationality is of instrumental value, those who are in the original position would most likely choose principles of justice that are of instrumental value, too.

But let us suspend our suspicions and consider what principles of justice the persons in the original position choose. We shall ask, Do they choose principles of rightness or fairness? Rawls argues that they decide in favor of two principles. The one is the principle of equal liberty, and the other is the difference principle. The equal liberty principle is not our present concern. This principle states that we ought to have "equality in the assignment of basic rights and duties" (*Theory* 1. 3. 13–14).[22]

Our concern at present is with the difference principle. This principle determines the distribution of wealth and authority. It asserts that inequalities of social and economic benefits are just "only if they result in compensating benefits for everyone, and in particular for the least advantaged members of society." The principle permits a few persons who are more fortunate to have greater benefits only if persons less fortunate find their situation improved, too, Rawls states. The fortunate few are the more capable and the less fortunate, presumably, the less capable (*Theory* 1. 3. 13–14; 1. 13. 65–68).

Why, then, would people in the original position accept the difference principle for the distribution of social and economic benefits? Why do they think this principle a good criterion for the distribution of property? Rawls assumes quite simply that, whatever else they want, the persons in the original position will want more rather than fewer benefits of these kinds. Each person prefers a larger to a smaller share of benefits, he states explicitly (*Theory* 1. 1. 4; 2. 15. 79). This assertion would, presumably, apply to both the better-off and the worse-off.

He does consider that those who are deciding on the principles of justice might wish to divide social and economic benefits equally. An equal division seems reasonable, he argues, because each would not expect to have more than an equal share and would prefer not to have less than an equal share (*Theory* 3. 26. 130). But he asks, Why would they not accept an unequal division of wealth and authority if inequality would mean more benefits for everyone? They should take into consideration "economic efficiency and the requirements of organization and technology," he argues (*Theory* 3. 26. 130–131; see also 2. 11. 54–55).

Rawls also offers what he takes to be a decisive consideration in favor of the difference principle. This consideration is the maximin rule. This rule is a criterion for making decisions under conditions less than certain. No one in the original position, remember, knows his or her eventual position in society, and anyone could possibly end up among the worse-off. The maximin rule asks them to rank the alternatives under consideration by their worst outcomes. They surely would, he concludes, accept the principle with the worst outcome that is best (*Theory* 3. 26. 132–133 and n. 19). This outcome would garner the most benefits for those who end up in the worst position.[23]

We can see, then, that persons in the original position preoccupy themselves with the distribution of social and economic benefits. They choose a principle of distribution that they think would provide everyone with the most benefits of this kind. They choose the difference principle because it guarantees that even those who are in the worst-off social and economic position would have more than they would otherwise have.[24]

One can also see that Rawls has no theory of acquisition. He does not even take up the topic, as far as I can tell, of how we originally acquire property. He simply assumes that we have possessions. He argues only that we must acquire our possessions through social cooperation if we are to have a satisfactory life. Society is marked by both cooperation and conflict, he explains, or, more succinctly, by an identity and a conflict of interests. We cooperate because we each gain greater benefits by doing so, but we are in conflict because we each differ over how these benefits are to be divided (*Theory* 1. 1. 4; 1. 22. 109).

Why does Rawls think cooperation essential? Rawls explains with a turn to what he calls the circumstances of justice. These circumstances he claims to borrow from David Hume. Hume, he tells us, recognizes that the essential circumstances are a conflict of interests and a moderate scarcity of resources. We have a conflict of interests because we each have our own plans of life with differing claims upon our resources, he explains. Moderate scarcity gives rise to our cooperation because resources are neither so abundant nor so scarce that cooperation becomes superfluous or futile (*Theory* 1. 22. 109–110).

Rawls takes for his primary concern, then, to show that we divide the benefits resulting from social cooperation in a way such that everyone is willing to cooperate, "even those less well situated" (*Theory* 1. 3. 13–14). Any distribution of property ought to allow all persons to obtain a maximal share in its benefits, especially those in the worst-off social and economic position. The difference principle, combined with the maximin rule, assures that those worse off will be in the worst-off position that is best.

I would now ask, Does Rawls offer a theory of justice that is right? More specifically, is the difference principle right? Rawls himself argues that the difference principle is a principle of rightness though it is incomplete. But he argues that rightness would simply extend the application of his principles of justice. A theory of rightness would apply the principles acknowledged in the original position not only to a political society but also to international law and to individuals (*Theory* 1. 2. 15; 1. 18. 93, 95–96).

Are, then, the principles chosen in the original position principles of rightness if we extend their application? My answer must be, They are not. Rightness, I am arguing unabashedly, is for the sake of happiness in a eudaimonic sense. Happiness in this ancient sense, again, is a rational activity of value for its own sake. Only if we act from our rationality, if we act in accordance with a principle of our rationality, and if we act for the sake of our rational activity, can we be happy.

In his original position Rawls offers us an impoverished concept of justice. He is quite correct to make a moral appeal to the fact that we are free and rational beings. But when he does so, he leaves out a key component of rightness. He does not make his appeal to a rationality that can engage in an action of value as an end in itself. Instead he appeals to a rationality that is merely one of means and ends. He fails to take into account the distinctive trait that makes our rationality human, and he grants us only a rationality that we share with other animals.

Perhaps we can see this unfortunate omission more clearly if we consider more closely the veil of ignorance. This veil is, as is any veil, translucent, and we can see through it if obscurely. The persons in the original position do have a general concept of their goodness even though they do not know their specific concept. Their general concept is a concept of fairness only. Rawls assumes, recall, that they would only "prefer a larger to a lesser share" of social and economic benefits (*Theory* 1. 1. 4; 3. 22. 109).[25]

Yet Rawls might seem to offer a theory that would allow for human happiness in a eudaimonic sense. Why could his theory not permit someone to engage in a rational activity for its own sake? After all, the principles of justice enable one to pursue goodness of different kinds. Rawls implicitly allows that someone might wish to pursue happiness when he points out that anyone who wishes may decline to accept more rather than fewer primary goods (*Theory* 1. 22. 111–112; 3. 25. 123). A person who seeks happiness would only desire primary goods sufficient for happiness and would have no desire for more.

Again, his assumption about human rationality would preclude this possibility. How could a person who possesses by hypothesis a rationality merely of means and ends value rational action as an end in itself? His theory rests on a mistaken assumption about what our rational nature is. Human rationality can perform an activity of intrinsic value as well as an activity of merely instrumental value, can it not?

Nor does Rawls recognize happiness of the kind that is a rational activity of value for itself. Our happiness, he does argue, is "the satisfaction of rational desire." This concept, he proudly claims, one can trace back to Aristotle. But he fails to argue that we have a rational desire for rational activity itself. Our desire is rational when we have a plan of life, he asserts. But a life plan enables us merely to satisfy harmoniously our various desires. We schedule them so that we can satisfy them without interference from each other (*Theory* 1. 15. 79–80; *Theory* 3. 25. 123–124).[26]

I would also argue that Rawls misinterprets Hume and misconstrues a crucial circumstance of justice. Rawls has what we may call a selfish theory of property distribution. He states that he does not presume persons to have egoistic or selfish ends. Though their ends are interests of a self, they need not have interests only in a self, he argues. They may find that they have altruistic interests in others, and that they wish "to advance the interests of others and to see their ends attained" (*Theory* 3. 22. 111–112).

Yet he clearly assumes that the persons in the original position have not only ends of a self but merely selfish ends. That the assumption of mutual disinterest in the original position excludes ties of natural sentiment, he explicitly states (111–112). They apparently may choose to act altruistically only after they leave the original position and enter a political society. They may then discover that they have altruistic ends after the veil of ignorance is removed.

If he were to avail himself of it, Hume would characterize the original position and the persons in it quite differently. He would no doubt argue that the persons in the original position are possessed of "humanity" within their breasts. We are "naturally partial to ourselves and to our friends," he argues, but we are also capable of "a more equitable conduct." This more equitable conduct justice works in us (*Morals* 3. 1. 188).

When he discusses its circumstances, Hume in fact shows that justice would vanish if our humanity were complete. He employs hypothetical situations to support his assertion. Imagine, he invites us, that we feel "an extensive benevolence," and that we feel "the utmost tenderness" for every one and "no more concern" for our interest than for the interests of another (184–185). Or imagine the golden age of poets, in which we find only "cordial affection, compassion, sympathy" within our breasts (188–189).

Justice would disappear, too, if our humanity were to cease to be. He appeals again to hypothetical situations. Imagine, he asks, that we have fallen into a "society of ruffians" who engage in a "desperate rapaciousness" (187). Or imagine a state of nature, not Lockean but Hobbesian, in which exists a "perpetual war of all against all," and only might makes right (189).

But you might object, Does Hume not wish to show that justice has its "sole foundation" in its utility (*Morals* 3. 1. 183)? Justice would surely serve our self-interest, then. I would respond by asking: what does Hume think our self-interest to be? The answer is that he recognizes self-interest of two kinds. The one kind rests on a social interest, and the other on a selfish interest. A social interest is the basis for his concept of justice.

He argues that our self-interest and our social interest are not opposed. Why, he asks, are not "the virtues of humanity, generosity, beneficence" desirable "with a view to happiness and self-interest"? The utmost that we can gain in our lives is "the indulgence of some affection." The benefactor and the miser both spend their wealth in the gratification of their desire (*Morals* 9. 2. 281).

Hume's concept of justice does, then, rest on selfishness but only a smidgen. But he rests his concept of justice on a selfishness that indulges the satisfaction of a social desire and not a selfish desire. The satisfaction of our benevolence, he writes, is especially "sweet, smooth, tender, and agreeable." It also entails "the agreeable reflection" that we have done our part for society (*Morals* 9. 2. 281–282; also see *Morals* App. 2.).

Hume further explains that utility pleases because we take satisfaction in the happiness of others and dissatisfaction in their unhappiness. We feel approbation for everything that "contributes to the happiness of society" (*Morals* 5. 2. 219). By the happiness of society he would appear to mean the happiness of others. Whatever "presents us with the view of human happiness or misery," he argues, "excites in our breast a sympathetic movement of pleasure or uneasiness" (221).

Nevertheless, he assumes, as you may have noticed, that our happiness is the satisfaction of desire. Our self-interest, whether selfish or social, rests "on an original propensity of some kind," and it gives "a relish to the objects of its pursuit," he argues. He continues that "the utmost" that we can attain is "the indulgence of some affection" (*Morals* 9. 2. 281).

I would, of course, modify the Humean theory. I agree with Hume that political activity ought to take happiness as its end. Our political principles ought to aim to make all those in political society happy. But I differ from Hume in that I advocate a rational happiness not a passional one. Happiness is a rational activity and not an emotional passivity, I cannot but assert.

I would appeal to our rational nature for a foundation of our politics. Hume appeals to our animal nature for its foundation. He is quite cheerful and explicit about his view that we have a passional nature quite similar to other animals (*Treatise* 2. 2. 12.). We do share these traits with other animals, I agree. But our rationality makes us specifically human. Our passions, tender and agreeable though their satisfaction might be, do not.

Though he does not use the term, Hume does have an implicit principle of rightness in human happiness. He indicates rather clearly that human happiness, albeit defined passionally, serves as a criterion for the distribution of property. He argues that the laws concerning property ought to be "*useful* and *beneficial*." But useful and beneficial to whom? Ultimately, "to human society" and to "the general *interest* of mankind" (*Morals* 3. 2. 194–195 his italics).

Rawls, then, does not have a principle of rightness even on a Humean view. He attempts to establish his theory without regard to what Hume calls the general interest of mankind. But Rawls would likely deny that he does. He asks us to distinguish the motivations of persons in the original position and persons in political society. A person who acts on the principles of justice in society is not egoistic, he claims. Why? This person takes on the moral limitations that these principles express (*Theory* 3. 25. 127–128).

He supports his claim with a discussion of a Humean concept--benevolence. He worries that someone might possibility think the omission of benevolence in the original position is a defect in his theory. Not so, he argues. The assumptions of mutual disinterest and the veil of ignorance taken together "serve much the same purpose as benevolence." The persons in the original position are thus "forced to take the good of others into account" (128–129).

But I must ask, Why do the persons in the original position take the good of others into account? Not everyone who does so is benevolent. All depends on their motivation. Do they consider the good of others for the sake of others? Or do they do so for their own sake? I believe that we can say, can we not, that the persons in the original position take the good of others into account for the sake of their own desire satisfaction. They primarily use others as a means to their own end of gaining more rather than fewer primary goods.

We see, then, that the difference principle is a principle that is neither right nor fair. The hypothetical persons in the original position, though they agree on this principle, are indifferent about any social interest, and they want solely to advance their own interest. How right or fair can this principle be if they do not consider the happiness of others in an ancient rational sense? Or if they do not consider the happiness of others even in a modern passional sense?

They distribute property for the sake of a concept of goodness that is only nominally the pursuit of their happiness but actually the pursuit of pleasure. Happiness is an ability to act rationally for the sake of rational action itself. Our rational activity has its own end of intrinsic value. Happiness is not an ability to act rationally for the sake of desire satisfaction. If it were, our rationality would be instrumental only.

A person who is happy needs material goods necessary for the sake of eudaimonic activity. But a person with more rather than fewer material goods is too often given to life of indulgence if not overindulgence. A person with fewer rather than more material goods is too often reduced to a life of subsistence. But whether rich or poor, neither person lives a good life but merely a life.[27]

5. We ought to remember that equality is of two kinds. These kinds are geometric equality and arithmetic equality. We tend to forget geometric equality and think of arithmetic equality only. We do so quite possibly because we tend to neglect rightness

and to seek only fairness. We consequently do not think that geometric equality can be equality, but that equality of this kind can be only inequality.

Rightness, you may recall, is a concept of justice that defines a principle of political happiness. I am arguing that a concept of justice in our era ought to rest on a principle of artisanal happiness because most people can without undue difficulty attain happiness of this kind. But a principle of happiness, artisanal or not, can be a basis for geometric equality, and this principle can determine how we ought to distribute property.

With a geometric distribution the ability a person possesses to engage in happiness determines what resources a person ought to receive. Those persons who are able to perform an intrinsically valuable political function requiring more resources ought to receive more property than those who are able to perform a function requiring fewer resources. Those persons who are more able to fulfill for its own sake a political function ought to receive more property than those less able.

Arithmetic equality does not take into account what political function a person exercises in the distribution of property. Nor does arithmetic equality take into account what ability a person has. Equality of this kind would be for each individual to receive the same distribution of property.

Nozick and Rawls do not recognize a principle of rightness. That they do not is apparent in what they omit from the philosophers who inspire them. Nozick claims to advance a mixed-labor theory or property, but he leaves out the animal functions that Locke thought the basis for a theory of this kind. Rawls claims to rest his concept of an original position on Humean circumstances of justice, but he leaves out the human compassion that Hume thought a crucial circumstance.

Yet these two philosophers do employ a concept of geometric equality to distribute property. They recognize not a eudaimonic principle but only a pleonectic principle of geometric equality. They admit only one function in their theory for their distribution of property. This function is to acquire property, and this acquisition is not political but personal. An entrepreneur may procure as much property as he or she desires provided only that others less entrepreneurial have their property either augmented in the slightest or not diminished in the slightest.

Who would be happy in a polity of this kind? Neither those who are rich nor those who are poor have a political function truly eudaimonic. Their polity is essentially a contemporary consumer society in which persons engage in action for the sake of personal ends. Are its corporate oligarchs happy? Not likely, I should think. Their desire is to maximize their profits, and their profits they lavish on vain luxuries. Are its mass consumers happy? Not likely, either. They are more likely than not to squander their meager earnings on mere amusements.[28]

What Nozick and Rawls offer, then, is a Calliclean polity. Their polity is Calliclean because its principle for property distribution is primarily pleonectic. They recognize only one political function for the persons in their polity, and this function is the acquisition of personal wealth. True, their oligarchy is not an unmitigated one. But can we say that it is more than mildly mitigated? They agree that the purpose of a political state is to enable persons to seek personal wealth with only negligible restrictions.

Are their theories not sophistry of the moral variety? They attempt to rationalize mitigated greed. Callicles would no doubt be pleased. They recognize what he calls the natural law of the more capable. But they strike a better bargain than he thought possible with the less capable. They propose a conventional law of inequality and forego a conventional law of equality. The more capable are content with more than an equal share though not as much as they could had have, and the less capable are content with less than an equal share though not as little as they would have had.

Rawls and Nozick, we might note, do not appear to be aware that natural law can place a limit on conventional law. Because they are not, they argue only that conventional law must limit natural law. Why? Natural law, if seen to be eudaimonic, provisions us with a cause for cooperation. If seen to be expedient, natural law yields only a cause for competition. A eudaimonic law is rational, and its ends we can share. But an expedient law is passional, and its ends, when selfish, we cannot share.

But a concept of natural law can provide us with a criterion for conceiving and implementing conventional law. We can see in both Locke and Hume how this criterion works, though I disagree with their concept of natural law. Locke offers our life functions as a criterion for property acquisition and its limits. Hume offers a social function, but a passional one, as a criterion for distribution of property.

Alexis de Tocqueville, we might note, has one fear for American democracy greater than any other. His fear is that this new democracy would give rise to what he calls an industrial aristocracy. An aristocracy of this kind arises through the division of labor. It consists of entrepreneurs and employers who enjoy wider activities and greater wealth and independence and of employees and workers who are left with more dependence and narrower activities (*Democracy* 2. 2. 20. 645–647).

He argues that this new aristocracy is "a monstrosity within the general fabric of society." The American society is becoming more democratic and its equality is increasing, but the industrial class is becoming more aristocratic, and its inequality is increasing. Some "industries inside the immense democratic whole" contain "some men who are very wealthy and a multitude who are wretchedly poor."

He asserts that this aristocracy, though "one of the most restrained and least dangerous," is yet "one of the most harsh ever to appear on earth." The new aristocrats, unlike the landed aristocrats of the past, feel themselves under no obligation of law or custom to care for their workers. They instead leave their workers, "having impoverished and brutalized" them, to rely on "public charity" in times of difficulty (647–648)!

He cautions that we ought constantly to take care to fix our "anxious gaze" in its direction. If "aristocracy and the permanent inequality of social conditions were to infiltrate the world once again," this "is the door by which they would enter" (648).

Tocqueville articulates a fear of an industrial aristocracy that has proven, I fear, to be not entirely without warrant. I fear, too, that this nouveau aristocracy in our era has proven to be less restrained and more dangerous than it apparently was in his era.[29]

5

Public and Private

1. I would now pose an indelicate question, Why are corrupt constitutions so common? Why, in other words, do corrupt constitutions appear so attractive to so many people? My question expressed in this rather straightforward manner might seem less than answerable and even less laudable. Who would argue in favor of corruption? Who would wish to live under corruption?

Perhaps we might ponder a question less vexing. Why do so many people choose to live under an oligarchic or a democratic constitution? Democracy is today taken to be the more common constitution, in which the many are thought to rule. Why do people wish to live under a constitution of this kind? Its citizens would no doubt reply that they choose to live under a democracy because everyone is equal and free to live as they see fit.

An oligarchy is thought the less common constitution, in which literally a few rule. The many are excluded from rule or, at least, from any effective rule. Why do people prefer to live under an oligarchy? Its denizens are likely to reply, Who does not wish to be wealthy? The few, who are wealthy, generally wish to retain their riches, and the many, who are not wealthy, wish to attain their riches.

But democracies and oligarchies are both corrupt, I dare say. I assume the classic definition of corruption. A constitution is corrupt when its rulers rule for their own sake. In a democracy the people are evidently the rulers, and they obviously rule for the benefit of themselves. The rich obviously rule in an oligarchy, and they, too, evidently rule for their own benefit.

Our question becomes, then, Why do people so often believe that rulers ought to rule for their own benefit? I submit that they are of this opinion because they do not seek human happiness. Democrats and oligarchs surely overlook happiness in a political sense as well as in a personal sense. They do not pursue an action prized for its own sake, but they engage in an action performed for the sake of augmenting their wealth or of gratifying their desires.

But why do oligarchs and democrats not seek happiness? They are mistaken about our goodness. Though they think that they do, they do not pursue a goodness that is human. I defer to Aristotle. Oligarchs and democrats, he argues, do not seek whole justice, which would be for the sake of happiness. They aim only at partial justice, which is for the sake of property or pleasure. They mistakenly take the part for the whole (*Politics* 3. 8. 1280a7–1280b6).

This difference in purpose has consequences of no little import. In a correct society people seek their political happiness. When they do, they seek a good that they can share with others. To pursue happiness in this sense is to pursue a good that is public. We wish to perform a political function that has value for its own sake. We act without an ulterior motive. I speak of a political function in a wide sense, which includes intellectual, martial, and artisanal roles.

But to perform a function for its own sake also has value for its consequences, to be sure. To pursue our political happiness is to assist others in the pursuit of their political happiness. When we fulfill our role in society, our fellow citizens can more easily fulfill their role.

People in a corrupt society are neither happy, nor do they help one another to be happy. The oligarchs and the democrats among us pursue goods primarily private. We may say that one person shares property with another by giving another, say, money. But the money that the one gives is not really shared because it now belongs to the other. We may say, too, that people can share pleasures, such as eating or drinking. But they merely enjoy together pleasures felt separately.

I would suggest, then, that rulers in an oligarchy or a democracy are mistaken in principle. They are mistaken in not permitting themselves to recognize a principle of goodness truly first. They rest content with a secondary principle, which they take to be primary. They are unable to see a good that we can share in common. They seek instead goods that cannot be shared.

We now might wonder, Why would people prefer to follow not a principle enabling them to engage in cooperation but a principle causing them to engage in conflict? Why would they take for their political principle a pleonectic or hedonic principle? The answer, I think, is, again, that they do not truly know themselves. They do not pause to ask themselves, What kind of creature am I? Am I essentially a rational animal? Or am I essentially passional?

What is at issue is a deeper question, then. Out of what do we wish to create our society? Obviously, we ourselves constitute the material out of which a political society arises. Indeed, our activities, both rational and political, are, I would argue, what ought to constitute a society. Or ought we to make a society out of our emotional passivities?

Alexis de Tocqueville recognizes that human goodness divides into two kinds. The one kind he calls beautiful virtue, and the other kind useful virtue. We can act on beautiful virtue if we forget ourselves and "do good without self-interest," he explains (*Democracy* 2. 2. 8. 609–610). But we act on useful virtue if we cannot forget ourselves and do good that serves our "own interest." By helping others we help ourselves (610).

He finds that American democracy falls short in beautiful virtue. He argues that democracy in America rests solely on useful virtue. Americans do not argue that they sacrifice themselves for their fellows "because it is a fine thing to do." They make sacrifices of this kind because they are "as necessary to the man who makes them as to those gaining from them" (610).

Tocqueville finds, too, that our desire for material comforts and enjoyments entail for us, if not conflict, anxiety. Americans, he states, are constantly seeking or safeguarding their "precious, imperfect, and fugitive delights." The American middle class has a fundamental passion for "material prosperity." But this passion extends to the rich few and the many poor as well. The rich fear to lose comforts, and the poor hope to obtain them (*Democracy* 2. 2. 10. 617–618).¹

2. What is now at issue is the idea of a community. Our rational and political nature, if we acknowledge it and accept it, can serve us as a foundation for a political community. Our actions, when rational and political, can constitute a political society prizeworthy for its own sake. If we fail to acknowledge and to accept our nature, we forsake any possibility of a community, and we constitute a society doomed to conflict and eventually to failure. Our humanity is our destiny, one might say.

That we ought especially to establish a political community, I unabashedly proclaim. A community of this kind should be our primary political goal! Within it we can aspire to happiness in any political activity that we might undertake. We ought not to subordinate our political activity to private interests. If we do, we corrupt, if not destroy, our community and its value, and our activity becomes little more than chicanery.

I assume, then, that we are essentially rational and political animals, and that we can enjoy, at least in a reasonable simulacrum, political happiness. In other words, we can fulfill a desire that we can reasonably take to be both rational and political. We fulfill a desire of this kind if we act from our rationality in accordance with a political principle, albeit hypothetical, for the sake of our political action itself.

What political principle ought we to act on? Our principle ought to define a political function for us. What ought to be our function? Our function in general should be a philosophical, a martial, or an artisanal activity. With Plato and Aristotle I take these general functions to be essential for any society. Unless a society should be so providentially provisioned that it would be without any need for cognition, action, or production on our part.

What specific function our principle defines, however, depends on our particular society and on our particular place within it. Both societies and persons can possess different opportunities and resources, and they both can have different uses for their opportunities and resources. Societies once defended themselves with infantry, cavalry, and triremes, for example. We can now defend ourselves with battleships, submarines, warplanes, and ballistic missiles.²

Again, I speak of political functions not personal functions, and I speak of political functions in a wide ancient sense. Any activity that we perform as a member of a political society, be it thinking, doing or making, I take to be political. A political function we need not restrict only to citizenship in a modern narrow sense of voting or holding office though in this sense citizenship is political, too.

My intention, then, is to argue that a political society is essentially a cooperative endeavor. Or, perhaps, I should say that a political society ought to be essentially a cooperative endeavor. Justice, recall, has value both for its own sake and for its consequences. If we fulfill a political function, we can engage in an action that is primarily an end in itself though it is also a means to other ends. These other ends are secondary, and they would include acquiring property and satisfying desire.

I assume that our political functions, if truly defined, are activities that complement and complete one another. We can provide a service or product for other persons who live within our society, and they can provide a product or service for us. Or, at least, we ought, and they ought. If we fulfill our function, we can benefit our fellows by doing our part in society. Our fellows benefit us by doing their part if they fulfill a function. Yet our purpose ought to be to act for the sake of others and not for ourselves.

A political society, then, can be primarily a public good and not a private good. We can create a political community of value for its own sake if we perform our function for its own sake. If we do so, we share a eudaimonic constitution of human activity. A just function can be eudaimonic, you may recall, though it is not always. We can share, one might say, in a community of happiness, by happiness, and for happiness.

We create a private good if we act merely for the sake of an ulterior end. We can hardly attain political happiness if we act primarily for the sake of benefits received. We create at best a joint exchange for trading in possessions and pleasures. We do not truly benefit others, but we act primarily for our own benefit. We act so that we might receive a benefit from others. They can easily be politic enough to return the favor.

A society constituted for the sake of exchanging property or pleasure is a zero-sum game, in other words. We cannot possess or consume an object that another consumes or possesses. Not to mention the fact that our resources are limited. Nor is a society of this sort likely to endure long. And no wonder! It disdains and denies our humanity itself.[3]

Readers not unacquainted with philosophy and its history may well recognize that I follow the ancient Greeks once more. Both Plato and Aristotle argue that we can create a political community if we form what they call a correct political society. They agree that a political society consists of functions that together can constitute an end in itself. Neither would permit these functions to succumb to private interests.

Do these ancient philosophers explain for us how a political society can come have a value primary for itself? After all, many persons even today are accustomed to think that political society has value primarily for its consequences, which are invariably its benefits for us. We can best see what answer these ancients have for this question, I think, with the aid of the distinction between what I shall term a naïve origin for justice and a philosophical origin.

We shall see again that we begin our philosophical and political life in a state of naïveté, but that we can free ourselves from our naïveté through education. Both Plato and Aristotle so argue. Education marks a turn from a preoccupation with sensible objects to an appreciation of intelligible objects. When we make this turn, we forego passional goods among sensible things, and we pursue a rational and moral good among intelligible things.[4]

Plato and Aristotle implicitly place the distinction between a naïve and a philosophical origin for justice at the foundation of their political philosophies. Let us begin with Plato. Plato recognizes this distinction implicitly when he undertakes to determine what value justice has. Socrates demonstrates to Glaucon and Adeimantus that justice is of value for itself as well as for its consequences against those who hold that only its consequences have value (*Republic* 2. 368c).

We shall see that to take justice to be of value for itself is to acknowledge its philosophical origin, and that to take justice to be of value only for its consequences is to acquiesce in its naïve origin. In other words, a naïve origin for justice arises from a desire for sensible objects, but a philosophical origin arises from a desire for an intelligible object. The one desire is passional, and the other is rational.

Plato presupposes the distinction between a naïve and a philosophical origin for justice when he expounds what one might call a natural history of political society. He rather obviously begins his history with a naïve explanation for justice. Justice is initially of value, he implies, for its consequences. Its consequences are the satisfaction of desires, and the desires to be satisfied turn out to be our most basic needs.

How does Plato account for the origin of society, then? A political society arises from the fact that we are separately non-self-sufficient. We each have needs for many things, and we must seek help from each other to satisfy our needs. We must turn to commerce or barter, he suggests. We exchange things with one another and supply each other with food, clothing, and shelter (*Republic* 2. 369b-e; but also 370c-371e).

He finds that we best become self-sufficient together if we help one another through a division of labor. We all ought to work to provide one service or one product for others. The usual arguments apply. We have each of us a different nature suited to a different function, we are better able to fulfill our function if we practice only it, and we can fulfill our function at the proper moment if we do not have other functions (369e-370c).

The society arising from this beginning is rather bucolic. Its inhabitants satisfy what Plato calls their necessary desires (see *Republic* 2. 373a; also *Republic* 8. 558d-559d). They desire plain foods, simple clothing, and adequate shelter though they also enjoy wines and sing hymns. They do not permit themselves more children than their resources allow lest they fall into war or poverty. They consequently live their lives in good health, and they die at a ripe old age (*Republic* 2. 372a-d).[5]

Unfortunately, this bucolic society appears to be short-lived. A society of this pastoral kind before long develops into a more urbane society. Our necessary desires are not our only desires. Those who live in this original society soon seek to satisfy unnecessary desires, Plato argues. Desires of this kind are for luxuries of various and sundry sorts (again *Republic* 8. 558d-559d). The inhabitants want a higher standard of living, we might say.

The original society changes from what Plato calls a healthy society to what he deems a fevered society. Its denizens want furniture and flatware, and they want sauces and desserts. With these desires come others for embroidered clothing, gold and ivory jewelry, and fine dining, and yet others for singers, dancers, and actors, and also for doctors and nurses. Not to mention less savory desires (*Republic* 2. 372d-373d).[6]

But this fevered society cannot long endure, either. Its denizens find that their unnecessary desires in their turn lead them to develop aggressive desires. To service their desires for luxuries, they eventually use up their resources, especially land, and they begin to encroach on the land of their neighbors. But their neighbors, if also in the thrall of unnecessary desires, may likewise start to encroach on their land (*Republic* 2. 373d-e).

Their society must now muster a martial class. This new class ought to be specialists, too, Plato argues. The division of labor again applies. Weapons would be marvelous things if anyone who picked them up would be skilled in their use, Glaucon remarks. To acquire their martial skill, their guardians must have the requisite psychological spiritedness and physical strength, they must continually practice with their weapons, and they must be free from other activities (373e–375b).

We can see, then, that these three societies each have a naïve origin. The bucolic, the luxurious, and the imperial society all rest on their desires for sensible objects. The imperial society with its martial class arises initially for the proximate purpose of defending and perhaps of acquiring resources for its society but also for the ultimate purpose of using its resources to satisfy its unnecessary, and presumably its necessary, desires.[7]

The next and last society in this natural history is a society with a philosophical origin. Its philosophical origin, one might surmise, lies in a desire for intelligible objects. The inhabitants of this society are those who are able to fulfill a rational and political function. They desire to act justly, in a word. But to act justly is to perform an activity of value for itself. They pursue, therefore, a happiness at once rational and political.

This philosophical society the class seemly least likely to establish it is the one to establish it. The martial class must become philosophical, Plato argues. The guardians, he observes, present a danger to society because of their naïve origin. Why would they wait for their enemies to plunder their society? asks Socrates. Why would they not plunder it themselves (*Republic* 2. 375b–c)? They are, after all, the best trained fighters and the best equipped.

Plato uses an analogy to argue in favor of philosophy and its importance for averting this calamity. His analogy is a watchdog. A watchdog, he argues, is both gentle with those whom it knows and harsh with those whom it does not know. Its knowledge determines how it acts toward others. The guardians similarly must have knowledge. They must be gentle with those whom they know, and with those whom they do not know they must be harsh (375c–376c).

The guardians require an education, then. Initially they receive an early education in right opinion. Their education prepares them to become the auxiliary guardians, who fulfill the function of defending society. This education is the traditional curriculum of music and gymnastics. Literature especially teaches them whom they are to fight, and whom not to fight. Stories about the gods, for example, ought to show them that family, friends, and fellow citizens do not fight with one another (377e–378e).

The guardians who prove worthy receive a higher education in knowledge proper. They become philosophical guardians, who rule society. Their curriculum less famously consists of the quadrivium and of dialectic. This curriculum has for its primary purpose to turn their souls to intelligible things. Arithmetic, geometry, astronomy, and music, all direct them to hypotheses about the ideas of the good, which govern the visible and audible world (*Republic* 7. 522e–525b, 526d–527c, 528e–530c, or 530d–531c). Dialectic takes them from the hypotheses of these sciences to the first principle of the good itself (531c–534d).

The guardians who are able to study philosophy must especially grasp the principle that constitutes knowledge about political society in its entirety. This principle would be justice, of course. With this principle they know what is good for their society as a whole (*Republic* 4. 428c–d). They accordingly rule their society for the sake of all its various functions (433a–434d). They are able to rule best, Plato concludes, because they are rich in a good and rational life, and they do not seek to be rich in gold (*Republic* 7. 520e–521b).

Plato shows us, then, how a correct political society finds its origin in philosophy. The guardians come to fulfill their political function primarily for its own sake though also for its consequences. The philosophical guardians do rule their society, after all, and the auxiliaries defend it. But because of their education, the guardians forgo any temptation to indulge their aggressive or appetitive instincts even though they initially arise at the behest of these instincts.

He argues, recall also, that the guardians, if they are to fulfill their function, ought not to indulge in any frivolous activities. They ought not to lead a festive life of feasting and drinking (*Republic* 4. 420b–421c). He famously requires that for their service they are to receive by way of compensation only their room and board and only what property might be necessary, presumably their armor and weapons (*Republic* 3. 416c–417b).[8]

Aristotle is at once more explicit and more concise. He begins the *Politics* with the assertion that a political society is a community, and that a community aims at a good. He argues that a political community is the most sovereign of all, and that it aims at the most sovereign good (*Politics* 1. 1. 1252a1–6). But the most sovereign good would be our political happiness. The implication is that a political community, because it aims at happiness in the ancient sense, has a philosophical origin.

But Aristotle finds that a political community initially arises from a naïve origin. He, too, offers a natural history of political society, and his history also originates in desire satisfaction. But he assumes that our most basic need is for reproduction. Society finds its origin in the coupling of male and female for the sake of generation, he argues. This coupling is not deliberate. By nature we come together to leave behind another of our kind, as do other animals and also plants (*Politics* 1. 2. 1252a26–30).

Next arise the family and the village. The family is first, and it exists for the sake of "daily" needs. These needs would appear to be necessary desires for food, clothing, and shelter (1252b9–15). An extended family, consisting of children and grandchildren, constitutes the earliest village. What those who live in a village desire Aristotle does not say. He states only that the village exists not "for the sake of everyday needs" (1252b15–18). Perhaps villagers concern themselves with some unnecessary desires for luxuries.

When several villages come together, a political society arises, Aristotle continues. We can now see a transition from a naïve to a philosophical origin for society. A political society, Aristotle argues explicitly, exists not for the sake of a life but for the sake of a good life (*Politics* 2. 1. 1252b27–30; also *Politics* 3. 6. 1278b17–24). But a good life would be a rational activity of value for its own sake. It would be a happy life.

Aristotle does not explain as explicitly as one might wish how those in a political society come to seek a good life. But he does argue that a political society for the sake of a good life is natural. As do prior communities, so does a political society arise by nature. Its citizens find their end in their political society, and their end is their nature. A thing, "when it has completely come to be," has fulfilled its nature, he states (*Politics* 1. 2. 1252b30–1253a3).[9]

But we might recall that law together with education is paramount for our political happiness. The law in fact trains us for a moral education, Aristotle asserts. It must habituate us to undertake good actions and not to engage in bad actions (*Ethics* 10. 9. 1179b20–1180a24; and *Politics* 8. 1.). Education, he argues, has the task of training and instructing us for a virtuous life (*Politics* 7. 13. 1332a38–1332b11). Gymnastics and music he commends less for their utility than for our leisure, and our leisure, he implies, is our happiness (*Politics* 8. 2–4.; and also 5–7.).[10]

Aristotle also points out that we are more political animals than insects or herding animals. We differ from these other creatures because we possess speech. We make sounds that are articulate, but other animals make inarticulate sounds. With an articulate sound we can distinguish good and bad and justice and injustice as well as expedience and inexpedience. This ability of ours is what enables us to form a political society (1253a7–18).[11]

I would note that Aristotle, as does Plato, finds a political society to be self-sufficient. Without society we are separately non-self-sufficient, he argues. A person stands to a society as a part to a whole. He presents an analogy to our body and its organs. Our hand or our foot by itself, for example, cannot be self-sufficient. Apart from our body neither one would be able to function, he argues, and it would be a hand or foot in name only (*Politics* 1. 2. 1253a18–29; also see *Ethics* 1. 7. 1097b8–11).

Aristotle recognizes a division of labor as well. He does so rather explicitly in his discussion of aristocracy, for example. He finds that a political society has to be able to fulfill several functions. These functions include the production of food, instruments, and arms, the acquisition of wealth, the cultivation of religion, and the conduct of deliberation and adjudication (*Politics* 7. 8. 1328b2–23).

But not any person can fulfill any function (*Politics* 7. 9. 1328b24–1329a2). He argues that no person ought to fulfill different functions at the same time. But he concedes that at different times one person can fulfill more than one function. For example, when younger, because they have strength, men ought to serve in the military, but when older, because have practical wisdom, they ought to serve in the assembly (*Politics* 7. 9. 1329a2–1329a17).

We again see, then, that we establish a society initially for the sake of desire satisfaction but ultimately for the sake of our happiness. A political society has a origin naïve initially but ultimately philosophical. In a political society we come to act for the sake of a rational and political function because of our very nature. But to fulfill a political and rational function for its own sake is to attain political happiness.[12]

I now wish to turn to the middle class. The middle class, after all, is the bulwark of any polity. Plato and Aristotle agree that a philosophical class, either of one person or a few persons, would be the best rulers in a political society. A constitution of this kind would be a monarchy or an aristocracy. But Aristotle, though Plato does not, would also permit the middle class to rule. They rule in a polity, which, he finds, is the most practicable for most societies.

We shall consider Plato first. Plato argues that the guardians ought to hold political office, but that they are not all eligible for office. Only the guardians who are older and have knowledge qualify for rule. They would care for their society because they know that what is beneficial for society and for them is the same (*Republic* 3. 412b–e). He is, however, obliged to concede that the guardians would likely attain rule only through divine inspiration or blind chance (*Republic* 6. 499a–499c).

Plato does not discuss a middle class. But the auxiliary guardians might make up a middle class. They, though, have very little property. But the auxiliaries do not qualify for rule apparently because they do not have knowledge but right opinion. Their right opinion is sufficient to enable them to fulfill their function of defense. It indicates to them who are the friends and the foes of their society (*Republic* 4. 429a–430c).

With the philosophical guardians, the auxiliary guardians have the task of ruling over the artisans and agrarians. The artisans and agrarians, Plato informs us, are not at all fit to rule. The guardians, though few, have simple and moderate desires that rest on understanding and right opinion. But the artisans, though many, have desires, apparently irrational, of many and diverse sorts. The few, who are thus superior, ought, Plato concludes, to rule the many, who are thus inferior (*Republic* 4. 431b–d).

Plato implies that the artisans and agrarians would rule poorly because they are naïve. They apparently lack both understanding and reason. He suggests that they have "knowledge of some sort," but their knowledge would appear to be, strictly speaking, opinion. They have right opinion not about their function in society but only about their function apart from society. A carpenter, he states, knows how to make furniture, and a farmer how to raise a crop (*Republic* 4. 428a–429a).

But Plato does require that the artisanal class do what is just. He shows that the guardians through their education improve not only themselves but also the artisans. He does so at the end of his discussion of music. The topic is, curiously, musical instruments. Not all instruments are appropriate for the education of the guardians. Only the lyre and the cithara are permissible in the city though the panpipes are allowed in the county (*Republic* 3. 399d–e).

With this stricture Socrates points out that the auxiliaries purge their society of its luxuries (399e). The guardians have no need for other musical instruments nor for those who make them, he argues (399c–d). This purge applies not only to musical instruments but apparently to most, if not all, products. Architecture, painting, weaving, and embroidery he mentions explicitly. Those who produce these objects must make them beautiful and graceful (401a–401d).

We might surmise that we could extend these strictures to the agrarians as well. They produce foodstuffs for the guardians. But the guardians have rather stringent dietary requirements (403c–404e).

Yet one might wonder, Why does Plato not think that the artisans can rise to a philosophical level of at least a rudimentary sort? Can the philosophical guardians not train and educate them to act justly? Through music and gymnastics, one would think, the artisans could attain, if not knowledge proper, right opinion about justice. They would need especially right opinion about what products would be beneficial for their society and what products would not.

We are all rational and political creatures, are we not, and we all are guardians, we might say, when we act justly. We act to preserve our society when we fulfill our function within it. I do not deny a role for a philosophical class or a martial class, but I would not deny a role for an artisanal and agrarian class, either. Could the artisans and agrarians not grasp that they do well when their society does well, and that their society does well when they do well.[13]

Aristotle takes us a step further. He would appear to agree with Plato on a very basic point. The rulers, he implies, ought to know that what is good for their society and for them is the same. Knowledge of this kind is the basis for a constitution correctly formed. He draws on analogies to the coach of a team and to the pilot of a ship. A pilot or a coach looks out for the goodness of his or her crew or team. But a pilot also benefits because he is a part of his crew, and a coach benefits if he takes part in his training regimen (*Politics* 3. 6. 1279a2–8).

Rulers in a corrupt constitution would appear to think that what is good for them is good for their society. Aristotle observes that in earlier days rulers used to look out for the interests of others when they ruled. But he complains that rulers in his day take care only for their own interests. They cling to rule for the sake of the profits to be gained (1279a8–16). They behave like a coach or a pilot who seeks, say, only to advance his own career.

Aristotle agrees, too, that a philosophical society is the best (see *Politics* 7. 3. 1325b14–23). He suggests that society of this kind would be either a monarchy or an aristocracy, which he thinks better (*Politics* 3. 15. 1286b3–7). But he argues that monarchy or an aristocracy is a constitution less than feasible. Either constitution rests on cultural and natural assumptions hardly acceptable. They would require that their rulers have a status akin to the divine when compared to other humans (*Politics* 7. 14. 1332b16–27).[14]

Aristotle argues at length that artisans and agrarians ought not to rule. His argument is harsher than that which Plato offers. He distinguishes between a political community and its conditions. A natural organism has parts, but these parts do not include those things without which it would not exist, he explains with an analogy. So, too, a political society requires property, for example, but its property is not among its parts even if its property includes living beings (*Politics* 7. 8. 1328a21–37).

A political community, if it aims at the most happiness, cannot include among its parts all those who are necessary for it, he continues. Its parts include only those persons who have virtue. Neither the craftsmen nor the farmers nor the businessmen can participate. The businessmen and the craftsmen lead a low life opposed to virtue, he informs us. The farmers do not have the leisure to become virtuous or to engage in politics (*Politics* 7. 9. 1328b33–1329a2). The farmers, he would appear to think, are either migrant workers or slaves (see 1329a17–26)!

Yet Aristotle would grant sovereignty to the middle class. He explains that the people rather than the few more often than not ought to rule (*Politics* 3. 11. 1281a40–42). The people, though they cannot separately, can together form a better judgment than the few about their society in its entirety. The many can judge better because they can each judge a part, and together they can all judge the whole. He relies on analogies to the criticism of poetry or of music (1281b7–10).

He implies further that the people can together judge better the success of their constitution and its laws. He employs more analogies to make his point. A pilot is a better judge of a rudder than a carpenter, a homeowner is a better judge of a house than a contractor, and guest a better judge of a dinner than a chef (1282a17–23).

Aristotle does make a qualification, however. The people must have an education in a modicum at least. Otherwise, his arguments would fail. He argues that the many, taken not separately but together, are likely to be better than the few. But that each person must have a portion of virtue and practical wisdom, he explicitly assumes (1281a42–1281b7; also 1281b10–15). He concedes that not all peoples meet this requisite qualification. Some are no better than beasts (1281b15–20).[15]

What political society can the people rule, then? They cannot rule in a monarchy or an aristocracy. But they can rule in a polity. The people, Aristotle implies, cannot have philosophical virtue. Only one person or a few persons can have every virtue. But the people can attain martial virtue and, presumably, its happiness. The citizens of a polity are those who defend society, and they are the ancient hoplites (*Politics* 3. 7. 1279a37–1279b3).[16]

Does Aristotle not assert, one might object, that a polity is a mix of oligarchy and democracy? He states further that a political society is usually thought to be a polity when the mix inclines toward democracy, and that it is thought an aristocracy when it inclines toward oligarchy (*Politics* 4. 8. 1293b31–42). He even goes on to offer various suggestions on how set up a polity by mixing democratic and oligarchic elements (*Politics* 4. 9.).

But a polity of this mixed kind clearly cannot be a eudaimonic polity. This polity can only be what I call an expedient polity. Why? Citizens of eudaimonic polity aim at happiness albeit of the martial variety. But citizens of a mixed polity aim at the acquisition of wealth, if oligarchic, or at the pursuit of pleasure, if democratic. The one polity seeks a good that is intelligible, and the other goods that are merely sensible.[17]

I would respond that Aristotle recognizes both a eudaimonic and an expedient polity, and he implies that a polity composed of the middle class would constitute, or at least approximate, a eudaimonic polity. Every society, he explains, has three parts. These parts are "the very rich," "the very poor," and "those in the middle" (*Politics* 4. 11. 1295b1–3). But those who are in the middle are well suited for rule, he implies, because they lie on a mean and possess the goods of fortune in moderation (1295b3–5).

Why does moderate wealth suit the middle class for rule? Those who have moderate wealth are more amenable to reason, he argues. The rich become grand criminals, and the poor petty criminals. The middle class is also less likely to seek or to shun office, and they are more likely to obey the law. But the rich are too coddled to be ruled, and the poor are too destitute. Neither does the middle class covet the goods of others, nor do others covet their goods. And they do not plot against others, and others do not plot against them, he argues (*Politics* 4. 11. 1295b5–1296a21).

But I now find myself again obliged to ask, Why cannot the artisans and agrarians participate in a polity? Would not the arguments about the people and their rule apply to them, too? If sufficiently virtuous and prudent, could they not together, though not separately, judge of their society as a whole? Could they not together judge as well the success of their constitution and its laws?

They would not need property sufficient to purchase heavy armor. They would need only moderate property sufficient to enable them to engage in their occupations. Their property would be their tools and raw materials. If they find their happiness in their occupations, would they not also be amenable to reason? Would they be likely to seek or to shun office, or would they likely disobey the law? Would they be covetous or given to plots? Not likely, I should think.[18]

I would observe that Aristotle himself all but arrives at this very conclusion. He implies that those in the best democracy or in the best oligarchy are nearly virtuous. His observations all but repeat his arguments about the middle class in a polity. The farmers or the herders rule in the best democracy. They have only moderate wealth, and they govern by the law (*Politics* 4. 6. 1292b25–29). They do prefer their own function to public office, but they do not covet the property of others (*Politics* 6. 4. 1318b10–16).[19]

He explicitly states that the best oligarchy approximates a polity though he likely refers to a mixed polity. He argues that this oligarchy has a high property requirement for higher offices, and a lower requirement for lower offices (*Politics* 6. 6. 1320b22–26). An oligarchy of this kind, he indicates, would likely rise out of the heavy infantry, who, recall, make up a eudaimonic polity. The cavalry, however, makes up a "strong oligarchy," and the light infantry or navy is "entirely democratic" (*Politics* 6. 7. 1321a8–14). The best oligarchy also governs by law (see *Politics* 4. 6. 1293a12–20).

We see, then, that the citizens in the best oligarchies and the best democracies would take a step toward virtue. They are law-abiding citizens. Their laws, admittedly, are not the best. They aim not at happiness but at acquisition of property or the attainment of pleasure. What these persons lack is moral education. But with an education they would quite likely seek a virtuous and happy life and establish laws with the same end.

How difficult would the requisite education be for those in moderate democracies and oligarchies? This question is one of value. In a democracy the agrarians and the artisans, admittedly, rule for the sake of their own class, and the heavy infantry in an oligarchy likely rules for its class. But the heavy infantry in a polity learn that their function is but a part of a whole with intrinsic value. Why could not the artisans and agrarians learn that their function has intrinsic value of its own within a whole?

I would conclude, then, that a political society finds its best material in a virtuous and happy population. I speak, again, of virtue and happiness in a political sense and in a broad political sense that includes philosophical, martial, and artisanal functions. These functions, if felicitous, citizens perform primarily for their own sake. They have a value intrinsic to them as well as any instrumental value.

But a felicitous population need not be philosophical or martial. Plato concedes that the philosophical part of society is but a few and can rule only with the martial class. Aristotle contends that the martial part of society in his day is many and can form a polity. But a martial class in our day would be too few to maintain a stable rule in a polity. Ought we not to educate the artisanal and agrarian class for rule, then? They are today the middle class in most societies if not all.

Does a political society require a full-fledged philosopher to see that a people can together constitute a whole and its parts? I would ask. With philosophy in a modicum can the artisans and agrarians not discover this insight adequately enough for political purposes? With right opinion about their society and their functions within it can they not rule together for the sake of their society in its entirety? They need not rule for the sake of themselves only.[20]

Happiness is of the political variety and is both yours and mine if we can but see our rational activity to be an intelligible good of intrinsic value. Happiness is of the passional sort and is either yours or mine if we take our rational activity to be a good of instrumental value only for purchasing and consuming material things.

Alexis de Tocqueville recognizes that education is of paramount importance for a political society. He argues that "freedom, public peace, and social order" will not prevail without education because we are now distant from "the century of blind sacrifice and instinctive virtues," which would presumably be the eighteenth century. Without education "ignorant and coarse citizens" would follow their selfishness to "ridiculous excesses" and to "shameful depths of wretchedness" (*Democracy* 2. 2. 8. 613).

Yet, alas, he favors an education not in what he calls beautiful virtue but rather in useful virtue or what he calls self-interest properly understood. Self-interest of this kind is the doctrine of "enlightened self-love." This self-love leads us to help others and to devote some time and wealth to the state and its welfare, he argues (611). But this self-interest allows that we do these things ultimately for the benefit of ourselves (610–611).

He thinks that a philosophy of proper self-love, though not sublime, is "clear and unambiguous." It does not aim at great things, but it attains its aims "without too much effort." It is, he claims, "the one best suited to the needs of contemporary men" and "the most powerful guarantee against their own nature" (611–612). He also finds that Americans universally adopt this philosophy. We weave it into everything we say, he states, whether we are rich or poor (611).

I would like to think that Tocqueville would be willing to allow an education for the sake of beautiful virtue could he but hear my arguments. He does observe, almost despite himself, that Americans do themselves an injustice when they espouse enlightened self-interest. Though they only rarely admit it, they do at times yield themselves to "disinterested and spontaneous impulses natural to man," he concedes (611).

Why, I would ask, could we not educate ourselves in these disinterested impulses so natural to man? Or, better, could we not endeavor to understand our rational and political nature and to act in harmony with it?[21]

3. Both John Rawls and Robert Nozick, our paradigmatic contemporary philosophers, develop a theory of polity for contemporary society though they do so apparently unawares. What is less fortunate is that neither Rawls nor Nozick advances a concept of a correct polity. Though their theories differ, they both advance a theory of polity that rests not on a eudaimonic principle but on a mixture of oligarchic and democratic principles.

Rawls and Nozick do not think that a political society has primarily intrinsic value though they acknowledge its intrinsic value. They both hold, albeit implicitly, that a political society has instrumental value primarily. Rawls does not take fully into account that we are by nature rational and political animals. That he does not, we can see in his analysis of a well-ordered society. People in a well-ordered society do what is just, but they do so for their own benefit. They each gain more rather than fewer primary goods.

Nozick fares no better than Rawls. He also fails to acknowledge fully our rational and political nature. His analysis he focuses on what he calls a utopian association. He argues expressly that any utopia is no more than a market, and that by joining a utopia people each seek their own good. They join up only if they can each receive in return their marginal contribution.

Rawls and Nozick, then, subordinate the public good to the private. A political society is not a *res publica* for either philosopher. There is no political community with a value essentially its own. Both philosophers find that a political society is in effect little more than a *res privata*. They argue that it has essentially instrumental value for individuals living within it.

We shall begin with John Rawls. Rawls clearly recognizes that a political society can have intrinsic value. He, indeed, characterizes this value very nicely for us when he discusses a social union. Human beings, he argues, have a "social nature." They have "shared final ends," and these ends they value "as good in themselves." He rightly asserts that we "need one another as partners in ways of life that are engaged in for their own sake." Citing Wilhelm von Humboldt, he argues that we enjoy the realized natural abilities of each other in a social union and its activity (*Theory* 9. 79. 458–460).

This concept of a social union he uses to define what he calls a social desire. A social desire is a common desire, but a common desire need not be social. Those who have a social desire have a shared end. They "have an agreed scheme of conduct in which the excellences and enjoyments of each are complementary to the good of all," he explains. But those who have a common desire may desire merely to have the same thing. Ulysses S. Grant and Robert E. Lee, for example, had a common desire to hold Richmond (460–461).

A political society can be a social union, Rawls continues. A well-ordered society on his theory has two features of a social union. Its members find that the activity "of the carrying out of just institutions" to be a final end, and that they value these just institutions "as good in themselves." The first feature of being a final end enables its members to share a common aim "of cooperating together to realize their own and another's nature," he explains. "This collective intention" citizens define by acting on principles of justice (462).

The second feature of being good in itself he explicates with what he calls a Kantian and an Aristotelian explanation. The Kantian explanation is that by acting to uphold their political institutions as good in themselves, citizens are able to express their nature "as free and equal moral persons" (462–463). The Aristotelian interpretation is that their political institutions provide "the most complex and diverse activity of all," and enable each person to have "a more ample and rich structure" for their plan of life (463).

He also appeals eloquently to the division of labor. We can overcome servile dependence on others with its monotony and routine though we cannot entirely overcome our dependence on others, he argues. We rely on others to do things that we cannot do or that we do not do. But in a social union "we cease to be mere fragments," and we join ourselves to "a wider and just arrangement the aims of which we affirm" (463–464).

Rawls thus offers a concept of a social union that expresses quite well the concept of an intrinsically valuable political activity. One would be hard pressed to improve upon his concept or its expression. A social union is truly a political community. Its concept shows that all persons in a political society can appreciate their shared activities as good for their own sake, and that our political activities can complement one another.

Nonetheless, Rawls does not give his concept of a social union the priority within his theory that one might wish. We can see that he does not if we consider how he establishes his concept of moral virtue. To place virtue within his theory, he distinguishes a full theory of goodness from a thin theory of goodness. The full theory, he explains, uses principles of justice to define moral concepts, such as moral worth and moral virtue (*Theory* 7. 60. 349–350). The thin theory concerns only the concept of a rational plan of life (347–349).

The full theory of goodness applies both to society and to persons, he argues (*Theory* 7. 66. 381–382). When applied to persons, the theory includes, among the concepts of moral worth and moral virtue, the good of justice and the good of a person and an action. This theory also concerns, less significantly for our purposes, other concepts, such as those of beneficence and supererogation. But these concepts would be amenable to a similar analysis (*Theory* 7. 60. 349–350).

The thin theory rests on a concept of a rational plan of life, Rawls explains, and it provides a foundation for the original position (*Theory* 7. 60. 347–348). The original position, you may perchance recall, is a hypothetical situation in which persons decide on principles of justice (*Theory* 1. 3. 10–11). The persons in the original position are "rational and mutually disinterested." They possess a rationality of means and ends, and they do not take an interest in the interests of one another (*Theory* 1. 3. 12).

The thin theory provides "the bare essentials" of a motive for deriving principles of justice (*Theory* 7. 60. 347–348). The instrumental concept of rationality Rawls uses to derive principles of justice that would provision the persons in the original position with the "prerequisites for carrying out their plans of life." He assumes that these persons would want more rather than fewer of what he terms primary goods. They would "prefer a wider to a narrower liberty and opportunity, and a greater rather than a smaller share of wealth and income" (*Theory* 7. 60. 348; 7. 66. 380).

We come now to the key problem. This problem is what Rawls calls the congruence question. It concerns what connection, if any, might lie between our rationality and justice. Is our rationality congruent with justice? His answer is that a "rational plan of life" does provide support for a "sense of justice." But he limits his answer, he explains, to a well-ordered society, in which persons act justly. In a well-ordered society, he asserts, a "match exists" between "the principles of rational choice" and "the principles of justice" (*Theory* 7. 60. 350; 9. 78. 450–451).

Rawls does not appear to appreciate that his congruence question is less than unambiguous. He rightly argues that justice can have intrinsic value, and he rightly thinks its intrinsic value significant. But he fails to take into account that it can have intrinsic value either primarily or secondarily. Unfortunately, his arguments for congruence imply that justice has an intrinsic value secondarily, and that it has an instrumental value primarily.

One would expect, then, that any political desire so derived would take for its object a political activity of value not primarily intrinsic but primarily instrumental. This expectation, if it holds, suggests further that our political activity could not constitute political happiness but would likely serve private interest. Our political society would no longer itself be an object of value to be cherished essentially for its own sake. It would be only an instrument to be employed if and when we find it serviceable.

Before he answers it, Rawls formulates the congruence question more explicitly and pointedly. He asks, Is it rational in the thin sense of the good to affirm a sense of justice (*Theory* 9. 86. 496–497)? Presumably, one would affirm a sense of justice by acting justly. So his question becomes, Is it rational instrumentally to act justly? After all, in the thin sense of the good our rationality is instrumental. The question, thus formulated, all but answers itself.

There are three "chief reasons," Rawls informs us, why we would be rational in the thin sense to act justly (*Theory* 9. 86. 501). These reasons turn out to be strikingly similar to those which account for our participation in a social union. They are so similar, I would assume, because a social union and a well-ordered society exhibit on his theory the same basic features. Those persons who live within a well-ordered society also value their just activities both as final ends and as good in themselves.

The first reason stems from the concept of a free rider, who resorts to acting unjustly when he can get away with it. A free rider, Rawls explains, would deny his moral psychology. He would subject himself to psychological costs that come with being deceptive (499). Moral psychology, he continues, inclines us to be fair and just with those whom we care for. A social union embodies bonds of "affection and fellow feeling" that extend widely. A free rider would deny himself these extensive social ties (499–500).

One can surely agree that deception has its psychological costs. But I must ask, Are there not psychological costs in the bonds of affection and fellow feeling of a social union? Would we feel affection for a well-ordered society and for other persons as good in themselves? Not on the Rawlsian theory. We would forgo any community feeling in a well-ordered society. We would feel affection for our society and for others for our own sake. A well-ordered society and its members are merely means to our ends.

A second reason that Rawls offers is, he claims, Kantian. The Kantian interpretation, he argues, is that we can express our nature as free and rational beings when we act justly. The desire to act freely and rationally and the desire to act justly are one and the same, he explains. Why are they the same? The principles of justice, because chosen in the original position, are principles of rationality and freedom (501).

How sound is the Kantian interpretation? The interpretation is untenable, I must argue. Kant argues that we express our free and rational nature when we perform an action from a moral imperative (*Grounding* 2. 415–417). But a moral imperative is categorical, and a categorical imperative demands that we perform an action for its own sake. A hypothetical imperative requires of us an action of value for its consequences (413–415).

Rawls relies, thirdly, on what he calls the Aristotelian principle. This principle is that we enjoy the exercise of more capacities and more complex capacities (*Theory* 9. 79. 374–376). A well-ordered society, he argues, enables its members to realize and to appreciate their manifold human potentialities. Because it is a social union, a society of this kind can enable everyone to enjoy a "greater richness and diversity of the collective activity." But to participate in a well-ordered society, we must accept and follow the principles of justice, which regulate our joint activity (*Theory* 9. 86. 500–501).

I fear that this social union leaves out what Aristotle takes to be the most important value. This value is our happiness. Our happiness is an activity of value primarily for its own sake (see *Ethics* 1. 7. 1097a24–1097b6). Our political happiness includes just actions, obviously (*Ethics* 5. 1. 1129b14–25, e.g.). What Rawls calls the Aristotelian principle cannot find its full realization in a social union. He does claim that this principle recognizes activities of value for their own sakes (*Theory* 3. 65. 378–379). But he takes an activity of this kind to be not primarily but secondarily of value for itself.[22]

We can now see why a social union lacks an essentially intrinsic value. At least, why it does on the Rawlsian theory. No person values participation in a social union for its own sake. Each person finds a motivation for participating in the benefits received. No one values a social union primarily as an end in itself, but everyone values it primarily as a means to more rather than fewer goods. Everyone finds the human potentialities expressed in a social union ultimately to be of value not for public but for personal ends.[23]

One might object that Rawls takes into consideration a concept of a private society, which, he argues, contrasts with a social union. I would reply that his concept of private society contrasts less than he apparently thinks. He argues that persons in a private society have ends that are not "complementary" but are "competing or independent" (*Theory* 9. 79. 457). I would point out that persons in a well-ordered society have ends primarily competing and independent though their ends are complementary. They remain, after all, mutually disinterested.

He also argues that persons in private society view just institutions not as having value in themselves but as "an efficient scheme that gives him the largest share of assets" (457). Though they view them as having intrinsic value, persons in a well-ordered society also take just institutions to be primarily not an end in themselves but an efficient means to gain for themselves more rather than fewer primary goods.

Finally, he argues that a private society is a power struggle. A society of this kind is held together by the calculation not that its institutions are "good in themselves," but that changes in its institutions would reduce the resources by which they seek their own ends (457–458). But, once again, a well-ordered society is primarily a means by which persons through public institutions pursue private goods in what they deem to be a fair manner though they also value society itself as a good.[24]

Rawls, then, presents a theory of justice in which persons use political means to pursue personal ends. Unfortunately, this theory offers a concept of political society that fits the classical definition of corruption. Rawls implicitly subsumes a concept of a correct constitution and its value under a concept of a corrupt constitution and its value. A well-ordered society may not be purely but it is primarily a private society that has a self-seeking instrumental value albeit with mitigating intrinsic value.[25]

How, then, might the middle class fare in a well-ordered society? The middle class is, after all, the mainstay of any polity. A eudaimonic polity, we have seen, takes for its end the middle class and its political function. This function constitutes happiness in the ancient sense. But an expedient polity, we shall see, need not promote a middle class. It instead promotes a compact between the rich and the poor.

One can easily see that Rawls offers an expedient polity. He concerns himself only with provisioning the rich and the poor classes with more rather than fewer primary goods and ultimately with the pleasure of enjoying these goods. The principles of justice, he explains, form the basis for "the willing cooperation" between the better-endowed and better-situated and the others (*Theory* 1. 3. 13–14). The others are the worse-endowed.

The middle class on the Rawlsian theory does not seek happiness in an ancient sense, neither martial nor artisanal. No class does. Perhaps persons could pursue happiness in a rational sense. But Rawls would imply that they do not. He assumes that we do not wish to perform an action for its own sake, and that with a plan of life we prefer to satisfy more desires rather than fewer. We consequently seek more rather than fewer primary goods.

He would forgo any consideration of the middle class and its advantages. Martial or artisanal happiness can set a limit for the acquisition of property. We would require only the resources needed for our function. Rawls has the notion that any limit of this kind is but personal preference (see *Theory* 3. 25. 123, e.g.). Why does he so think? Persons in the middle class on his theory would have no political function proper to them. All persons have in fact only the private functions of acquiring property and satisfying desire.

Rawls prefers to focus his analysis on the rich and the poor classes. Herein lies the danger, I think. The middle class resides in a political society in which the rich and the poor classes divide the spoils of political cooperation. The difference principle permits the rich to gain whatever benefits they can if only they grant benefits to the poor. Those of moderate means are not part of the bargain. Why would they not fail to receive any benefits at all and be left behind?[26]

Rawls would no doubt respond that any consequences of this sort are less than likely. To suggest that they would be unlikely, he makes two assumptions about political society. These assumptions he deems "plausible." The one is chain connections and the other close knittings. Chain connections assume that to raise the benefits for the better-off and the worse-off is to raise them for all classes in between. Close knittings assume more strongly that to raise the benefits for any class is to raise them for every class (*Theory* 2. 13. 69–72).[27]

I must point out in response that not only is it not unlikely, the scenario that the middle class loses out is quite likely. In fact, this scenario is not merely probable but actual. Has Rawls not heard of a dual economy? A dual economy is one divided between the rich and the poor classes with a very small, if any, middle class. Cosmopolitan elites enjoy a luxurious life on the backs urban and rural workers who are impoverished if not destitute. The middle class, if not whipsawed, is at best stagnant.[28]

Rawls, then, has a society essentially unjust because his society is not a polity resting on a eudaimonic principle but a mixed polity relying on oligarchic and democratic principles. Rawlsian citizens act not on desires of a political nature but on desires not at all political. They essentially seek not to assist one another in attaining any shared ends, but they seek to take advantage of one another in attaining of their separate ends. They view each other not as ends to be respected but as means to be exploited.[29]

In his attempt to prove that a political society is a social union, Rawls, I think we can see, begs the question though he denies that he does. If we use a concept of instrumental rationality to derive political principles, and if we use the principles so derived to define moral concepts, we ought to find that our presumed rationality is congruent with our moral concepts so defined. Justice, I suggest, would have not moral value but instrumental value only.

Rawls argues that the derivation would fail only if we use our concept of rationality directly to define moral virtue. He claims that we can use our rationality to define virtue indirectly through the original position and the principles of justice (*Theory* 7. 66. 380, 381–382). I fail to see the difference. We begin with an instrumental theory of rationality, and we end with an instrumental theory of morality, do we not? No matter how many intermediate steps our inference might take.

I would conclude, then, that we ought not, in Rawlsian terms, to use a thin theory of the good to derive a full theory. We ought better, I should think, to use a full theory of the good to derive a thin theory. Intrinsic value surely ought to take precedence over any instrumental value.

4. I shall now argue that Robert Nozick develops a polity similar in its general features to the polity of John Rawls. He, too, offers a polity not of eudaimonics but of expedience. His polity also rests not on a principle of happiness but on oligarchic and democratic principles. Its aim is not a good of political action of value for itself but a good of personal preference.

Nozick does recognize that political activity can have value for its own sake, and he argues that we can appreciate the varied activities of others, especially the activities that we ourselves cannot perform. In other words, he recognizes what Rawls calls a social union and its value. But, unfortunately, Nozick, too, reduces this intrinsic social value to a value merely instrumental.

Nozick thus fails to offer a true concept of a community of value for itself. A political society includes no common activities that we all share without an ulterior motive. Though he recognizes that it can have intrinsic value, he takes the position, implicitly I admit, that political activity has an instrumental value that he takes to be primary, and that its intrinsic value is secondary.

Any reader acquainted with Nozick would by now likely have objected, if only silently, that I have not taken into account what he says about utopia. I concede the omission. I would rejoin, however, that I had to take into consideration what Nozick calls a protective association and a minimal state before taking up his concept of utopia. We shall now see that Nozick extends his analysis of a state of nature to include not only a protective association and a minimal state but also a utopian association.

Utopia, Nozick argues, ought to be "a framework for utopias." This framework would give persons the liberty to realize their own view of a good life in their own ideal community (*Anarchy* 3. 10. 311–312). The framework grants everyone a right to realize a particular utopia by imagining a world to inhabit. The only condition is that everyone also has the option of leaving one imagined world for another imagined world. A utopia becomes stable when no one who inhabits its world can imagine another world more preferable (297–300).

Nozick calls these particular utopias associations. He shows that a utopian association is very much like a social union. He even cites Rawls. Each person benefits "from co-existing in the world with others and being part of the normal social network," he explains. Every person also finds others useful or delightful, he continues, because of their complementary talents and abilities. We cannot realize all our potentialities as human beings, but we can all appreciate others who develop capacities that we do not (*Anarchy* 3. 10. 306 and n3).

But could he argue that a utopian association is a political society of intrinsic value? He could not likely do so, I am afraid. He offers no argument in favor of a rational activity of value for itself. Any rational activity would most likely be subordinated to imagination and to desire. Those who inhabit a utopian association live in a world that they imagine, and their imagined world, though it must be feasible, can approach the fanciful. That some utopians have in fact blurred the line between reality and fantasy, he concedes (*Anarchy* 3. 10. 307–308; also 316–317).

Indeed, Nozick suggests that we do not have a social nature or even a nature. He argues explicitly that there are no objective values either for persons or for their associations. He provides a lengthy and colorful list of famous persons, including philosophers, scientists, politicians, artists, entertainers, and athletes, among others, to suggest that there can be no objective values. Is there one life best for all these individuals? he asks. That there might be one best community for them, he avers, seems incredible (309–311).

Nor do we have a social desire. Nozick clearly implies that a utopian association has a value primarily instrumental. A social union is merely one benefit among others (306). We join a utopia with the same motivation we have when we enter "a competitive market," he argues. Utopian associations seeking members are analogous to business firms competing for employees. Persons join an association when they receive their marginal contribution from their imagined world (301–302).

He declares quite earnestly that his economic model for utopias yields distinct advantages. The model brings to bear on utopian theory theoretical tools not only from economic theory but also from decision theory and game theory (302, 306).[30]

But we ought to take a closer look at Nozick's concept of utopia and its foundation. This foundation we can discover if we examine the derivation of a utopia. Our examination will take us back to a state of nature and the law of nature. As he takes a state of nature and transforms it into a political realm of a protective association, so Nozick transforms the state of nature further into a personal realm of a utopian association.

We ought to ask, How does the utopian framework enable one to imagine a utopian world to inhabit? One can see without undue difficulty that Nozick applies to a utopian association an analysis similar to his analysis of a protective association. A utopia is also a specification of perfect freedom for oneself and freedom from harm by others. But the utopian variation rests less on natural law than on personal liking (see *Anarchy* 1. 2. 10).

Nozick argues that one can form a utopian association with what he calls design devices and filter devices (*Anarchy* 3. 10. 312–313). Design devices people use to think about what the best society might be. They result in a model that can be a pattern for a utopia. But these devices are less than satisfactory, he argues. Human beings are far too complex and their institutions too complex for someone to invent a single ideal pattern for a society. Imagine, he asks, cavemen sitting around and trying to think up for all time a concept of the best possible society (313–314).

Filter devices people use to eliminate alternatives. They secure conditions that people want by excluding persons who would violate them. These devices are more satisfactory, Nozick argues. They are appropriate for people who have at best limited knowledge about what society would be best. We require more knowledge to determine what we want and less knowledge to determine what we do not want. These devices also become more selective when they have winnowed out more undesirable alternatives (314).

Design and filter devices one can use together within the framework for utopian experimentation, Nozick explains further. The best method for imagining a utopian association is in fact to combine both devices. Design devices generate concepts of specific utopias to be tried out, and filtering devices reject or modify concepts of utopias that people do not like. There thus arises an interaction between designing and filtering concepts (315–317).

This utopian framework, I would argue, presents an extension of a state of nature quite similar in its fundamentals to a protective association. Recall how people join together to form a protective association. In a state of nature we have perfect freedom to dispose of our persons and our possessions as we see fit. We also have a right by the law of nature not to be harmed in our life, health, liberty, or property (*Anarchy* 1. 2. 10).

Unfortunately, some people violate the law of nature and do us harm. We each have the right to redress these violations (10). But our ad hoc attempts to enforce this law are less than satisfactory. Individual attempts at enforcement are subject to what John Locke calls inconveniences. We may find that the law of nature is not sufficiently specific, we frequently make erroneous judgments in our own case, and we often lack adequate power to enforce the law (11–12).

Because of these inconveniences, persons soon find themselves obliged to form an association for their mutual protection. When they do, they would likely have recourse to design and filter devices. Design devices could enable them to establish proper procedures for determining what offense, if any, has occurred and, presumably, what reparation or punishment, if any, is appropriate. These devices could also serve to suggest that they ought to employ agents who have the power to apply their procedures and carry out their policies (compare *Anarchy* 1. 2. 13).

Filter devices determine who is a member of the association and who receives protection from the association. Initially an association rests on volunteer participation, and only persons who participate are protected (*Anarchy* 1. 2. 12–13). After an association begins to hire agents, only persons who help pay for the protective agents receive protection (13, 24–25). Eventually a protective association becomes a minimal state, and even those who do not pay receive protection when they interact with those who do pay (*Anarchy* 5. 110–113, 113–114).

A protective association, then, is a specification of the state of nature. Design and filter devices, Nozick implicitly indicates, can specify in part what perfect freedom is and to whom the law of nature applies. Persons in an association use their freedom to hire protective agents and to define procedures for determining offenses and redressing them. They also use association membership to exclude those who do not receive protection though they allow for exceptions.

One can now see that a utopia develops and specifies what goods a protective association would protect. Nozick clearly implies that a utopian association presupposes a protective association since developed into a minimal state. That the minimal state is in fact the framework for utopia, he declares explicitly. The minimal state regards its members "as inviolate individuals," he explains, and this state allows them to realize their ends and themselves as far as they can (*Anarchy* 3. 10. 333–334).

But do these individuals know what their ends and their selves are? Apparently not. They would know only that they retain their "perfect freedom" from a state of nature to do with their persons and their possessions as they think fit. Indeed, they cannot know what their purposes and their persons are. There is no objective principle of goodness. Or so Nozick argues. They must specify their goodness by imagining a world that they think to be good.

Nor can they know what harms they seek to prevent. The law of nature is not sufficiently specific. They know only in general that they have a freedom from harm to their life, health, liberty, and property. They must imagine for their utopia a more specific good that they find desirable. They allow into their utopia only those who subscribe to the imagined good that they attempt to realize. Those who imagine a different good would not be able to enter. Not that those excluded would likely be clamoring to get in.

A utopian association, then, bears a general similarity to a protective association. Persons in a utopia pursue what they take to be good, and they protect their good by imposing constraints on others. But the law of nature protects natural goods—life, health, liberty, and property. At least, Locke so thought. An imagined utopia protects what are imagined goods—personal preferences.

We find, then, that Nozick does not offer a community that has an intrinsic value primarily. Both a protective association and a utopian association have primarily an instrumental value. Neither association is a social union of value for its own sake. A utopia is not a political society of activities naturally of value for themselves but merely a society of activities imagined to be of value for its members.[31]

The middle class would fare little better within a Nozickian utopia than they would within a Rawlsian well-ordered society. They would not likely enjoy a eudaimonic polity. Surely, they do not require a eudaimonic principle to imagine a utopian association or to inhabit one. An oligarchic or a democratic principle would be more likely. They do not act on their rational nature and would likely imagine a pleonectic or hedonic world.

But a polity of expediency could foster a middle class of sorts. The middle class, Nozick suggests, would become a prize contested in a political and economic arena. A danger for Nozick appears to be a conflict between the rich class and the poor class. He worries that the poor could vote to expropriate the property of the rich. But to succeed, they would need, he argues, the votes of the middle class, at least in part, to gain a majority.

The rich class can prevent this expropriation of their property by garnering the middle class votes themselves, Nozick continues. The rich could co-opt the middle class. They could do so enacting programs for the benefit of those with moderate wealth. Because they have more resources, the rich would obviously find the task of winning over the middle class easier than the poor class would (*Anarchy* 2. 8. 274–275).

Nozick in effect presents a Rawlsian difference principle. But this difference principle, if we may so call it, would extend down only to the middle class and not even to all of this class. The rich would benefit only those who are moderately well-off in a quantity sufficient to secure a stable majority. They need not trouble themselves, unless they are of sufficient largesse, to benefit those who are worse-off.[32]

But I wonder whether the utopias that Nozick envisions might not fall out into associations resting more on class interests. Would not each class be likely to design a utopia solely for its own sake? Would they not wish to exclude other classes that do not share their interests or do not wish, at least, to cooperate with them (see *Anarchy* 3. 7. 193)? I believe that these classes historically often have done so. Plato and Aristotle saw class interests as the foundations for constitutions of the corrupt varieties, not excluding oligarchy and democracy.

I would argue that a eudaimonic polity has a middle class much harder to co-opt. An artisanal class who value their activities for their own sake would wish to have little beyond what they need to engage in their eudaimonic activities. I would also wonder if a eudaimonic middle class might themselves co-opt the rich and the poor classes by their example. One would like to think that the other classes might see the benefits of activities of value for themselves and of a community of activities of value for itself.

A utopia, then, is a more sophisticated, not to say sophistical, state of nature. Its goal is merely an imagined good to be enjoyed exclusively. But if a minimal state remains in a state of nature, so, then, does a utopia remain in a state of nature. We do not so much leave our natural state as we change it to suit ourselves. But we remain ignorant of any objective goodness resting on our human nature. Our ignorance gives rise to the pursuit of a good merely imagined to be desirable.

I must argue against Nozick that our happiness can provide us with an objective value, and that our happiness rests on our rational nature. Our eudaimonic activities embody the same rational concepts for all those who choose to engage in them. You may have a talent for brewing beer, for example. If you do, you must then brew your beer within certain parameters. You may invent a new recipe for your beer or a new process for brewing. But other brewers, if you let them in on your secret, can brew beer with the very same, or nearly the same, qualities. Your recipe or process is objective.[33]

I cheerfully concede, however, that one could use design and filter devices to establish a eudaimonic polity. Our design devices would stipulate that we ought to pursue happiness in the sense of a rational activity of intrinsic value. This device can advocate both happiness in general and happiness of particular kinds. Everyone can appreciate what value happiness generally has, but no one can predict what specific form happiness will take.

I thus agree with Nozick that there is no one best society. Plato argues for an ideal society of philosophical happiness, and Aristotle for a society of martial happiness. But I am arguing in general for a society of artisanal happiness. I would also argue for artisanal happiness of various specific senses for its members. Any society, even an artisanal one, needs brewers and bakers if not candlestick makers. Though they seek artisanal happiness, its members must perforce seek artisanal happiness of different kinds.

We might note, too, that even cavemen could surely recognize rational activity as good for its own sake, but they obviously could not anticipate the specific rational activities that humans pursue in our day. They surely could recognize eudaimonic activity if they were *Homo sapiens*, and they might even be able to do so if they were another species, say, *Homo neanderthalensis*.

Filter devices one could use to deny a primary place to hedonic and pleonectic activities. These activities can play no eudaimonic role within a polity but only a subordinate role. They do not constitute artisanal activities, not to mention philosophical or martial activities! Artisanal activities require that we act in accordance with a principle for its own sake, and they require that we do not aim at pleasure or property, especially not in excess.

I concede, then, that a polity resting on artisanal happiness might be a possible utopia within a Nozickian framework. The inhabitants of a utopia may accept certain general principles, Nozick informs us. He gives the example of an equal distribution of goods produced (*Anarchy* 10. 304). A principle of eudaimonic happiness could surely be among these possible principles. But artisanal happiness would focus on productive activities rather than on the enjoyment of things produced.

I am cautious, however, about the likelihood of a eudaimonic polity. My fear is that a society of this kind would not be apt to arise under the aegis of the utopian framework. The framework itself rests on no objective principle of human goodness, and it allows any notion of goodness to be pursued, not merely those known to be good but also those imagined to be good. Even if it did somehow arise, an artisanal polity would still be but one correct political society among many corrupt societies within a corrupt framework.

But justice, if eudaimonic, would be, one could say, utopian. Its utopia would be essentially a political community of intrinsically valuable activities. It would be a social union, in other words, and a social union primarily of value for itself. It would not be a community, so-called, of primarily instrumental value for the purpose of doing whatever one might please without hindrance from others.

5. In a eudaimonic polity we find what is truly fraternity. Where does a political constitution exist if not in our character and in our conduct? Our political virtue and our political happiness are public goods shared with others within our society. Nay, they are public goods made possible only within a society. We can, if we so choose, acknowledge and accept each other and our political roles to be ends valuable for their own sake. We are, after all is said and done, creatures with a rational and political nature.

Fraternity cannot arise in an expedient polity. Though common in our era, an expedient polity is little more than a compact between its denizens to exploit one another even if in a mitigated manner. This compact would permit us to take each other and our political roles to be a means valuable merely for our own sake. The compact does no more than set the rules of engagement. Its presumption is that we have not a rational and political nature but a nature solitary and passional.

John Rawls and Robert Nozick both fail to theorize about a political constitution worthy of the name. They do not make the transition from a naïve origin to a philosophical origin for justice. Rawls offers a theory that in effect permits naïve origin for justice to subsume what would otherwise be a philosophical origin. The persons in the original position use an instrumental rationality to decide on the principles of justice, and they further use their instrumental principles to define a social union for themselves.

Nozick in a similar fashion derives from a naïve origin of justice what pretends to be a philosophical origin. He assumes a state of nature with perfect freedom and a law of nature, and he implicitly assumes that this freedom and this law provide a foundation for a utopian framework and its utopian associations. We may imagine whatever social union we please, he claims, and we may exclude from our social union whomever we please.

Rawls and Nozick do not give sufficient priority to the intrinsic value of justice. They and other philosophers of their ilk do not recognize that we can pursue goods essentially intelligible. Plato would argue that they are not full-fledged philosophers because they fail to turn their intellect toward an intelligible good. They remain no more than benighted, admittedly not unsophisticated but yet sophistical, seekers of sensible goods.

I concede, though, that Rawls and Nozick are right to take the position that moral rationality and economic rationality can be the same. Or, rather, that an intrinsically valuable and an instrumentally valuable rationality can be the same. But I must aver that our moral rationality ought to subsume any economic rationality. They argue that our economic rationality ought to subsume moral rationality.

We find ourselves obliged, then, to decide what value we wish to place on our liberty and on property. Shall we employ of our freedom and our wealth for purpose of establishing a community with intrinsic values all its own for ourselves and others? Or shall we deploy our wealth and freedom for the purpose of taking ever more profits and pleasures from our community or what passes for a community? Far too often, I submit, we pursue community values because we find in them an instrumental value all our own.[34]

Rawls and Nozick would have us choose a political society essentially hubristic albeit not unmitigatedly so. They wish to promote a political society without any natural foundation in our rational and political goodness. They offer only a social convention for procuring goods private and irrational. But a political society of this sort denies and degrades our very nature.

One could conclude, though I shall not, that Rawls and Nozick advocate and advance political philosophies that are so far from being eudaimonic as to be, philosophically speaking, kakodaimonic. Justice for them is but an external constraint imposed upon pleonectic and hedonic doings.

Part Three

The Cave Again: The Daunting Prospect of Political Tragedy

6

Poetical Animals

1. Politicians are liars all. Or so people say, especially during election season. But we ought not to be too harsh on our politicians, I submit. Their falsehoods are not always voluntary. The more popular arguments will suffice. During a campaign even candidates who otherwise display integrity often speak off the cuff and can misspeak. Before elected to office, they may also make sincere promises, but their promises may prove difficult to keep. They may find after taking office that the situation was not quite what it had seemed.

Political philosophers are liars, too. Our lies, I dare say, are nothing less than endemic to our enterprise. But we ought not to be too harsh on ourselves, either. Our untruths are hardly voluntary. The usual philosophical arguments are the more apposite. We are but mortals, and our faculties, even our rational faculties, are feeble. We can have recourse only to hypotheses, whether we reason or understand. But our hypotheses at best only approximate any absolute truth, and a political world, on which they can shed light, only approximates them.

I would go so far as to declare that natural as well as moral philosophers are less than truthful. All our theories, natural or moral, are hypothetical. To this thought we ought by now to have become accustomed. But are we accustomed to its consequences? Have we thought out its consequences? A theory, I submit, concerns intelligible objects, but these objects are our own ideas. With our ideas we can at best attempt to formulate a grander, unifying, hypothesis and employ it for a first principle.

Nor can our theory, because it concerns intelligible things, express any truth about sensible things. Sensible things are merely images of a theory, Plato would insist. Sensible things only approximate a theory, we would say. Any physicist or chemist would tell you that their theory has its limits. They cheerfully accept for a satisfactory confirmation of a hypothesis an experimental result deemed an adequate approximation to it.

I would venture to assert, then, that any theory is a myth. My assumption is that a myth concerns less than necessary ideas but more than contingent impressions. Perhaps Aristotle put the matter best. He in effect asserts that myth concerns a realm that lies between what is more intelligible and what is merely sensible. Explicitly he compares poetry to history. Poetry is more philosophical than history because it concerns more a universal and less a particular (*Poetics* 9. 1451b5–11).

Theory at its best, then, can be no more than logically cogent. We can rise from narrower hypotheses about intelligible entities to broader hypotheses, and we can descend from broader to lesser hypotheses and to their conclusions. But, again, we cannot presume to glean an absolute truth, nor can we presume to grasp an empirical truth. At its worst theory is emotionally congenial. With our reasonings and understandings we can, perhaps unawares, keep ourselves tethered to sensible entities. These entities might include our reputation, our employment, or our enjoyment.

Political theory can obviously be no exception. Indeed, a political theory often rests explicitly on a myth. Consider the allegory of the cave. Socrates himself doubts whether its truths are truly true, especially our idea of the good. But the allegorical cave does represent a truth more universal than historical fact, which it does not pretend to represent. Political knowledge and opinion are only approximate because we can never escape our ideas and our impressions. And our ideas and our impressions are no more than images.

Both the state of nature, which philosophers invoke to explain a social contract theory or even an invisible hand theory, and the original position, which expounds a contract theory in an idiosyncratic manner, are also myths. No philosopher would deny that they are hypothetical situations, and that they do not represent historical facts. These situations are presumed to rest on assumptions deemed sufficiently true to warrant analyzing their consequences for political thought and action.

America, too, is a myth! Any political society is. America rests on a constitution of political hypotheses presumed to be true, and on these presumptions we find ourselves obliged to act. We take our political hypotheses to be first principles, declared to be self-evident, and we act out their consequences. We are but the stuff dreams are made on. Indeed, we do speak of the American Dream, and we all acknowledge it to be more ideal than real.

Nor can we escape the fact that a political society is a myth. We create a political myth *ex nihilo* in every moment of our lives. We create our myth out of our actions and our passions with our forebodings and our yearnings. We ought, therefore, to ask, What myth do we wish to live out? We naturally have aspirations and look beyond ourselves. But we must also find time for reflection and look within ourselves. Are we living out a rational or an irrational tale?

We now find ourselves obliged to enter poetry and its realm. We are poetical animals (ζῷον ποιητικόν)! We live within a poetical world because we live ineluctably within a world of images. We cannot forgo our images, be they ideas or impressions. Our images are themselves objects, but they are not the objects purportedly imaged. They are thus real and yet not real.

What is more, within this whorl of images we find what we take to be our humanity. Our humanity is but a wispy thing of dreams and daydreams. Or a weird thing of nightmares and insanities!

2. We humans face a choice ineluctable and unenviable. We have no adequate theory of politics, and yet we are obliged to engage in politics. We know, if we are given to reflection, that a theory is no more than a myth, and yet we must act on a theory. We can only ask ourselves, On what political theory do we wish to act? Shall we act on a theory that inspires us to pursue an intelligible good, or shall we acquiesce in a theory that permits us to indulge in sensible goods? Ought our theory to rest on a hypothesis rationally cogent or passionally congenial?

I would urge, yet again, that we ought to entertain a rationally cogent hypothesis in our political endeavors. I wish to advocate a hypothesis setting out a new polity of a kind that is eudaimonic rather than expedient. A eudaimonic polity is a polity of rational activity rather than emotional passivity; a polity of this kind is for the sake of human happiness rather than for the sake of property or pleasure; and it arises out of cooperation with one another rather than conflict.

That a political theory can be no more than myth, Plato would surely agree. We might remind ourselves, if we could possibly have forgotten, that Plato writes in dialogues. He does so even when he reflects on political philosophy. His dialogues are not purely conceptual expositions, nor are they merely historical accounts. The *Republic* itself, though not obviously tragic, is a myth. It is an image made out of words.

I would remind you, too, that within the *Republic* Plato portrays Socrates telling Glaucon and Adeimantus that they are in effect constructing a myth. Socrates explains that they are making a paradigm for a political society in theory, and that they cannot expect their political paradigm to be exactly established. He does not state that their theory does not contain absolute truth, but he does state that it attains more truth than does practice (*Republic* 5. 473a–473b).

Socrates also draws an analogy to suggest that a political theory is no more than an image. He compares himself and his companions in the dialogue to a painter. As a painter might make a paradigm of a most beautiful human being who could never come to be, so they are making a paradigm of a good political society that could never come to be. His analogy implies that they are making in theory an image only, as a painter makes only an image in oils or now in acrylics (*Republic* 5. 472d–e).[1]

Perhaps we ought, then, to turn to what Plato tells us about poetry and about tragedy specifically. To do so, we must once more return to the allegorical cave. We shall now contemplate the shadows on the cave wall. Plato will provide us, we shall find, with a philosophical analysis of the shadows. Its shadows, he implies, include the images of the liberal arts. These images, I wish to argue, include political theory as well. When we theorize, do we not think in verbal images or speak and listen to them or read and write them?

With his analysis Plato would appear to resume an earlier discussion of poetry. He initially analyzes and critiques the liberal arts when he develops an elementary education for the young guardians of his political society. He focuses on the literary arts, especially epic poetry. This art can produce myths that are, he argues, true lies. Its myths can have a truth within them, but as a whole they are false (*Republic* 2. 376e–377a).[2]

He criticizes Homer and Hesiod for not telling their myths well. They make up epics that do not have truth within them, he implies, because they make bad images of gods and heroes (377d–e). Their myths ought to imitate types, presumably those appropriate for the young guardians to follow, and they ought not to imitate the gods and heroes fighting and feuding with one another, he argues (377e–379a). Yet these epics must remain false because we do not know the truth about these ancient events (382c–d).

Plato emphasizes that these epic poems are about gods and heroes. He promises to take up myths about human beings later. Their myths, he tells us, are about justice and injustice, and they also are, he adds, badly told (*Republic* 3. 392a–c). We shall now encounter these promised human myths. Plato explicitly argues that myths about humans are the stuff of tragedy, and he shows us implicitly that tragedy concerns justice and injustice. Might not his analysis of tragic poetry inform us about political myth, then?

Plato begins his analysis of poetry with a discussion of imitation. His assumption would appear to be that imitation includes, among other images, tragedy. What is an imitator? he asks. To answer this question, he returns again, though implicitly, to the figure of the divided line. Recall that this line is divided into two sections, and that these sections, each subdivided into two segments, represent intelligible objects and sensible objects (see *Republic* 6. 509d–510b).

He now acknowledges the intelligible section of the line, but he does not concern himself with its segments. He asserts merely that a god furnishes one idea for the many things that we sense. A god makes an idea for the many couches that we see, for example, and he makes another idea for the many tables that we see (*Republic* 10. 596a–b; see 597b).

I would ask you to set aside any anxieties about Platonic forms or metaphysics. We need not worry about absolute ideas. For our purpose we need focus only on our hypotheses about our own ideas. Your anxiety may arise because we are more often accustomed to think real not intelligible objects and their images but sensible objects and their images. Perhaps Plato wishes to humor our customary thinking because he now considers primarily the visual and aural images encountered in daily life.

Plato in fact reminds us of the lower section of the divided line, and he takes into account its division into segments. The one segment, recall, concerns sensible objects, and the other their images (see *Republic* 6. 509d–510a). He explains that the various artisans, such as a carpenter, look to what he holds to be a divine idea, and with it they make an image. They make, using an intelligible idea, a sensible object. This object is a thing of our quotidian experience. It is, again, a couch or a table (*Republic* 10. 596a–b, 597a, 597d).

Those whom Plato calls imitators make yet another image. The imitators, such as a painter, do not take an intelligible thing and make a sensible thing with it. Instead they take a sensible thing, and of it they make an imitation (597d–e). A painter resembles, he argues, someone who holds up a mirror to any and every thing and makes of them an appearance (596b–e). A better example today might be a camera, perhaps one in a mobile phone.

What is worse, an imitator actually makes an image not of a sensible thing itself but of its appearance. He continues with his example of a painter. A painter imitates a sensible thing, such as a couch. But he imitates a thing of this kind not as it is but as it appears. When we look at it, we find that a couch appears differently from different perspectives, for example. A painter imitates a visual appearance of one perspective (597e–598c).[3]

We have, then, three products, Plato concludes. A god makes the idea of a couch, a carpenter makes of this idea a sensible couch, and a painter makes of a sensible couch a visible image (597b). One could say, I think, that a carpenter is in a more general sense an imitator, too. But he imitates an intelligible object rather than a sensible one.

I would observe that the political painter whom Socrates mentions would differ from what he calls an imitative painter. A political painter creates an image of an intelligible object, an ordinary painter an image of a sensible object. A painter of politics would resemble more a craftsman. But a painter of oils or acrylics, too, could resemble a craftsman if he imitates an idea.[4]

We may now turn to tragedy. All poetry, Plato argues, is imitation. Poetry imitates a human being who is performing an action, who thinks that he or she is doing well or ill, and who is feeling pleasure or pain (603c). Tragedy would, presumably, imitate a person who is engaged in an action and doing badly and feeling pain. A tragedy might imitate a person who loses a son, for example, or a dear companion, perhaps a comrade in arms (see 603e).

A person in a situation of this sort feels a conflict within his soul, Plato argues. The rational and irrational parts of his soul, he implies, are at odds (603c-d). A good person would be able with his rationality to control his passions. He knows that fortune, bad or good, is of no great concern. We do not know how things of this kind will turn out, nor do we make the future better when we lament about them. Human affairs are also of little or no consequence, and any suffering only makes deliberation harder (603e-604d).

But a tragedian, Plato suggests, prefers to imitate someone who is acting not rationally but irrationally. A tragic hero, he implies, is more likely to be someone who is acting passionately, dwelling on and bemoaning a stroke of bad fortune (*Republic* 10. 604d-605c). Homer himself portrays personages of this sort. Achilles, for example, grieves excessively over the death of Patroclus (see *Republic* 3. 388a-b). Thetis, too, excessively laments the death of Achilles (388b-c).

Tragedy, and presumably other imitative arts, can, then, present a grave danger to the human soul. Because it is imitative, a tragic drama can thwart our reason and whet our passion in an untoward manner.[5]

But we can watch a tragedy and maintain our reason if we have knowledge of what thing is imitated, Plato continues. Knowledge of this kind can apparently serve for an antidote to tragedy and can counteract its potentially deleterious affects (*Republic* 10. 595b). Our knowledge of the object imitated, he implies, can help us preserve the organization within our soul (608a-b).

If we can preserve our inner organization, we would, presumably, preserve our rationality and its function. We would know that we ought, if we are to be happy, to act for the sake of our rational function itself. Our intellect, recall, ought to rule, and our aggressive and our appetitive impulses ought to obey (*Republic* 4. 441e-442b). We would likely know, too, I should think, that fortune with its vicissitudes is of little significance (see *Republic* 10. 604b-c).

Persons who lack knowledge of what is imitated, he asserts, permit tragedy to become the ruin of their reason (*Republic* 10. 595b). A tragedy imitates bad characters, who take sensible things seriously. It can easily weaken our reason, he implies, and it can stir up our passions. A tragedian produces plays of this kind because they are easier to write, he explains, and these plays the crowds going around to festivals more easily understand (604d–605a).

But a tragedy at times can captivate even those among us who might think ourselves of good character. We can too easily find tragic characters and their lamentations pleasant. We may permit ourselves to sympathize with the characters and to enter into their sufferings. We may then make them objects of our passions and through them satisfy our passions. They can become objects of our pity (605c–606b).[6]

We see, then, that tragedy concerns human beings and our justice and injustice. The knowledge needed to inoculate ourselves against tragedy would be none other than the knowledge of what justice is. Justice writ small, recall, is to have a soul so organized that its rational part and its irrational parts can each fulfill their own function (*Republic* 4. 443c–444a).

We see, too, that Plato provides us with a principle for criticizing poetry and especially tragedy. The principle would be justice. I would note that this principle permits us to see that not all poetry need be imitative in a pejorative sense. Despite his shortcomings, even Homer, if properly censured, can imitate persons with just souls. These persons are types for the guardians to follow when they fulfill their function.

Plato, in fact, allows for the possibility that poetry could be rational (*Republic* 10. 607c–e). He also is willing to permit hymns and encomia in his ideal political society (607a). Then, too, the denizens in his bucolic society, which is the first society of his natural history, sing hymns to the gods (*Republic* 2. 372b).[7]

Recall now the shadows on the cave wall. With his principle Plato shows us what these images ought to be. The shadows ought to be images of just persons, who face their misfortunes rationally. Though they ought to imitate justice, the shadows can, unfortunately, more easily imitate injustice. They can, alas, be images of unjust persons, who bemoan and bewail their misfortunes. They can be bad tragedies.

I would conclude, then, that a political society is a theatrocracy! Any political society must rest on a political philosophy, but all political philosophy is merely a myth. Any theory is a myth because we construct our theory out of our own ideas and images, and our ideas and images are merely approximations to any truths empyrean or empirical. Perhaps we ought to speak more appropriately not of political philosophy but of political poetry.

A philosophical politician, we might also conclude, is more of a poet politician. Or perhaps an artist or an artisan politician. A political philosophy can be only a myth, but a myth can provide a type for a political society. A political society is an epic poem, one might say. It can be a society with justice or injustice writ large, and it can reflect souls with justice or injustice writ small. We live and breathe within a political allegory, in other words.

Unfortunately, we today take for reality myths that are even less refined than those of ancient epic and drama. We have, alas, for the most part lost our Homer! More mundane images, especially if they engage our passions, will do. We are left with our ubiquitous mass media. We do have the printed word, not to mention the spoken. But we may easily find ourselves enthralled by images from, for example, radio, television, or now the internet.

3. Plato would suggest, I now wish to argue, that poetry can give us a new perspective on an artisanal political philosophy. My argument will rest on the contention that poetry includes myth, and that myth includes political theory. We shall see especially that a political theory, though it surely need not, can all too often be tragic. A theory of this kind, though it can rest on our rationality and its activity, can also pander to our passions and their pleasures.

What is at stake, we shall see, is a theoretical image not only of our political society but also of its artisanal products. Who we are and what we produce, rests on what we take to be our goodness. We again come face to face with our fundamental political choice. Persons in a political society can pursue rational or irrational functions, and we can make things for the sake of our happiness or things merely for our pleasure.

I would now draw your attention to the fact that "poetry" in ancient Greek can refer to production of any kind. Poetry in this broad sense includes not only what we call the liberal arts but also what one might call the artisanal or mechanical arts. The allegorical cave would appear to concern more a liberal than an artisanal art. The cave is, after all, a theater albeit a puppet theater. Or, we might better say, the cave concerns an art potentially liberal. A dramatic production can also be illiberal.

Plato takes advantage of this broad usage both for his initial analysis of imitation and also for his extended analysis. When he initially explains what imitation is, he does so by introducing us to an artisan. The artisan to whom he introduces us is a carpenter. A carpenter, recall, looks to a divine idea, and of it he makes an image. This image is a sensible object, perhaps a couch or a table (*Republic* 10. 596a–b).

He continues with more examples of artisans. He recurs again, though implicitly, to the divided line. The intellectual faculties and objects under consideration again lie on the lower section of the line. They are the artisanal arts and their products. He wishes to distinguish consumers from producers by their faculties and their objects. The consumers are an equestrian and a flautist, and the producers a flutemaker and a bronzesmith.

A consumer is a person who has knowledge, but a producer is a person with right opinion, Plato argues. An equestrian, for example, has knowledge of a bit and its function. Because he knows its function, he also knows how a bit ought to be made. A bronzesmith does not have knowledge but only right opinion about a bit. His right opinion he receives from an equestrian who explains him how to make a proper bit (*Republic* 10. 601c–d).

Or, again, someone who plays a flute, he argues, would know what function a flute has and how a flute is to be made. He would know what flutes play well and what flutes do not. He could accordingly tell a flutemaker how to make flutes if they are to be well made (601d–602a).

But an imitator, Plato adds, has neither knowledge nor right opinion. A painter, for example, neither uses nor makes either a bit or a flute. An artist of this sort only observes them and paints their appearances (602a–b).

Plato argues, then, that a consumer, because he has knowledge of its function, can critique a product. A producer can make a product because he obtains right opinion about it. But an imitator has neither knowledge nor right opinion, and he can neither critique nor make a product.[8]

What, then, do these examples tell us about the artisanal arts and their products? I wish to suggest that a philosophical guardian would be a person who knows the function of a product. A guardian who has studied philosophy knows what justice is, writ both large and small, and he rules in a political society. Because he knows what justice writ large is, a guardian of this rank would know the various functions within his society. Justice, recall, is that all parts of society fulfill their function (*Republic* 4. 433a–433b).

A guardian who rules would know not merely philosophical and political functions. He would also know martial functions because he must work his way up through the military ranks (see *Republic* 3. 412b–e). If he came up through the cavalry ranks, he would know what the function a cavalry regiment is and what the functions of an officer and a horse are and the functions of a saddle and a bridle. He would thus know how a bit ought to be made.

Only the philosophical guardians can inform an artisan about how to make a product. Not all guardians have knowledge of justice because not all are able to study philosophy. The auxiliary guardians do not have knowledge but only right opinion (see, e.g., *Republic* 4. 429b–c). Their opinion the philosophical guardians imbue in them through education. The auxiliary guardians would be less likely to give proper instructions about making a product.

We must now make a qualification. Recall the division of the divided line into its upper segments. Knowledge divides into understanding and reasoning. Plato distinguishes these faculties by how we use hypotheses. Understanding uses a hypothesis to induce a first principle or at least a higher hypothesis. But reasoning uses a hypothesis merely to deduce a conclusion (*Republic* 6. 510b–511d).

This distinction permits us to divide consumers into two kinds. Cavalry officers would have understanding, if philosophical guardians, of their political function because they know the principle of justice. But a flautist could not have knowledge of this kind. He could not have understanding about his function in society but at best reasoning about how to play his instrument. Why? A flute has no place in a just society. This instrument is not appropriate because it is polyharmonic, Socrates argues (*Republic* 3. 399c–d).[9]

We see again that Plato finds in poetry, now taken in the broad sense, a principle for evaluating the arts and their products, not only the liberal but also the artisanal arts. The principle is again justice. Justice constitutes an understanding of the functions of a political society and of the appropriate functions of their accouterments and instruments.

But let us not forget that justice rests on education. Education for Plato is nothing short of revolutionary. It requires that we turn our souls from sensible objects to intelligible objects. Through education we can gain an understanding of our function in society and of the objects needed to fulfill it. And through education we can give up any predilection for our passions and their objects.

I shall now argue that a political society has a potential to be tragic, but that it can also purge itself of its tragic potential. Plato, you may recall, offers a natural history to account for the origin of political society. If we examine his history, we shall see that a political society exists initially for passional functions, and that these functions can lead us to war and other evils. But we shall also see that through education a society can pursue rational functions, and that our rational functions can supplant our passional ones.

Plato, you may also recall, rests his account of the origin of political society on two principles. These principles are those of non-self-sufficiency and the division of labor. We are obviously not separately self-sufficient, he argues. We come together in society for the sake of satisfying our desires, and we call upon one another to help satisfy them (*Republic* 2. 369b–c).

But, he continues, persons in society can best help each other through the division of labor. In this way each person provides one service or good for all. He reminds us that we each have different natural abilities, that we can improve upon these abilities with practice, and that we must be able to exercise our abilities at the right moment (369e–370c).

These two principles account for justice in an ambiguous manner. The principles have not only a passional sense but also a rational sense. Most, if not all, philosophers overlook this ambiguity. But Socrates hints at it when he tells Glaucon not that the first bucolic society has justice, but that "perhaps" this society has justice (*Republic* 2. 371e–372a; also see *Republic* 4. 443b–444a). He goes on to suggest that they continue to look for justice and not shrink from doing so (*Republic* 2. 372a).

To begin his natural history, Plato takes the principles of non-self-sufficiency and of the division of labor in their passional sense. Justice is initially of value, he implies, for the sake of its consequences, and its consequences are our desire satisfaction. At first we seek to satisfy ourselves with products that are the necessities of life. For example, we obviously have need of food, clothing, and shelter (*Republic* 2. 369c–d).

But in our pursuit of the necessities we can before long, perhaps almost unawares, begin to pursue the luxuries of life. What, no fish sauce? Glaucon asks (*Republic* 2. 372c). Socrates concedes to Glaucon our desire for sauces and desserts and for even more luxurious products of sundry sorts (372c–373b). But he explains that with these products come great evils and war. We can easily become aggressive and take resources from our neighbors, and our neighbors, if also given to luxuries, are likely to covet our resources (373d–e).

Plato argues, then, that we constitute a political society at first out of actions with instrumental value rather than out of actions with intrinsic value. With these actions we seek to satisfy our desires. Indeed, we form a society in this way because each person thinks it better for himself (*Republic* 2. 369c). Could one deny that we depend on one another for our desire satisfaction? Or that we best satisfy our desires by dividing our labor? No one could deny, either, that we can fall into conflict over objects so desired.

What, then, is the rational sense of these two principles? The martial forces in society, though at first mustered to be defensive, and perhaps imperialistic, discover that their actions have not only instrumental value but also intrinsic value. With their education the guardians learn that they have a political function to fulfill in society, and that they can fulfill their political function for the sake of itself and their society. They discover, Socrates implies, that their happiness is part and parcel of societal happiness (*Republic* 4. 419–421c).

I would observe that we obviously are not self-sufficient when we fulfill a rational function. The guardians, for example, require not only an education but also weapons and again food, clothing, and shelter. The guardians obviously benefit, too, from a division of labor. They could not likely hone their martial skills if they had to make their own weapons and to supply themselves with the necessities of life (*Republic* 2. 373e–374e).

How does a political society purge itself, then? The guardians are obliged not only to purge themselves but also to purge their fellows of unnecessary desires (399e). They must in particular rein in the artisan and agrarian class (401a–d). This class also has a function to fulfill. They must provision the guardians and other citizens. But, if they give themselves up to luxury and frivolity, the farmers will no longer be farmers, nor will the potters be potters (*Republic* 4. 420e–421a).

If they cannot purge it, the guardians might well discover that they no longer have a society. They would likely find that their society eventually is not one but two or more. A rich class and a poor class can come to be within a political society, and these two classes can be at war with each other (422d–423b). The guardians, Socrates cautions, ought to take care to secure only resources sufficient for their society to remain one (423b–c).

Socrates indicates that the guardian ought to purge the artisans and agrarians through external restrains. Their society is temperate, he argues, when the rulers and the ruled are of the same opinion about who ought to rule. The superior few with their knowledge and desires ought to control the inferior many and their desires, he explains. The few, who receive an education, have understanding and true opinion with desires simple and moderate. But the many, presumably without understanding or true opinion, have desires of diverse, and likely immoderate, sorts (*Republic* 4. 431b–e).

But I must ask, again, Why cannot the agrarians and artisans receive an education? If they cannot have understanding or reasoning, can the artisans and agrarians not have right opinion? The auxiliary guardians rely on right opinion for fulfilling their function. Can the agrarian and artisan class not receive an education in right opinion as well? Their education would instruct them not about the defense of their society but about the products requisite for the functions of society, including defense.

When he discusses imitation, Plato implicitly concedes that an artisan can have an education though perhaps limited. He suggests that an artisan can have knowledge. If so, an artisan would have, if not understanding, at least reasoning about his product. What he argues explicitly is that a carpenter has a divine idea, and that with it he can make a couch or a table (*Republic* 10. 596a–b)!

He also concedes explicitly that an artisan can obtain right opinion about his products. He argues that an equestrian, for example, can instruct a bronzesmith in right opinion about how to make a bit![10]

We begin our political lives in a manner potentially tragic, then. We can allow ourselves to become preoccupied with our appetites and their pleasurable objects. If we do, we live lives that can come to actual tragedy. We can embody injustice writ both large and small. We can no longer fulfill our political functions because we allow ourselves to be preoccupied with goods frivolous and fortuitous. We may become wealthy and lazy, and we may leave others poor and unfit (*Republic* 4. 421c–422a).

Our soul would then have parts that also fail to fulfill their functions. Our rationality no longer fulfills its function of ruling, and our aggressive and appetitive instincts are no longer ruled. Our reason becomes, in the words of a modern philosopher disarmingly perspicacious, the slave of our passions.

But we need not live political lives that are tragic. Plato indicates how a society can purge itself of its tragic inclinations though, unfortunately, not all societies do. Through a philosophical education we can learn what justice is, and we can learn to perform our political function for its own sake. We can dedicate our lives to the pursuit of an intelligible good, which is none other than our happiness.

With an education we can also order our soul so that our intellect rules our passions. In our pursuit of happiness do we not need but little to satisfy our passions? We need not become entangled in the competitions and conflicts arising from the unnecessary pursuit of luxuries assorted and sordid.

4. Political philosophers in our era more often than not are not cognizant of the fact that their theories are myth. Few philosophers are. Yet these philosophers do frequently rest their theories on what is tantamount to myth. They imagine a hypothetical situation to account for the origin of a political society. A situation of this kind reflects a hypothesis, but it is not reflected in historical fact. It is true to type and yet false. It is, in a word, a myth not unlike those told to the young guardians (see *Republic* 2. 376e–377e).

Nor do these philosophers recognize that their theories can be tragic. With little or no fanfare they grant themselves the assumption, for example, that human goodness is to gratify our desire. John Rawls and Robert Nozick both do, to recur to our conspicuous examples. But to take the gratification of desire for our goodness is to court tragedy. To do so is to subordinate reason and its intelligible objects to passion and its fortuitous objects.[11]

Rawls and Nozick both begin their theories with assumptions that are obviously mythical. Their assumptions are neither absolute truths nor empirical truths. Consider Nozick, for example. He rests his theory on a state of nature. A state of this kind is obviously a myth. Though he does not use the phrase, he implies that a state of nature is a hypothetical situation. He argues that "a theory of a state of nature" can serve to explain "how a state would arise … , *even if no actual state ever arose that way*" (*Anarchy* 1. 1. 7–8, his emphasis).

But a state of nature, he indicates, need not reflect a true hypothesis. He acknowledges that he employs assumptions that are emotive. He explains that he rejects the most pessimistic assumptions and the most optimistic, and that he settles on assumptions that are "not wildly optimistic." He focuses on a situation in which people "generally act as they ought" (*Anarchy* 1. 1. 4–5).

These preferred assumptions he makes more explicit when he specifies his concept of a state of nature. Quoting John Locke, he asserts that persons in a state of nature possess a perfect freedom bounded only by the law of nature. Their perfect freedom enables them to do "as they think fit … without asking leave or dependency on the will" of another. The law of nature requires that they ought not "to harm another in his life, health, liberty, or possessions" (*Anarchy* 1. 2. 10).

I agree that these presuppositions about the state of nature are not wildly optimistic. But are we by nature creatures whose political life consists in leaving each other alone? I would ask. Are we so self-centered that our sole political concern is that we do not harm anyone, and, presumably, that no one harm us? Most persons, if not most philosophers, would find a solitary political life of this sort rather dreary. Do we not by nature wish to do things together with one another and even wish to help one another?[12]

Nozick continues, with a nod to Adam Smith, that a state of nature gives rise to an invisible hand explanation for political society. An explanation of this kind is what he calls a fundamental explanation. Fundamental explanations supposedly yield a "greater understanding" than "straightforward explanations." Why? They explain something in terms of something else (*Anarchy* 1. 2. 18–19). In particular we ought, he argues, to explain a political state in terms of a nonpolitical state (*Anarchy* 1. 1. 6–7). A nonpolitical state would be a state of nature, he informs us (8–9).

I cannot but wonder why in general a fundamental explanation, so-called, offers greater understanding than a straightforward explanation. Must we always explain something in terms of something else? A regress is surely lurking in the background. But ought we in particular to explain a political society in terms of a remote cause instead of a proximate cause? We can obviously form an intention to establish a political society, and we can fulfill our intention by acting on it. To deny these facts is to deny us any purpose of a political kind.

Nozick assumes an explanation of the same kind when he discusses method. He claims that one can back into a state without trying (*Anarchy* 1. 1. 1). We can do so, he again argues, by means of an invisible hand. He explicitly asserts that an explanation of this kind makes no appeal either to beliefs about a complicated pattern or to desires to bring about a pattern (18–19). The complicated pattern in question would, presumably, be the constitution of a political society.

Individuals in a state of nature, he argues, can, separately or in a group, produce and maintain "an overall pattern or design" through a process that does not require them to have a pattern or design "in mind." He explains, now quoting Smith, that a process of this kind appeals merely to the presumption that each individual "intends only his own gain," but that an invisible hand leads each individual "to promote an end which was not part of his intention" (18–19).

I must ask, Why would anyone want to back into a political state? Would one not better establish a political society consciously and intentionally? I would think that we can better constitute a political society if we act with a concept of its organization in mind. Our concept would, of course, be a principle of justice. With this principle we could establish a political constitution for the sake of rational and political functions. We would not be very likely to form a constitution of this kind if we act solely for our own gain.

Nozick, then, offers a political myth that is not rationally cogent but rather passionally congenial. His basic assumptions he does not establish cognitively but emotively. His explanation and method would also appear to be less than rational. They are not proximate to political theory, and his reliance on an invisible hand finds its basis in mere desire. Each person seeks only his own gain.[13]

Now consider Rawls. He explicitly acknowledges that his theory relies on assumptions that are hypothetical. He stipulates that people ought to decide on principles of justice in his original position. This position, he explicitly states, is "a purely hypothetical situation." He assumes that his original situation presents no necessary truths, and he acknowledges that this situation is untrue to historical fact (*Theory* 1. 3. 11; *Theory* 1. 4. 18-19). The original position is, in a word, a myth.

Rawls prides himself on the fact that the original position relies on what he takes to be appropriate assumptions. He claims that he has introduced "no controversial ethical elements," and that he employs "stipulations that are widely accepted" (*Theory* 1. 3. 12). He emphasizes that his assumptions are "commonly shared" and "widely accepted but weak." They are "natural and plausible" and "innocuous or even trivial" (*Theory* 1. 4. 16).

What are these assumptions? They are that the persons in the original position concern themselves exclusively with their own interests. Rawls characterizes these persons as "rational and mutually disinterested." They are rational because they have an instrumental rationality "of taking the most effective means to given ends." They are mutually disinterested because they take no interest in the interests of each other (*Theory* 1. 3. 12).

Why not use presuppositions known to be true? I cannot but wonder. Even if known hypothetically to be true. The assumptions that we have an instrumental rationality, and that we are mutually disinterested, are hardly incontrovertible. That we have a rational nature, and that we can act for the sake of our rational activity itself, even our practical activity, are truths that many philosophers would go to some length to defend.

The ancient Greek philosophers would surely find the presuppositions espoused by Rawls quite questionable. Recall that Plato portrays Glaucon and Adeimantus initiating their discussion of justice with Socrates by extending to him a challenge in effect to defend justice without these presumptions. They especially wish him to prove justice to be not of instrumental value but of intrinsic value (*Republic* 2. 358b, e.g.).[14]

Rawls himself argues that truth is what he calls the "first virtue" of a theory, not that acceptability, plausibility, or triviality is its virtue. No matter how "elegant or economical" it might be, we must reject any theory that is not true, he states (*Theory* 1. 1. 3-4). Are our truths, in particular our political truths, always so incontrovertible, innocuous, and trivial that we may substitute these criteria for truth? I have my doubts, and no doubt you do, too.

But Rawls would object. He claims that the assumptions underlying the original position are confirmed by the method of reflective equilibrium. Equilibrium of this kind is a method of testing principles of justice. We deduce from the principles conclusions about particular cases, and we see whether the conclusions reached match our "considered convictions." These convictions we "make intuitively" and we have "the greatest confidence" in them (*Theory* 1. 4. 17-18; also *Theory* 1. 9. 42-45).

I submit that reflective equilibrium begs the question. Rawls would have us begin with widely accepted assumptions and end with intuitively accepted conclusions. I fail to find the difference significant. Callicles would no doubt declare that Rawls does a better job than he of explicating and defending a concept of justice espoused by the many. Would he not admire the systemic exposition of the conventional concept?[15]

To the fact that Rawls and Nozick rest their theories on myths, I do not object. I do object to the fact that their myths rest on dubious hypotheses. Rawls relies on political assumptions that are conventional, and Nozick relies on assumptions that are not even political. They attempt to rest their theories on their assumptions because they find them to be not rationally cogent but emotionally congenial.

These two philosophers would, then, appear to present political theories that follow from assumptions that one might well deem tragic. Perhaps they do so because they in effect offer rationalizations of contemporary societies. Could anyone deny that societies today are tragic? Do they not rest on the assumptions that our rationality is a means to another end, that our end is basically self-interested, and that our end is merely desire satisfaction?

That Rawls and Nozick do present theories that are tragic, I shall now argue. To see how they tragic are, I propose that we consider what implications their theories have for our natural abilities. Plato implies that our abilities ought to be cultivated for the benefit of one another. He argues that we establish a political society because we are severally non-self-sufficient, and because we can together best attain self-sufficiency through a division of labor (*Republic* 2. 369b–371e).

But we are non-self-sufficient and divide our labor in more than one sense. We can become self-sufficient by dividing our labor in a rational sense. No one separately can form a political society of value for the sake of itself. We can do so only if we divide our labor and we each perform a political function for its own sake. We then live a good political life together, and our political life is its own end.

We can also overcome our non-self-sufficiency for the sake of satisfying our desire. We are non-self-sufficient in a passional sense, too. By dividing our labor and working together with others we can more efficiently satisfy our desires. But when we do, we fulfill a political function for the sake of its consequences. We do not live a good political life together, but our political life is a mere means.

We can, then, use our natural abilities to contribute to a just society. We can perform a political function in the broad sense of philosophical, martial, or artisanal activities for its own sake. With our abilities we can act for the sake of our function itself and participate in society for its own sake. We can all engage in and enjoy what contemporary philosophers, including Rawls and Nozick, call a social union.

Our political activities in turn produce and preserve within us a just soul. Our rational activities, theoretical, practical, or poetical, find their end in these very activities and not in an ulterior aim. Our reason rules for the sake of these activities over the aggressive and appetitive parts of the soul, and these three parts thus interact harmoniously as if they were high, middle, and low notes of a chord (*Republic* 4. 443c–444a).

Unfortunately, both Rawls and Nozick take the naïve position that we ought to use our natural abilities for the sake not of rational but of passional functions. Neither do they take into account the fact that we are separately non-self-sufficient. They simply assume that we are individually self-sufficient. Nor do they recognize rightly how we ought to divide our labor. They imply that we divide our labor in a manner rather superficial.

Rawls is concerned that our natural abilities and talents are distributed in an arbitrary fashion. Our abilities and talents are "the outcome of natural chance," and we cannot be said "to deserve" them (*Theory* 1. 3. 11, 13–14). He asserts again that "the natural distribution of abilities and talents" is no more than "the outcome of the natural lottery," and that their distribution can only be "arbitrary from a moral point of view" (*Theory* 2. 13. 63–64).

One could hardly disagree that our natural talents and abilities are the result of chance. Indeed, our very nature is the result of chance. But one might wonder why this fortuitous fact ought to be thought morally arbitrary. Rawls attempts to explain. The natural lottery, if left unchecked, is morally arbitrary because our natural abilities affect what distribution of income and wealth we receive. This distribution in its turn is "arbitrary from a moral point of view" (*Theory* 2. 12. 62–62, 64–65).

Notice that our natural abilities have a moral import only for property distribution. Indeed, Rawls offers four interpretations for the difference principle, which, you may recall, is his principle for distributing primary goods, including income and wealth. Each interpretation only considers a different way of determining how much income and wealth individuals are to receive from exercising their natural abilities.

The interpretations concern both our natural abilities and their cumulative social effects. What he calls natural liberty does not attempt to mitigate either natural or social contingencies. Liberal equality, he argues, seeks to mitigate social but not natural contingencies. Natural aristocracy mitigates natural contingencies but not social (*Theory* 2. 12. 62–65). Only democratic equality, which rests on his difference principle, mitigates contingencies both social and natural (*Theory* 2. 13. 65–69).[16]

Rawls does not argue, I would have you notice, that those with natural abilities ought to employ them for the sake of rational functions within a political society. He does not argue that those with intellectual ability ought to hold office in their society, for example, nor that those with martial ability ought to defend their society. He concerns himself not with the appropriate function of those more able but only with the material benefits that they might gain.[17]

Rawls would imply, then, that we are self-sufficient in a passional sense. But he does not argue that we come together to form a society to help one another satisfy our needs. He argues for the weaker proposition that we can each have a better life through social cooperation than "any would have if each were to live solely by his own efforts." We form a society only to determine how to distribute "the greater benefits" of cooperation (*Theory* 1. 1. 4).

He does not appear to recognize a division of labor in any significant sense. He does not distinguish philosophical, martial, or artisanal functions for what he takes to be a just society. Instead, he restricts a division of labor, if we may so call it, simply to being more or less able to obtain more rather than less income and wealth. He attributes to us only an acquisitive function albeit in different degrees.

We can now see that for Rawls persons who live within a political society do not and cannot have a just soul. Their intellect does not rule within them. They do not perform a eudaimonic function. They apparently have no rational function to perform. They possess souls that are tragically unjust. Their intellect works to obtain for them more rather than fewer objects of desire.

Rawls, then, offers a tragic theory of justice. His theory rests not on our rational nature but on our passional nature. He does not with his theory take cognizance of the fact that our rationality and its function can overcome fortune and its fickleness. On his theory we would crave the goods of fortune and most likely lament their loss. He does not see how morally insignificant these goods are.

Is Rawls right that the distribution of our abilities and talents is morally arbitrary? I would argue that their distribution is naturally arbitrary but need not be morally arbitrary. Fortune determines what qualities we have, but what we do with these qualities determines their moral value—good, bad, or indifferent. Our abilities can be morally commendable if we use them rationally for the sake of a political function. If we do not, they are not.[18]

What does Nozick think about the distribution of our natural abilities? Nozick is harsher and even more tragic than Rawls. He agrees with Rawls that natural abilities are arbitrarily distributed. He in fact quotes Rawls to the effect that they are. But he favorably cites Rawls at length on what he says about the system of natural liberty, which does not mitigate natural or social contingencies. He frankly admits that this system comes closest to his own (*Anarchy* 2. 7. 213–214).

He continues by disagreeing with Rawls about the moral arbitrariness of this natural distribution. Rawls, he complains, has lost sight of our "human dignity." He makes no mention of "how persons have chosen to develop their own natural assets." He would appear to argue that by developing them we can have property in our abilities. In other words, he implicitly applies the Lockean theory of mixed labor to them (*Anarchy* 2. 7. 213–214).[19]

How does Nozick keep sight of our dignity, then? Nozick has for his sole concern that we do not harm others with the property that we have in our abilities or with the property we acquire through them. He appeals to the law of nature and its Lockean proviso. We cannot acquire or utilize property in any way that would "violate the proviso by making the situation of others worse than their baseline situation." We cannot, for example, appropriate the only water hole in a desert and charge what we will for water (*Anarchy* 2. 7. 180).

But we are under no obligation to assist others. The fact that one might own the entire supply of a product, need not entail that we leave others in a worse situation than the baseline, he argues. We would be free to charge whatever we wish for a new cure for a disease, for example, if we were to synthesize our cure from readily available resources. Why? Our synthesis does not rely on appropriating materials that others are not free to appropriate. We have not in any way worsened their situation (181).

Nozick, too, fails to take into account a rational function for our talents. We are under no obligation to engage in a political function for its own sake. Our abilities serve us to garner what income and wealth we please so long as we do no harm to others. But he does, admittedly, ameliorate his position slightly. He implies that that our property right in our new cure for a disease, for example, might expire with time because someone else could eventually make the same synthesis. Patent rights are properly limited, he explains (181–182).

Nozick, then, would also deny us a just soul. Our rationality is most likely subordinate to our passionality. Our intellect has no intrinsic value but only an instrumental value. We are not obliged to employ our intellect for its own sake. We can use our intellect to develop our abilities, but we would most likely subordinate our abilities to our passions because we have the freedom do with them as we please.

Nozick goes so far as to declare explicitly that we are separately self-sufficient. He suggests that the law of nature is a side-constraint, and he argues that this side-constraint rests on the "root idea" that we are "different individuals with separate lives" to lead. We are, he reiterates, "distinct individuals each with his *own* life to lead" (*Anarchy* 1. 3. 33–34, his italics).

He implies that a division of labor rests solely on the function of acquiring wealth, which we can fulfill with greater or lesser ability. He argues that each individual, even when cooperating, works "separately" and is "a miniature firm," and that each makes a product "easily identifiable" with its value determined "on the open market by prices set competitively." In other words, our function finds value in its "marginal product" (*Anarchy* 2. 7. 186–187).[20]

I would conclude, then, that our natural abilities and their exercise, whether theoretical, practical, or artisanal, are morally ambiguous. We can view them in light of our rational nature, or we can see them in terms of our passional nature. They can be resources for rational or passional functions, and their products can serve rational or passional functions as well.

I would also conclude that Rawls and Nozick can offer only a tragic criterion to evaluate artisanal consumption and production. They would have us value the beautiful and useful arts and their products solely for the sake of benefits to be received from them, and these benefits they take to be only the income and wealth to be had from society. This income and wealth in turn serves merely to gratify our desire.

Plato argues that we ought to employ the principle of justice, writ large and small, to evaluate artisanal consumption and production. But Rawls and Nozick do not concern themselves with a political criterion for artisanal abilities and their products. No one has a truly political function to fulfill in society. Everyone has essentially private functions—to acquire and to secure wealth and income and to take pleasure in its consumption.

With their theories Rawls and Nozick, then, appear to offer tragic myths to rationalize contemporary society. We might do well to remind ourselves that their theories have terrible consequences for people in the billions who fall victim to brazen exploitation and suffer in abject deprivation. These consequences need hardly arise from acts of commission but can arise from acts of omission and indifference. In our affluent era indifference issues in degradations not often spoken of and too often unspeakable. But indifference itself no doubt occasions the greatest pain of all.

Plato tells us that we ought to pity the prisoners pilloried in the allegorical cave and enamored of the shadows on the cave wall. The prisoners have no knowledge of the things imitated by the shadows, and they preoccupy themselves solely with the imitations of things in the shadows. They pass their days, he states, remembering the past comings and goings of the shadows, and imagining their future comings and goings (*Republic* 7. 516c).

I would say, too, and Plato would surely agree I think, that we ought to fear the prisoners in the cave. We ourselves, even if we have knowledge of the things imitated, can unwittingly fail prey to the imitations of things. We are, after all, sympathetic creatures (see *Republic* 10. 605c–d). We can easily lapse in our knowledge and become enthralled by the characters imitated and by their doings and sufferings and by their thoughts of being better off or worse off.

5. Political philosophy can be nothing more and nothing less than a lie. Philosophy of the political variety can be a noble lie at its best, but at its worst philosophy of this kind can be an ignoble lie.

Plato argues that the guardians of his ideal political society ought to tell their fellow inhabitants a noble lie. A lie of this kind, he explains, is a lie not in the soul but a lie in words (*Republic* 3. 414b–c). A lie in the soul is ignorance about what is, but a lie in words is ignorance about what is ancient. A lie in words includes, for example, the myths told to the young guardians about the gods and heroes. A lie of this kind, he implies, contains truth about what is but not about what is past (*Republic* 2. 382a–d).[21]

The noble lie is a Phoenician myth, he informs us. The myth is that the earth molded within herself the inhabitants of his ideal society with their weapons and other equipment, and that, when their gestation was complete, she let them spring forth from her. The myth also states that the god mixed different metals in the inhabitants. She put gold in those who ought to be philosophical guardians, silver in those who are to be auxiliary guardians, and bronze in the artisan and agrarians (*Republic* 3. 414d–415c).

This myth would appear to imitate the principles that account for the origin of political society (see *Republic* 2. 369b–371e). That the earth is our mother, and that we all are brothers and sisters, apparently reflects the truth that we are not self-sufficient and that we ought to care for one another. That we have different metals within us obviously reflects the truth that we ought to divide our labors, and that those with different abilities ought to fulfill different functions.

But the myth is an allegory. The guardians and the other citizens did not literally rise up from the earth fully armed and equipped. No one truly knows what origins we came from though anthropologists in our day know more than the ancients did. Nor can we account for our different natural characters by means of different metals in our composition though finer biochemical distinctions can now yield some insights.[22]

An ignoble lie is a lie in the soul, I would argue. A lie of this kind can be banausic in a rather pejorative sense. An ignoble lie does not contain a truth about what is but a notion about what we might like to imagine is. A lie of this sort frequently rests on the presupposition that we are individuals who are separate and independent, and that we differ from one another only in our ability to acquire and to secure more or fewer resources.

A lie of this sort does not distinguish philosophical, martial, or poetical functions within society. It presumes that persons with a greater ability to accumulate more and more wealth somehow enable persons with a lesser ability to acquire and to retain more wealth. An invisible hand, perhaps forging chain connections or knitting closely, insures that wealth trickles down to all. *Mirabile dictu!* What we see at work is the hand of a *deus ex machina* most astounding!

An ignoble lie presupposes that we all are better off within any society than we would be without any society. Perhaps we are. But are we not still better off in a society that enables us to devote ourselves to a good life than in a society that consigns us merely to a life? Ought we to give up our hopes for happiness in exchange for a glimmer of trinkets and baubles?

We stand, then, at a crossroads, to borrow an expression from a modern philosopher. But we see a crossroads obscured in myth, both noble and ignoble. Live out a myth we must! But let us strive to live out a philosophical myth and not a myth naïve and tragic. Let us strive to play a role within our community and not to spend our time feasting and drinking.

We must endeavor not to mistake our animal nature—philosophical and political and poetical—for more or less than it is. We ought not to presume to necessary truths, nor ought we to spurn contingent truths. We are but mere mortals, and to us a fate has been allotted. To forget these humble facts is to risk suffering at once pitiable and fearful.

The American Dream is a dream of a better life. Who does not share this dream, American or no? But what is a better life? we must never forget to ask. Is it a life of intrinsically valuable activity that we can share with others? Or a life of property and pleasure that cannot be shared and cannot but deprive others?[23]

We ought also to remember that to take a myth literally is to take a dream for reality. Not to take a myth literally is be aware that our dream is but a dream, and that our dream is but a flickering image most faint and frail.

To take a dream for reality is also to forget that we dream. But to forget that we dream is to forget that how human we mortals be.

Notes

Preface

1. Conversely, one half of the adult population owns less than one percent of the household wealth (Shorrocks et al., 9).
2. Happiness studies has become a burgeoning field of inquiry today. Despite obvious sophistication, its research programs and its policy recommendations would, however, appear to rest unquestioningly on a passional definition (see, e.g., Helliwell et al.).
3. That a utilitarian might sacrifice the interests of the many for the benefit of a few, Rawls and Nozick do not, curiously enough, appear to give due consideration.
4. Because I wish to focus on my contemporaries, I am obliged to omit any extended discussion the utilitarians of the Scottish Enlightenment. Adam Smith and David Hume, for example, with a principle of sympathy offer a more refined concept of deferred gratification. Nonetheless, one could show, *mutatis mutandis*, that a similar analysis and critique would apply to their political philosophies.
5. I would note that, when he later offers some emendations, Rawls himself informs us that he leaves his initial theory unchanged in its essentials.

Chapter 1

1. Ferguson is the bête noire residing within the recesses of the cave. He apparently denies any reality to the images on the cave wall. He implies that they are only illusions. Color, he argues, is a perfection in our eyes occasioned by sunlight, and it is not an existent thing ("Again," 192, 196–197; Part I, 135). I can agree that color is not an existent thing. But I would also point out that color more likely than not has a cause in an existent thing or in an image, such as a shadow or reflection. It may or may not resemble its cause, of course.

   Either Cross or Woozley is hesitant to think that the prisoners could take sensible images seriously. One of them, they tell us, thinks that our normal human condition is not illusion, to use their term, but belief (Cross and Woozley 9. 227–228). I wonder if this assumption about our normal condition is in fact so. Do we not quite frequently take visual and aural images on television or the internet, for example, or verbal imagines in newspapers or magazines to be real? I think that we do more often than we might care to admit.

   Annas argues that the images in the cave "are literally shadows and metaphorically are any ordinary opinions about things like justice, taken over unreflectively and based on acquaintance in the way things appear rather than effort to find out how they really are" (255–256). She likely means to say, I would think, that the images are objects of ordinary opinions about these things.

Annas also explains how *The Conformist* of Bernardo Bertolucci shows that a society can become concerned more with public images and public opinion than with the truth (257-258).

2 Ferguson is famous for denying that cave and its fire represent the visible world and its sun. He argues that the obscure firelight stands for the opinable, and that the sunlight "constantly" stands for the intelligible ("Again," 196 n5). The firelight, he claims, cannot coherently represent a sunlight that stands both for opinion and for knowledge ("Again," 202-203, 210; Part I, 152 postscript). It can only represent an obscure light less than sunlight "in which vision is obfuscated" ("Again," 208-209; also Part I, 139-141). This obfuscated vision he identifies with "*accepted* standards other than the Good" ("Again," 206-207, his italics).

I would argue with most scholars that the cave and its fire do represent the visible world and the sun. Plato appears to state quite straightforwardly that it does, does he not (*Republic* 7. 517a-b)? I would counter Ferguson with the thought that the fire can be an image of the sun, and the sun can yet be an image of the good. But I agree that the firelight does produce an obscure, if not obfuscated, vision. Opinion is always more obscure than knowledge. But I would add that opinion includes not only opinion merely accepted but also true opinion.

Cross and Woozley agree. They argue that the cave is not merely illustrative but also contrastive. The cave with its fire bears an analogy to the world outside with the sun, but the cave and the fire also mark a contrast with the outside world and the sun. Plato both draws an analogy and makes a contrast between a world of opinion and a world of knowledge (Cross and Woozley 9. 224-226).

Ferguson also denies that the lower section of the divided line has any ontological significance. The lower section with its segments has the sole purpose of illustrating the difference in upper section between its segments (Part I, 146). I can agree that the lower section is illustrative. Ferguson offers insightful arguments to show that it is. But I must ask, Why cannot this section be ontological as well? Plato, again, appears to state explicitly that it is (*Republic* 6. 509d-510a).

Cross and Woozley disagree with Ferguson, and they offer cogent several arguments against his position. They point out, I would especially note, that Plato ascribes to the line four mental states and four objects, and he compares "a common scale of clearness applicable to the four states of mind" with "a common scale of reality applicable to their objects" (Cross and Woozley 9. 212-214).

Annas denies that there can be a correspondence between the images in the line and in the cave. She argues that the images of the line are to be taken literally, and that they are insignificant in our lives (Annas 10. 248-249, 250-251, 255). But the images in the cave represent our ordinary beliefs and are, presumably, significant. Her contention is that the contrast between images and beliefs in the line is too clear to support a correspondence (255). Annas appears to assume that the contrast between images and beliefs is less clear in the cave. But the contrast between images and beliefs in the cave is quite clear, too, I should think. They are objects of two distinct kinds, and a prisoner must turn from the one to see the other. Indeed, this turn is painful, as Annas reminds us (255).

3 Cross and Woozley agree about these methods. They observe that reasoning and understanding, if both faculties concern forms, might appear to have the same object and thus to contravene the tenet that different faculties have each an object proper to them. But they argue, rightly I think, that reason concerns forms "as

separate and unconnected," and that understanding concerns forms "in the light of the whole system to which they are seen to belong" (Cross and Woozley 10. 233–238).

The method of working toward a higher hypothesis they call "axiomatization." They favorably cite Bertrand Russell on its use. But they also point out that the hypothetical method and the non-hypothetical first principle "are not easy bedfellows." Their resolution is to grant a philosopher a "final flash of intuition" enabling him to grasp the non-hypothetical (Cross and Woozley 10. 249–254). My resolution would be to assert, cheerfully, that we mortals, though we can aspire to it, can never quite attain to the non-hypothetical. We may indeed gain a flash of intuition but only in the guise of a higher hypothesis.

4 Smith attempts to argue that geometricians do not hypothesize about mathematical forms. They cannot do so, he claims, because mathematical forms are not images ("Line," 33–34). But Plato asserts on several occasions, he explains, that the geometrician "employs visibles as images in his reasoning." He concludes, then, that "the originals of the visible realm" Plato recognizes to be "the images in the intelligible realm" (34).

I would argue that mathematical forms can be images. The fifth postulate of Euclid, for example, is only a partial approximation of a more ultimate postulate about straight lines. This postulate does hold on a flat surface, but the postulate does not hold on an elliptical or a hyperbolic surface. But I would also point out that, when he refers to mathematical images, Plato explicitly discusses geometrical diagrams drawn, I would imagine, on a tablet or on the ground. These figures, he explains explicitly, are visible originals of shadows and reflections, and they are also visible images that resemble intelligible forms (*Republic* 6. 510d–511a).

Smith recognizes that his position would appear to violate the basic distinction in the divided line between the visible realm and the intelligible realm. One could object that he moves visible images from the visible realm into the intelligible realm ("Line," 34–35). He responds by arguing that "sensibles can *in some way* or *to some degree* be made intelligible." If not, political rulers "would gain no political advantage from their acquisition and development of knowledge" (37–38, his italics).

I would agree that the visible can be knowable. But I would argue that the visible is an object not of knowledge proper but of opinion. Plato explicitly so states (*Republic* 6. 510a, 511d–e). Smith would appear to neglect the fact that a political ruler must love knowledge of all kinds. Knowledge in this wide sense includes not only knowledge, which concerns intelligible forms, but also opinion, which concerns their sensible images (*Republic* 5. 474c–476d).

Smith does agree, nonetheless, that geometers reason with hypotheses less clear than those of understanding. He points out, and this point is the one that I would make, too, that they do not see their hypotheses in the light of the good ("Line," 33–34).

5 That the prisoner who is released turns toward the puppets, Ferguson argues, is not "an important achievement." He points out that the prisoner cannot make out what the puppets are. The prisoner must leave the cave and he must adjust to the sunlight before he can make sensible objects out. That is, he must first "learn to apprehend the forms." He will then be able to see that sensible objects are images of intelligible objects ("Again," 203–204; Part II 23–24).

Ferguson is right to argue that the turn to sensible objects is not a terribly important achievement. The important achievement is the turn from sensible to intelligible objects. But he overlooks a not insignificant allegorical fact. The prisoner sees that the shadows are images, and that the puppets are their originals. He also sees that a shadow is less real than a sensible object. He thus becomes better prepared to learn, though he has yet to learn, that a sensible object is in its turn an image, and that it is less real than an intelligible object.

Ferguson is also right that the prisoner cannot truly opine sensible objects until he turns toward the intelligible objects and begins to apprehend them. But the prisoner can yet opine sensible objects, truly or falsely, before he can see them as reflections of intelligibles. These opinions, Ferguson reminds us, can make education a rather difficult process ("Again," 204–206).

Cross and Woozley would add that the prisoner who has turned from the sensible realm toward the intelligible realm must also turn from hypothetical forms, which would be dianoetic, to a purportedly non-hypothetical form, which would be noetic (Cross and Woozley 9. 227–228).

6   We may, I should think, identify the good with the demiurge, who is the artisan of the universe (*Timaeus*, e.g., 27c–29d).

Ferguson holds, and some readers may be tempted to agree, that we cannot identify the good with the demiurge. He claims that the simile of the sun is nothing more than an analogy, and that the good can be only a formal cause and not an efficient cause. That the sun is the offspring of the good, is not an assertion about causation, he claims. It states only that the sun resembles the good in its own sphere. The sun is merely "an observed cause of good" (Part I, 133–134; see Part II, 28 addenda).

But Plato, I am afraid, does state not only that the sun is "the child and offspring of the good" (*Republic* 6. 507a). He also states that the good "engenders both light and its sovereign" (517a–c). I must ask, Is a parent not the cause of its child, and Is a parent not the cause of what it engenders? Ferguson himself tells us that the point of resemblance between the sun and the good is their causality. But the fact that a child resembles its parent, I would point out, need not exclude the fact that a parent causes its child.

Ferguson questions how the sun, though itself not generation, can be the cause of generation (Part I, 133, 134). I take this proposition to mean merely that the sun itself does not come to be, but that it causes things to come to be—and to grow and to be nourished (*Republic* 6. 509b). The ancient Greeks, remember, thought that celestial beings did not come to be or cease to be. Plato in fact calls the sun a god (508a). We know now that our sun came to be about 5 billion years ago, and that it will cease to be in about 5 billion years. But I should think that 10 billion years or so sufficiently approximates divine status for our mundane purposes.

Cross and Woozley also appear to take the good to be a formal cause. They argue that the sun occupies "in the visible world a position analogous to that of the Form of the Good in the world of Forms" (Cross and Woozley 9. 201–202). But Plato draws an analogy not between the sun and the forms but between the sun and the good, and he denies that we can identify the forms of the good with the good. He asserts explicitly that the forms are other than the good, and the good is yet better than they (*Republic* 6. 508b–509a). Cross and Woozley take note of this assertion, but they do not, apparently, see its full implication.

Annas raises two important issues about the good and its forms that might be particularly pertinent for contemporary readers. She observes rightly that we like to think our knowledge to be "objective claims about something," and values to be "arbitrary expressions of personal preference." A reference to the good for an explanation of knowledge "seems out of place" (Annas 10. 243). We sharply distinguish between facts and values, in other words (246).

Annas wonders, accordingly, how Plato could use the good to account for knowledge. He seems to hold that "values are fundamental to explaining facts" (246–247). He does not, she claims, "talk of laws or generalizations," though he takes knowledge to be systemic (242–243). She also questions how Plato could use the good to account for the nature of things. If it is fundamental in our understanding, then the good must also be fundamental in nature itself, she argues (246–247).

I must reply that Plato offers a concept of the good and its forms that is objective and knowable. The forms or ideas of the good, I would point out, are akin to natural laws and generalizations. Plato argues in effect that they are universals. A form is the one beside the many (see *Republic* 5. 475e–476a; or *Republic* 6. 507a–b). Perhaps we might better call the forms the formulae of the good.

Plato explains that these formulae, if you will, are the causes both of things known and of knowledge (*Republic* 5. 508e). But we poor souls, alas, can attempt to grasp them only with our meager hypotheses. The good, or the demiurge if you prefer, is thus fundamental in nature itself. Plato declares explicitly that good with its ideas or forms causes "all things right and noble," including the sun and its light, as well as "understanding and truth" (*Republic* 7. 517b–c).

7   See Chapter 2.
8   Smith agrees. He argues that the guardians do not take for the proper objects of their study the visible and audible objects themselves. But they study them "as images of higher realities," which are "the intelligible originals (the Forms)" ("Line," 39). But he goes on to argue that the objects are not "wholly different objects to appear on each side of the division" between the visible and the intelligible realms. They somehow "straddle the division" between the visible and the intelligible and are "conceived wholly differently on each side of it" (40).

I would argue that the objects of the quadrivium remain in the visible realm and do not appear in the intelligible realm. They remain but objects of opinion. Yet these opinable objects can also appear to be images of forms. They appear to be images to those who are both able to opine them and to have knowledge of their forms. These persons are also able to distinguish these images from their forms (see, e.g., *Republic* 5. 476a–d).

Annas argues that the guardians study a mathematical curriculum in the quadrivium that does not prepare them for their rule. Plato unduly limits them to a restricted range of forms, she claims. Mathematics does not seem to prepare the guardians for rule a political society. "Philosophical knowledge is associated with impersonal disciplines" and not with "the desire to sort out actual tangled moral problems" (Annas 10. 260–262). Mathematical concepts, she protests, are not the only concepts that can "make the mind work out what experience does not settle" (250–251).

I am not so certain that mathematics is irrelevant. Plato frequently points out that the quadrivium does have relevance for military affairs. He, for example, ridicules

Agamemnon for not knowing how many feet he had (*Republic* 7. 522b-e; see also 526d, 527d). Annas herself takes note of these military applications though she finds them "grotesque" (Annas 11. 275-276). Mathematics might very well be useful for political policy and practice, too, I would think. At a minimum one would wish to have an ability to count votes.

But the study of mathematics need not preclude other studies. The guardians would undoubtedly study the principle of justice. They have to know what is good for their political society and for their souls. Annas is right that other studies can awaken the mind. The study of justice surely could do so. Socrates develops the principle of justice with Glaucon and Adeimantus in part by showing them that alternative principles lead to excess and war.

9 Other philosophers also recognize the hypothetical nature of this argument. Cross and Woozley, for example, observe that Socrates reminds Glaucon to take their definition of justice in a society to be provisional until they can confirm their definition with a similar definition in an individual (Cross and Woozley 4. 77). But they think that Plato gives priority of exposition to justice in the city, and that he gives priority of argument, apparently evidential priority, to justice in an individual (Cross and Woozley 5. 109-111; Cross and Woozley 6. 130-133).

Annas agrees with me. She reminds us that Socrates uses the analogy of starting a fire by rubbing sticks together. He proposes to his interlocutors, she argues, that they define justice in a society and then in a soul and see whether a just person and a just society are alike. If they are not, they will have to make adjustments in their definition. This procedure requires that neither justice in a society nor in a soul is prior to the other, she explains. The underlying assumption is that justice must be a single form in things of different kinds (Annas 5. 146-148).

10 The term "class" can be misleading to a contemporary ear. A class for Plato indicates less a hierarchy and more a function though a hierarchy is present. With this term we tend to place more emphasis on a hierarchy, especially one resting on possessions, and less on a function. This linguistic fact one could take for evidence of our philosophical and political naïveté.

11 Annas explains nicely. She compares the principle of justice to a discovery in natural science. The principle, she argues, corrects our ordinary concept of justice much as a scientific discovery can correct our initial concept of a subject under investigation. Our discovery can prompt us to refine and to clarify our concept. If, for example, we are investigating a disease, what we eventually discover might lead us to redefine the disease and to exclude some "original cases that we set out to explain" (Annas 5. 119-123).

12 Though they do not explain, Cross and Woozley aptly observe in general that the guardians have knowledge of their whole society and not merely of a part (Cross and Woozley 5. 105). But one can readily see, for example, that an oligarch would take his hypothesis of acquiring wealth to be an exclusive principle of justice. He is not aware that to possess property is only one function within a political society, and that a higher principle of justice ought to organize this function and others into a system of political thought and action.

Cross and Woozley note also that Plato has transformed the principle of the division of labor. The principle is no longer that one person has one function, but that one class has one function. A person in one class, they explain, ought not to usurp the function of a higher class, but he or she can change functions within a class. A carpenter cannot become a guardian without doing great damage to society though he can become a cobbler (Cross and Woozley 5. 109–111).

Smith would likely agree that a principle of justice in a constitution other than just is only partially true. He argues that what he calls vulgar definitions of justice, which the early interlocutors in the *Republic* offer, are inadequate definitions though he does not take class bias into account ("Prisoners," 193–198). But he also argues that a definition of justice approximates justice in a society, and that justice in a society approximates justice in a soul (192–193). Justice in a society is an image of justice in a soul (199–200).

I would argue rather that the definition of justice accounts for justice both in a society and in a soul. Plato in fact argues that justice in a society and justice in a soul resemble the same form (*Republic* 4. 435a–b). Hence, the form of justice has an image in both a society and a soul. A vulgar definition of justice would also approximate justice in a society and justice in a soul. But a vulgar definition in a soul or in a society remains justice not in its entirety but in part only.

13   Annas, for example, would appear to imply that Plato himself is a timocrat. She distinguishes "act-centered" and "agent-centered" moral theories. Plato, she argues, is an agent-centered theorist. A theorist of this kind holds that no "lists of rules or maxims" can tell us what actions are just. Only if we know what a just person would do can we tell what a just action is. But a just person is simply someone who receives an education in character (Annas 6. 157–160).

14   One can see why Cross and Woozley think that the philosophers and the military transform their society from a natural into an artificial community. They argue that the guardians and their auxiliaries have a new function of governing, and that this function maintains the unity of society. They have the function of supervising and regulating what they call the economic class. This class has the sole function of doing what they are told (Cross and Woozley 5. 99–101).

I would argue that the philosophers and the military have two new functions. Their functions are to rule society and to defend it. But these new functions aim at a natural and not an artificial community. They transform their society into one seeking an intelligible good from one seeking a sensible good. They rule with the concept of justice, which is for each class to fulfill its role. With this concept they give society its natural unity.

But I must concede that they do impose this intelligible unity on the artisan and agrarian class in what one might call an artificial manner. They fulfill their own functions with, we might say, an internal cause, which is their intellect. But they require the artisans and agrarians to fulfill their function of production with an external cause. Imposing this external cause one could call a governing.

I would obviously agree with them, though, that for Plato temperance is that the rulers and the ruled agree about who ought to rule. They explain that temperance requires that the better rule the worse, and that the better and the worse agree about this arrangement (Cross and Woozley 5. 106–107).

15   Cross and Woozley suggest that a philosopher might take a hypothesis of reason to be dogmatically certain because our sense experience seems to confirm it. What they argue is that a mathematician fails "to question and give an account of his assumptions" because his diagrams seem to bear them out. Euclidean geometry presents a keen example of this unfortunate naïveté, they point out (Cross and Woozley 10. 244–246).

Chapter 2

1. Ferguson captures the passional aspect of the cave. But he argues that persons inside the cave represent not a "naïve level of experience" or "a mere privation" but rather "a positive and perverted state" (Part II 15–16). He argues at length that the prisoners, infatuated with their images, engage in a political life deprived of philosophy. They pursue a human good. Their good is to seek out honor and victory to satisfy their aggressive instinct or spirit (Part II 16–19; "Again," 206–207).

   Ferguson goes too far, I think. The persons inside the cave can include both those who are naïve as well as those who are perverse. They would surely include the young guardians. They are obviously in a state of naïveté. What images they experience in their early childhood, Plato informs us, will determine how they develop. A censored Homer, for example, can properly educate them and prepare them for their function. But a Homer uncensored would very likely corrupt them (see "Again," 207).

   Annas agrees with me. She asserts that the cave represents "the human condition" and "not the degraded state of a bad society." We all begin in the cave, she continues, but we do not all end there (Annas 10. 252–253). I would add that those who leave can return to the cave with the benefit of philosophical enlightenment.

   Cross and Woozley agree that poetry as well as painting are imitations that constitute images of this kind (Cross and Woozley 9. 222–224). They also remind us that the sophists, rhetoricians, and demagogues can create images that seem desirable. They cite the passage in which Plato asserts that the philosopher who returns to the cave must contend in the courts and assemblies with the shadows of justice as well as the originals casting the shadows. They explain further that someone who looks at the originals casting the shadows would be someone who looks at the facts and draws his own conclusions (220–222).

2. Cross and Woozley remind us of this political fact (Cross and Woozley 5. 97–98).

3. Consider *The Bottom Billion*, for example, only one of many contemporary books on poverty today. Collier explains how conflict over natural resources can contribute to keeping an entire country in poverty (chap. 3, esp.).

4. Is the example of the guardians as improbable as it might at first seem? Many martial activities have become sports, and some activities of this kind have been sports since antiquity. Wrestling, boxing, fencing, and archery, and now pistol and rifle shooting, were all very likely martial activities originally and have since become sports as well.

   Kraut would appear to agree though he speaks only of knowledge not of opinion. He explains that to live well we must recognize the forms and "try to incorporate these objects into our lives by understanding, loving, and imitating them." The forms are "the preeminent good we must possess in order to be happy." We must forsake "the ordinary objects of pursuit—the pleasures, powers, honors, and material goods," he adds (Kraut 12. 204–205).

   The forms, Kraut argues further, possess a goodness in that "they possess a kind of harmony, balance, or proportion," and they are superior to other things in that they possess "a higher degree of harmony that any other type of object." His explicit assumption is that the goodness of anything consists in "the harmony or proportion that is appropriate for things of that kind" (208).

   If we study the divine order, we can make our soul "as orderly and divine as it is possible for a human soul to be" (208). One will be best able to live a life dominated by our love of the forms "if one trains the nonrational components of one's soul to serve one's love of philosophy" (209–210). Kraut would, presumably, agree that one would also wish to serve the divine order in our political life as well.

Cross and Woozley agree that our intellect has a desire proper to it, and they argue that its desire is twofold. It desires to know, and it desires to control and to care for our soul. Our intellect cares for our soul because it has "the function of controlling and harmonising the particular desires of all the elements (including its own)" (Cross and Woozley 6. 118–119).

I would agree with them that our intellect has a practical function of its own. But I would remind them that its practical function is primarily to engage in a rational activity that is an end in itself. With its knowledge that our rational and our irrational functions constitute a whole, our intellect can, admittedly, control and harmonize our other desires and their functions. But within this whole our intellect ought to give priority to our rational function over our passional functions.

Annas agrees with Cross and Woozley. She also argues that our intellect has two main functions. The one is "that of searching for the truth and increasing one's knowledge," and the other is "to rule the soul" (Annas 5. 125–126). But she apparently does not see, either, that our intellect can engage in an intrinsically valuable activity. She argues that reason cares for the soul by enabling us "to act in a co-ordinated way over our life as a whole without giving in to every short-term gratification." Reason "organizes and harmonizes other motives and makes it possible for us to attain all or most of our important ends without conflict" (133–134).

Cross and Woozley also recognize that the philosophical guardians have knowledge, and that the auxiliary guardians have only belief. They argue accordingly that the philosophical and the auxiliary guardians both have courage, but that they do not have courage of the same kind. Courage of the one rests on knowledge, courage of the other on correct belief (Cross and Woozley 5. 106).

Ferguson recognizes that the cave allegory has a political dimension. But he claims that the allegory represents a distinct "cleft" between incompatible lives of two kinds. The interior of the cave represents a political life, but the exterior of the cave a philosophical life, he explains. And the political life of the cave is less than optimal. This life is not merely one of opinion but one of corrupt opinion. It represents the corrupt political life of ancient Greece (Part II 18–19, 20–21).

I must reply that the interior of the cave need not be exclusively political but can also be philosophical, and that the exterior of the cave is not merely philosophical but is also political. The principle of justice clearly carries political consequences. This principle enables the guardians to rule, and it requires that they rule. They must return to the cave and fulfill their function. With the principle they must govern those who remain behind, both the auxiliaries and the artisans and agrarians.

The cave itself can be philosophical, then. Even the auxiliary guardians, though not educated in philosophy, have true opinions about courage that are steeped in philosophy. They receive an education in music and gymnastics to prepare them for their function of defending society. The fact that Plato censors their nursery stories, shows that even these images, though the most distant from reality and truth, can also reflect truth and reality.

Against Ferguson, Cross and Woozley argue that the cave represents the ordinary life of non-philosophical belief and not the corrupt life of perverse belief. Ferguson, they point out, implies that there could be no cave once the philosophical guardians assume their rule and establish an ideal state. But Plato clearly intends the cave to be "permanent feature even of his own state," and to represent "the world of the ordinary non-philosopher" (Cross and Woozley 9. 214–216).

5. Annas may share with a contemporary reader an anxiety about this idea of justice. She thinks that the good does not provide a concept of justice that is of worth for our good. Plato requires us to accept "what is simply just and good, and not what is just and good *for me*," she declares. Our knowledge of the good is "purely impersonal," and the good "has nothing to do with one's *own* good" (Annas 10. 259–260, her italics).

She is quite right to assert that our knowledge of the good is impersonal. What Plato asks of us is to accept an idea of human goodness and to reject our notion of merely personal goodness. The idea is a principle of justice, and this principle is the same for everyone. We all share a common human nature, and we all ought to act in concert with our nature. We can accordingly enjoy cooperation in political society for the sake of a public intelligible good, and we need not indulge in conflict for the sake of private sensible goods.

Annas is also reluctant to accept the proposition that the guardians would, allegorically speaking, return to the cave and rule in their society. Her reluctance may be typical of other scholars and students. Plato argues, she rightly states, that the guardians would return because justice requires them to return. They do so because they do "what is impersonally best." They consider their own interest to be "part of the workings of the whole." But their return is not in their own interest, she argues, nor is it in the interest of others (266–268).

I would respond that our interests may not be what we might have thought them to be. Our interests lie in a justice the same for all human beings and not in a justice, if we may so call it, particular to any one human being. Justice requires that each person in society fulfill his or her role in society. The interest and happiness of each part are the same as the interest and happiness of the whole. By engaging in the happiness of our part, we also engage in the happiness of the whole.

Annas considers this possibility. Justice demands, she rightly remarks, that I judge the happiness and interest of myself in the very same way as I judge the happiness and interest of anybody else. But, she asks, Why should I do so? If I did, I would cease "to care about my own happiness in a special intimate way" (269). Why should you do so? Because justice requires you to be impartial, I should think.

But we would have to stop being human if we are to be just! she exclaims. The impartial viewpoint is "not in the interests of any actual people" (269–270). I can only reply, No, we have to begin being human! The impartial viewpoint is in the interests of any and all actual people and of any and all potential people.

6. Cross and Woozley would likely agree. They argue in general that there is "not at any point a complete break" between the world of intelligible and sensible objects. The world of intelligibles is "more real," but the world of sensible is "not completely unreal" (*Republic* 10. 257–260).

7. Benoni agrees that the guardians undergo rather severe tests to insure that true opinions are deeply imbued in their souls, and he points out that they undergo these tests not only after their early education but also after their dialectical studies.

8. See Chapter 1.

9. Salkever speculates that Aristotle offers an analysis of aristocracy "strictly for theoretical clarification" and "not for practical emulation" (Salkever 5. 206).

10. Salkever denies that political activity can be eudaimonic for Aristotle. He argues that political activity "cannot be, as the best life must, an end in itself." The best life

is a philosophical one, and a life of this kind is, presumably, its own end (Salkever 2. 72, 78). I can only agree that a philosophical life is best, and that it is an end in itself. But I would argue that a political life, though not the best, is also its own end—at least, in part. A just action, if virtuous, is of value both for itself and for its consequences. All virtuous action we must choose for its own sake as well as choose knowingly and habitually, Aristotle argues. If we do not, we do not act justly, say, or temperately. We do only what a just or temperate person would do (*Ethics* 2. 4. 1105a26–1105b9).

11 Miller rightly reminds us that a lawgiver for Aristotle has more than one function. He argues that a lawgiver can fulfill three functions. A lawgiver ought to be able to establish the best constitution ideally, the best constitution under the circumstances, and the best under an assumption (Goodman and Talisse 1. 15–17). But he overlooks the fact that Aristotle grants a lawgiver a fourth function. A lawgiver also ought to be able to set up the constitution most suitable for any society (*Politics* 4. 1. 1288b33–39). A constitution of this kind turns out to be a eudaimonic polity, which is for the sake of martial virtue and happiness. Its rulers are those with moderate means (*Politics* 4. 11. 1295a25–1295b1; 3. 7. 1279a37–1279b4).

Perhaps because of his oversight Miller in effect dismisses a eudaimonic polity. He does recognize that Aristotle offers a concept of polity aiming at virtue and, presumably, happiness. He states rightly that its ruling class is in possession "of 'military' virtue," and that they are "moderately wealthy" (Goodman and Talisse 1. 19–20). But he goes on to argue that Aristotle redefines his concept of polity "as a *mixed constitution*." If it has some virtue, it becomes "an aristocratic polity." But if it has little or no virtue, it respects "the political rights of both rich and poor" (20).

Mulgan agrees with Miller. He argues that polity has a nature dependent on oligarchy and democracy. He does so because he takes polity to be only a mixture of oligarchy and democracy (Keyt and Miller 13. 311). But polity is prior, though derivative, because it is a "well-tempered constitution" (311–312). Polity is in fact "the perfect mixture" of the two (313). Incidentally, he also takes aristocracy to be a mixed constitution, different from polity but derived, apparently, from oligarchy and democracy (311).

12 Aristotle does refer to polity as timocracy in an extended passage in which he divides constitutions into their species (*Ethics* 8. 10. 1160a31–11. 1161a30).

13 Lear argues that an appetitive person in a just society will not have "the *virtue* of temperance" but "will be well disposed to temperance." An appetitive person, due "to his education," will have "only appetites for the bare necessities of life and for things which genuinely do him good." He "will be brought up so as not to have unnecessary appetites," which lead "to no good (or even to bad)." His intellect will tell him that "the best way to satisfy his appetites is to harken to the reason manifest in the laws of the philosopher-king" (Kraut 4. 72–75, his italics).

I think that Lear offers a persuasive argument. Unfortunately, I doubt that Plato would agree. Plato explicitly compares the rule of the guardian and auxiliary classes over the appetitive class within a society to the restraint of the better part over the worse part within a soul. The superior few with their understanding and right opinion and their simple desires ought, he argues, to control the inferior many with their diverse desires. Temperance in society is for Plato merely that those naturally better and those naturally worse agree about who should rule and who should be ruled (*Republic* 4. 430c–432b).

I would, nonetheless, want to take the argument one step further. Lear argues that a person in the appetitive class, if educated, would still seek to satisfy only his necessary appetites. I wish argue that with an education a person in the appetitive class could have right opinion about justice and not merely about who should rule and who should be ruled. With this opinion an artisan or an agrarian would be able to have virtue, though resting on opinion, and able to engage in an activity for its own sake and not for the sake of desire satisfaction. They could, in a word, be happy.

14   Bradley agrees that education for Aristotle is "the fundamental problem of politics." Aristotle, he argues, holds that education must be "*public* and *compulsory*" (Keyt and Miller 1, 39–40, his italics). He also argues that Aristotle requires education to be "*uniform* and *universal*." Aristotle, he explains, requires that women as well as men be educated because they make up one half the free population. Not to educate them would be to leave half the population "uncared for by the law." He reminds us that Sparta failed to educate its women, and that this failure was "a fatal error" in its constitution (40, his italics again).

I would ask, Ought not a political society to educate its artisans and agrarians as well? What portion of the population does this part of society make up? To neglect their education would surely be to neglect more than half the population. I am assuming, of course, that the artisans and agrarians are by nature free. One would think that, if left uneducated, they could very likely cause difficulties not unlike those which the Spartan women caused.

Sandel, too, recognizes the importance of legislation for forming good habits in citizens. He also reminds us that neither "rote behavior" nor rule-following behavior are sufficient for moral conduct. One must also have judgment in order to discern which habit or rule is appropriate in a given situation. He explains that we have judgment when we acquire practical wisdom, which concerns particulars (*Justice* 8. 197–199).

15   Sandel also commends Aristotle. He rightly points out that we cannot know what might be just unless we know what functions and abilities constitute a good life. That is, we need to know both the purpose of a social practice and the virtues it requires. He offers the example, taken from Aristotle, of flute distribution. We ought to present the best flutes to the best flute players not to those who might be wealthier or more beautiful (*Justice* 8. 186–188).

We need, then, to determine what purpose a political society might have. Sandel argues rightly that a political society ought to aim at the common good, which is a good life, and that it ought to cultivate virtue in its citizens (192–194). What might the common good and the good life be? Citing Aristotle, he states rightly that participation in politics enables us fully to "realize our nature as human beings," and that happiness is "an activity of the soul in accordance with virtue." He does state that virtue does not consist "in aggregating of pleasures and pains." But then he implies that happiness lies merely "in aligning" pleasures and pains "so that we delight in noble things and take pain in base ones" (195–197).

Nor does he define and distinguish our political functions in a broad sense. He states that politics has the purpose of enabling people "to develop their distinctive human capacities and virtues." But these capacities and virtues he defines only in the narrow modern sense of citizenship. They are "to deliberate about the common good, to acquire practical judgment, to share in self-government, to care for the fate of the community as a whole" (193–194). He considers no other functions than these few.

That is why, Sandel continues, "the highest offices and honors should go to people, such as Pericles, who are greatest in civic virtue and best at identifying the common good" (194–195). But he does not specify what might be the common good, which would, presumably, be the end of civic virtue. Aristotle himself takes us a step further. He suggests that Pericles deserved political office because he was able to see not only what is good for himself but also what is good for human beings (*Ethics* 6. 5. 1140b7–11). What is good for human beings, he explains, is an action that is itself an end (1140b4–7).

16 Cross and Woozley explain that "ideals are standards or patterns by which we can measure our actual human situation." But they caution that our thought can come closer to an ideal than our action can (Cross and Woozley 7. 136).

17 One might also compare a philosophical guardian to the demiurge, who with his own paradigm is the artisan of the universe (see *Timaeus* 27d–28b).

Lear agrees though without mentioning the demiurge. He argues that the philosopher king looks toward "a divine paradigm," and that he fashions first himself in its likeness and then his political society (Kraut 5. 66–67).

Cooper explains that "a just person is a devotee of *the* good, not *his own* good." He wishes "to advance the reign of rational order in the world as a whole." This person "can not only impose rational order on his own soul," but "he can help bring rational order to the souls of other individuals, and to their social life" (Kraut 2. 24–25). Hence, he would actually be happier leading a mixed life of philosophy and politics (25–27).

Cooper rightly asserts that Plato is "no egoist, and no altruist either." But he may go too far when he states that Plato is "a fanatic," albeit "a high-minded fanatic," with "permanent and deep interests" in the good (27–28). I would say that Plato is neither egoist nor altruist not because he is a high-minded fanatic but because he grasps the principles of non-self-sufficiency and of the division of labor.

Annas argues that with his emphasis on theory Plato does not see how different the contemplative philosopher is from the practical philosopher. If they are to rule, the philosophers must not have contemplative knowledge of the forms with "a desire to escape entirely from the world of practical affairs." They must have practical knowledge and judgment. Their knowledge must be "applicable to experience in such a way as to guide the person to make good particular choices" (Annas 10. 260–263).

True enough, Plato does give more consideration to knowledge than to opinion. He no doubt does so because his purpose is to define what justice itself is. But with his analogy to the artist Plato shows how knowledge and opinion can work together. The guardians require knowledge to see what the idea of justice is, and they require opinion to see how justice is reflected in those whom they rule. That the guardians have both knowledge and opinion, Plato makes quite clear. They love knowledge of all kinds (e.g., *Republic* 5. 475b–d; or *Republic* 7. 520a–d).

Annas would conclude that Plato does not allow that our theoretical and practical intellect could ever conflict because he thinks of our intellect as "a *single* faculty." He rejects "any distinction of practical and theoretical reasoning," she claims (Annas 10. 263–266, her italics). But Plato is very clear that our faculty of knowledge and our faculty of opinion are distinct. He argues at length that they must be distinct because they have different objects (*Republic* 5. 476d–480).

18 Cross and Woozley assert that these arguments show what antipathy Plato has for democracy and sophistry. They recognize that a true ruler must know the form of

justice. They do not explain further except to state that democrats are lost in a world of belief (Cross and Woozley 9. 197-199). But they do not ask themselves what the democrats believe and why they believe it. I would note that Plato also has an antipathy for oligarchy. Oligarchs, too, are lost in their beliefs.

19 Ferguson would appear to agree. He mentions in passing that "an actual state" does not permit "the natural division of labour" but causes "an absolute perversion of function" (Part II 17-18). He thus implies rather pessimistically, I would note, that actual states are corrupt.

Bradley does not refer to the division of labor. But he does argue that there is a "necessary equilibrium of the various elements of society," and that a "disproportionate development of one social function is hostile to the wellbeing of the whole, and may destroy the constitution" (Keyt and Miller 1. 32).

Chapter 3

1 In another dialogue Plato argues more explicitly that our intellect gives us an ability to move ourselves. He distinguishes between things that are self-moved and things that are moved by other things. And among the things self-moved, we find the human soul (*Phaedrus* 245c–246a). He also uses the famous image of a charioteer and his horses to show how our intellect within our soul can discipline our instincts (253c–254e).

2 Cooper agrees about reason and its role though he does not discuss freedom. He argues that reason knows what is good, makes decisions "in light of this knowledge," and, he adds, "its decisions are effective" (Kraut 2. 19).

Cross and Woozley express the odd worry that Plato cannot account for moral responsibility. Plato offers us a tripartite soul that does not seem to provide for a person "over and above" its parts to make moral choices. On one occasion reason may prevail, and on another appetite (Cross and Woozley 6. 128–130). I would aver that Plato does provide for one part to be a person responsible for moral choices. The person in question is essentially our intellect, and our intellect ought to rule our aggressive and appetitive instincts.

3 Cooper again agrees. He argues that the auxiliaries have courage "in a qualified sense." They lack "the fullest possible understanding of what is good," but they do have "a deep-dyed belief," and their belief enables them to be "fearless and selfless soldiers and police officers." He appears also to imply that the artisans and agrarians lack even "a reduced form of virtue." That they stick to their work indicates by itself nothing about their internal condition, he states (Kraut 2. 19–20).

4 To act voluntarily, we ought to have knowledge of particular facts, too. Ignorance of particulars occasions involuntary action. Action of this kind is a source of pity or pardon (*Ethics* 3. 1. 1110b31–1111a2).

5 That Aristotle holds our rationality to be the internal cause of our voluntary action, is, I am obliged to admit, not a proposition commonly held. Salkever, for example, agrees that Aristotle holds our voluntary action to have an internal cause. But he argues that our internal cause of action is "neither reason or will" but desire (Salkever 2. 65–66). To show that reason is not a cause of action, he cites the passage in which Aristotle asserts that "thought by itself moves nothing" (67). He would distinguish human from animal desire by the fact that our desire has greater variability than

animal desire (67–69), and that our desire is for "a coherent whole rather than a series of moments." It is for "a characteristic way of life" (69–70).

But Aristotle, I would point out, implies rather obviously that his statement about thought moving nothing applies only to the theoretical intellect. He immediately continues with the assertion that practical thought can move us. The intellect that "is practical and for the sake of something," he states, moves (*Ethics* 6. 2. 1139a35–36). I could, nonetheless, agree that human desire, albeit defined rationally, is for a characteristic way of life, and that our desire is more variable than animal desire. A characteristic way of life, I might add, ought to include our political function, and our political function varies from individual to individual.

6   Halper agrees. He argues that for Aristotle persons must act autonomously to establish and to preserve a political society and its end. The good in the state is "no different from the individuals in the state performing their tasks for the sake of maintaining the state in its fully functioning condition." The citizens find a good in "the exercise of human faculties in running the state." He states explicitly that a political society is itself "a fulfillment of human nature." To attain its good, its citizens must have "real insight into the state's end" as well as "the ability to advance it" (Goodman and Talisse 2. 34–35).

7   Sandel agrees about these two facets of Kantian freedom. He argues that we act freely when we act in accordance with the moral law and for the sake of the law (*Justice* 5. 109–112). We can so act, he explains, because we have a capacity to exercise our practical reason itself (107–108). We can also act on an appetite or a desire, but a desire or an appetite is "a determination given outside us" (108–109). Our rational capacity, he reminds us, is for Kant a spontaneity proper to an intelligible world, but our appetitive capacity is proper only to a sensible world (127–129).

8   Bellah et al. share with Tocqueville the fear that we face a danger of despotism. They argue that this danger arises from what they call "an invisible complexity" in our society. This complexity "has called forth special professions to try to understand it" and "special professions to run it: administrators, managers, and a variety of technical specialists and applied scientists." Hence, it can result what Tocqueville deems an "administrative despotism" or, paradoxically, a "democratic despotism" (Bellah et al. 8. 208–209).

They argue further that these professionals in contemporary America fail "to formulate a vision of the national polity," and they cannot articulate "a moral discourse of the common good" and "provide an alternative to a culture of individualism" (209–210). Theirs is a "professionalism without content." They do not think "of the massive disparities of wealth and power in our society" or of the efforts "to nurture ethical individuality and citizenship" (210–211).

Bellah et al. recommend with Tocqueville that we fight against this professional despotism by strengthening "all those associations and movements through which citizens influence and moderate the power of their government." These associations would have the purpose of "bringing a sense of citizenship into the operation of government," of discussing "positive purposes and ends of government," and of reappropriating "the ethical meaning of professionalism" (211).

They cite the Civil Rights Movement as an example of a particular civic association of this kind. Martin Luther King led the movement explicitly toward "broadening and strengthening effective membership in the national community," they argue, and he was able "to galvanize widespread political action, particularly among college youth, for reform in various quarters of the society" (213).

They also cite the Institute for the Study of Civic Values. They indicate that its founder Edward Schwartz all but articulates a concept of rational action of value for its own sake. He argues, they state, that justice is "securing the dignity of citizens through their participation in social and economic life as well as politics," and he contends that our capacity to organize our common life is "both an end and a means" (214–218).

In sum, they conclude that politics of this kind "depends upon a notion of community and citizenship importantly different from the utilitarian individualist view," and that we can find our "fulfillment in relationships with others in a society organized through public dialogue" (218)!

9 I take up the oligarchic principles in Chapter 4.
10 Anscombe would likely say that people of this sort are "calculating uncontrolled" persons though she might also deem them intemperate (Anscombe, 143–144).
11 Rawls assumes in addition that those in the original position have a sense of justice (*Theory* 1. 4. 17). But their sense of justice is simply a general ability to form a judgment that things are just or unjust and a willingness to act on their judgment (*Theory* 1. 9. 41).

Hare contends that Rawls advances a theory bearing a significant resemblance to utilitarian theories. He does not argue that Rawls advances a concept of human goodness that is desire satisfaction, however. He argues rather that persons in the original position could play the same role that an ideal utilitarian observer plays. A veil of ignorance, if denying them knowledge of their roles only, would make those in the original position effectively impartial and benevolent in their deliberations about their principles (Daniels 4. 89–90; 93–95).

But Hare points out that Rawls wishes to set up this theory so that it avoids any utilitarian implications. Rawls accordingly supplies those deliberating in the original position, he argues, with a more opaque veil of ignorance. A thicker veil denies those deliberating on principles any knowledge of objective probabilities. The result is that they are unable to make use of the principle of insufficient reason, and that they rely instead on an aversion to risk. Hence, they choose a principle that Hare takes not to be utilitarian (102–104).

Scanlon rightly argues that persons in the original position find their motivation in their goodness. But he goes on to argue that their goodness consists in their rational agency and their ability "to adopt and modify" their goals rather than in any particular goal that they might adopt (Daniels 8. 171). He explains that Rawls has a positive and a negative thesis. The positive thesis is "a sketch of standards of rationality" regarding choices between our life plans, and the negative thesis is "an attack on the idea that there must be some single overriding general goal" (173–174).

I would argue that Rawls does assume a single overriding goal. He argues that those in the original position have rational plans with the general goal of satisfying their desires, but that they ought to satisfy their desires in a rational manner lest conflict arise among them. What they do not have is a particular goal of satisfying this or that desire. Scanlon himself recognizes, though without seeing its importance apparently, that a life plan does have the aim of satisfying desires both current and future (173).

Dworkin argues that Rawls offers a theory based on rights and not on goals. The original position in fact relies on natural rights because it fundamentally protects individual choices without subordinating them to any goal (Daniels 2. 42, 45–46).

He even claims that a theory based on goals cannot be a contract theory. A contract theory is not the mere application of a goal but the pursuit of individual interest (42–44).

I am obliged to respond again that Rawls rests his theory primarily on his concept of a plan of life. The persons in the original position assume that they wish to promote a plan of life, and for this purpose they choose to have more rather than fewer primary goods. Their rights to basic liberties and to property are subordinate to their plan. I would also ask why a contract theory could not rest on a goal. The parties to the contract can have an interest in common, and they can choose the means to fulfill their interest together. These means could include their various rights.

12 Nagel elaborates suggestively. He explains that liberty for Rawls, because it permits us to review and to revise our ends, serves to determine our plan of life after meeting our basic material needs. Liberty thus enables us to utilize further increases in primary goods (Daniels 1. 14–15).

I cannot but wonder if one might not compare the persons in the original position with the democratic man of Plato (*Republic* 8. 561a–561d).

13 Mulhall and Swift would defend Rawls against the objections that the persons in the original position would not have an identity without a conception of their goodness, and that these persons would thus be deprived of the resources needed for deciding matters of justice (Freeman 13. 464–465). They respond that the original position is a hypothetical model, and that its purpose is to exclude "certain considerations or reasons" inappropriate for "thinking about social justice." They explain that the model respects the freedom and equality of persons because it denies them knowledge of their particular concepts of the good and of their social and natural qualities (465).

I would agree both that this hypothetical model does grant the persons in the original position an identity distinct from their own goodness, and that the model does exclude considerations thought to be inappropriate for deliberating about justice. But I would also argue that those in the original position do yet retain an identity tied to a general concept of their goodness. They know that they have a plan of life. What they do not know is the specific good that they might eventually seek. They do not know what their specific plan might be.

Unfortunately, I am also obliged to point out that they have a concept of goodness that, because it is false, prevents them from being truly free. Their concept makes them equal only in their bondage to a plan of life, whether general or specific, and to their passional desires, which they seek to satisfy.

Fisk accuses Rawls of attempting merely to reform a market society (Daniels 3. 58–59). He recognizes that individuals in the original position would want freedom to choose their life plan and freedom of thought. But, he argues, social institutions restrict their choice of life plans and of their beliefs. Indeed, freedom of thought is "a cover for the hidden persuaders that aid oppressing groups." "Genuine freedom of thought" would arise only from an awareness that human beings are "members of groups" and are subject to restrictions imposed by group conflict (59–61).

I would ask Fisk to take his analysis a step further. Why, he might ask, do groups fall into conflict and impose restrictions on thought? I would answer, Because they misconceive human goodness. The persons in the original position seek primarily a rational activity of value not for its own sake but for its consequences. Rawls presumes that they would restrict themselves to an economic rationality of means and ends. They each wish to fulfill only their own plan of life and to receive for themselves more rather than fewer primary goods.

Hence, I would have to agree, albeit for a different reason, that Rawls does indeed defend what is primarily a market society. He misconstrues what human rationality is. This philosophical naïveté entails consequences for a political community that are not insignificant. Not the least of these consequence is conflict with one another over resources social and natural.

Nagel goes so far as to argue that a contract sanctions nothing if "motivated by ignorance or fear or helplessness or a defective sense of what is reasonable"! What justifies a contract, he explains, is not mere agreement itself but "whatever justifies the agreement" (Daniels 1. 5–6).

14 I take up the difference principle in Chapter 4.
15 Halper is perhaps too generous to claim that the liberal state rests on autonomy. He argues that leaders and citizens who decide to establish and to preserve a liberal state require "a rational perception of the purpose of the state and the ability to act on that rational perception." They must exhibit "a capacity for free or autonomous activity" (Goodman and Talisse 2. 34–35).

He might argue better that the liberal state rests on what its citizens take to be autonomy. Indeed, he goes on to explain that a liberal state differs in three ways from an Aristotelian state. The liberal state has only the task of "preserving the individual good"; this state is "an artifice… that serves merely to preserve individual nature"; and it requires only collective action so that individuals can function "without interference from others" (35).

These differences, Halper explains, point to a crucial difference in the value of political activity. He asks, Is political activity "a mere necessity or a positive value in its own right" (35)? One might ask, in other words, does it have an instrumental value only or an intrinsic value?

Gutmann takes up the charge that Rawls subordinates political liberty to personal liberty (Freeman 4. 169–170). He does not, she claims. But she would appear to undermine her own claim. She begins by arguing that a free and equal person would require both political and personal liberties. But she implies that political liberties ultimately enable us "to choose among the good lives" possible within social cooperation. Political liberties "shape the context within which each can enjoy" personal liberties, which in turn enable us to choose a good life (171–173).

She continues to claim that neither political nor personal liberties are subordinated to the other "in a purely means-ends relationship" (175). But she then goes on to assert that political liberties enable individuals to become as free as possible to shape institutions within which "they can make personal choices about how best to live their own life" (175–176). The principles of justice chosen in the original position "satisfy our self-interest" (176–177).

Gutmann argues in addition that both political and personal liberty take priority over other considerations of justice. She offers three reasons for this priority. One reason is that the priority recognizes our nature as free beings. But two reasons are that political reason is "instrumental" to personal. "Political liberties are instrumental in helping people lead a good life," she explicitly states. They "create the context within which" people "can carry out their own (non-political) purposes." Political liberties, additionally, account for our sense of justice, she continues. But our sense of justice is "both instrumentally and intimately connected" with our own good. Justice "would have no purpose" if we did not know what good we sought to realize (178–180).

Gutmann wishes to argue, finally, that Rawls does not accept the general subordination of political to personal liberties. But she explains that, when they conflict, these liberties exhibit a conflict between instrumentally and intrinsically valuable liberties. The question for her is whether a specific political liberty with its instrumental value would outweigh a specific personal liberty and its intrinsic value (181–182).

16 Please note that in this chapter I am discussing what Rawls calls the thin theory of the good. Rawls also distinguishes what he calls the full theory of the good, which includes a concept of moral virtue. The full theory I examine in Chapter 5.

Nussbaum offers a capabilities approach that she holds to constitute an alternative to Rawls. She argues that her approach "takes *each person as an end*," and it asks "about the opportunities available to each person." The approach is "*focused on choice or freedom*." It requires that "the crucial good" promoted by society be "a set of opportunities, or substantial freedoms." These freedoms people "may or may not exercise in action: the choice is theirs" (*Capabilities* 2. 18–19, her emphasis).

I would ask, Does the capabilities approach advocate a freedom resting on the principle of a rational activity of intrinsic value? Does it require that each person have the opportunity to pursue happiness, in a word? I must answer that Nussbaum does not take into consideration an opportunity pursue happiness, political or personal, in the ancient sense. Yet her capabilities approach, though not advocating it, would apparently allow for an opportunity to engage in an intrinsically valuable activity.

Nussbaum argues that "capabilities are important" because "they may lead to functionings," and that a capability includes the "notion of *freedom to choose*" a functioning. This "freedom has intrinsic value," she states (*Capabilities* 2. 24–26, her italics). But does freedom in this sense issue in actions of intrinsic value? Not necessarily. She offers two examples of functionings that are not even rational activities. "Enjoying good health" and "lying peacefully in the grass" are her examples (24–25). And yet she offers two other examples of activities that "are not merely instrumental but partly constitutive of a worthwhile human life." They are "play and the free expansion of imaginative capacities" (*Capabilities* 2. 36). Obviously the fine arts and games are activities that can be rational activities of value for their own sake.

She argues further that the capabilities approach invokes "the notion of human dignity and of a life worthy of it." This notion "will dictate policy choices that protect and support agency" (29–30). She lists ten central capabilities that we ought to secure. The capabilities that she lists would be conducive to free agency though the list is minimal and provisional, she tells us (32–35). But she does not argue that human dignity rests on a nature capable engaging in a rational activity as an end in itself. Indeed, she denies that the capabilities approach "is a theory of what human nature is," and that it might "read norms off from innate human nature" (27–28).

Nor does Nussbaum argue that the functions under consideration are political activities. She develops her approach exclusively for individual activities though it could, again, allow for political activities. But she forcibly asserts that capabilities "belong first and foremost to individual persons, and only derivatively to groups." She continues explicitly that "group-based policies" can have a justification only as "effective instruments in the creation of individual capabilities" (35).

17 The idea of priority has occasioned considerable commentary. Nagel, for example, praises Rawls for giving priority to the right over the good. He argues that this priority is "an important element in Rawls's concept of liberty," and that it prevents a state from imposing "a single conception of the ends and meaning of life" on its citizens (Freeman 1. 72–73). But he does recognize, apparently without realizing its full implications, that the persons in the original position rest their choice of the principles of justice "on a thin, purely formal, conception" of the good (73).

Scanlon argues that Rawls offers a theory that is not teleological. A teleological theory would establish an end of some kind, and just institutions would "be appraised strictly on the basis of their tendency to promote this end." He also claims that a teleological theory raises problems for individual liberty. Institutions would provide individuals with opportunities to pursue their own interests "only to the extent that they are the most effective means to the promotion of the given end" (Daniels 8. 171–172).

But one can see that Rawls does offer a teleological theory despite his denial. His theory rests explicitly on his thin concept of the good. This concept is to have a rational plan of life for the sake of the general end of satisfying desire. And, obviously, his teleological theory constricts political as well as personal liberty. With his theory Rawls defends a principle of liberty designed explicitly to permit an individual to seek the satisfaction of his or her desires.

Mulhall and Swift would argue that Rawls offers a theory of political society that is neutral with regard to any concept of the good held by its citizens. But his theory is not value free, they explain, because he gives priority to the right over the good. The state acts to provide a framework that permits individuals to decide for themselves about what will make their lives better or worse (Freeman 13. 470–471).

But we can, again, see that the right for Rawls is not neutral about goodness. Rawls assumes that the right promotes a general concept of the good, and that we wish to have more rather than fewer primary goods. Mulhall and Swift themselves acknowledge, though without going into detail, that philosophers critical of Rawls hold a similar position. These critics, they report, think that the concept of the right smuggles in a concept of the good (470–471)!

Scheffler argues that Rawls distinguishes himself from the utilitarians with a distinction between monistic and pluralistic concept of the good. Rawls, he argues, thinks that utilitarianism is monistic as well as teleological because it attempts to define the good independently of the right, and that utilitarianism takes its concept of the good to be hedonistic. Yet Scheffler finds, to his consternation, that Rawls claims to have in common with utilitarianism the concept of the good as desire satisfaction. He also candidly admits that Rawls finds utilitarianism pluralistic because it recognizes that individuals pursue different pleasures (Freeman 12. 436–437 and n13).

This analysis suggests, I would add, that Rawls offers a theory similar to utilitarianism in significant respects. Rawls has a theory that advances the good of desire satisfaction, and this good is monistic in a general sense but pluralistic in a particular sense. He is in fact able to recommend the general good of desire satisfaction as a dominant end for deliberation in the original position. Scheffler himself points out that Rawls is aware of this implication for utilitarianism but denies the implication for his own theory (see Freeman 12. 437–438).

One final consideration on this topic. Daniels shows how Rawls leaves room in his theory for a "reasonable pluralism." We commit ourselves, he argues, to act within the constraints of the principles of justice, but we still have what he calls "a choice space" in which to pursue our plan of life whatever it might be. We are thus able at once to avoid violating the rules of a just society and to seek the means to fulfill our own plan. Any suggestion that justice must outweigh our personal commitments, he adds, would be to deny us our pluralism (Freeman 6. 267–268).

With his argument Daniels enables us to see how a eudaimonic principle would also allow for political and personal pluralism. A political theory with a principle of this kind rests on the general end of eudaimonic activity. Its principle would oblige us to perform a political function primarily for its own sake, but it would permit us to choose what political function we perform. Its principle would also permit us to choose what personal functions we might wish. At their best our personal functions would no doubt also be eudaimonic.

We might note that Nussbaum with her capabilities approach argues for a pluralism similar in this regard though her pluralism is not a political one. She offers a list of central capabilities that are "rather abstract." The capacities can be specified by each society in accordance with their principles and laws and their traditions and histories and their resources, she explains. The list is meant to be "aspirational" and to indicate a threshold of "an ample social minimum." But it is not meant to be indicative of an unworkable utopianism nor of a standard below human dignity (*Capacities* 2. 40–42).

18 Nagel agrees that those in the original position would act not autonomously but heteronomously. He argues that the principles of justice, because arising out of a desire for primary goods, could be not categorical but would be hypothetical and assertoric, and that our adherence to them, because resting "on gratitude for benefits received," would be hypothetical and problematic (Daniels 1. 4–5, n3).

19 Nozick does recognize, however, the crucial importance for us of activity when he takes up his hypothetical example of an experience machine. A machine of this kind would have the capacity to give us any experience that we might wish to have. What would be most disturbing about this machine, he argues, would be its "living of our lives for us." But he postpones further discussion of this moral fact and its implications (*Anarchy* 1. 3. 42–45).

20 Fried would appear to start out on the wrong foot when she critiques Nozick. She attempts to argue that the dominant protective association forces all those who are not members to become members (Bader and Meadowcroft 9. 235; also 238, 240). She also claims that the dominant association forbids independent protective associations from defending their members (236).

But the dominant association does not require anyone to join it. Nor does it prevent another association from defending its members. What the dominant association does is forbid other associations and nonmembers from using unreliable enforcement procedures to defend themselves against its members. An independent association or a nonmember remains free to defend themselves against any and all nonmembers (see *Anarchy* 1. 5. 109–110).

Fried rightly notes that Nozick holds those who are not members to have no right to exercise unreliable enforcement procedures (Bader and Meadowcroft 9. 236). But she apparently does not see why. Who is the victim of these unreliable measures? she asks. The dominant association protecting its members or the independent association deprived of its ability to protect its members? She argues that we cannot decide solely with a factual determination, but that we need a normative commitment. Nozick seemingly lacks a commitment of this kind (236–238).

But Nozick surely has a normative commitment. His commitment is to the Lockean law of nature. This law requires that no one harm another in their life, health, liberty, or property (*Anarchy* 1. 2. 10). Those who engage in an attempt to defend themselves with risky procedures, if they have the power to do so, would more likely than not cause harm to another. They would likely overestimate the harm done to themselves and exact excessive compensation or punishment (10–12).

21 That an ultraminimal state might transform itself into a minimal state, is a sticking point for many readers. Holmes, for example, argues that the transition to the minimal state is either illegitimate or unnecessary. It is unnecessary if independents are not wrongly derived of their defense. No compensation is required, and no minimal state arises. It is illegitimate if independents are wrongly deprived of their right to defend themselves. Then compensation is required, and a minimal state arises (Paul 3. 60–61).

Holmes overlooks a crucial distinction, I think. Nozick does not argue that the ultraminimal state arises in a morally impermissible manner. He argues that "for persons to maintain the monopoly in the ultraminimal state" is morally impermissible (*Anarchy* 1. 3. 52–53). The difference I take to be that to prevent independents from defending themselves in a risky manner is morally permissible, but that to prevent them from defending themselves in any manner is not. The assumption would be that an independent, perhaps due to ignorance or inability, is unable to muster any defense other than a risky one. A person of this sort the dominant association must protect with a defense that is not risky.

One could turn to other scholars for similar objections to the transition from the ultraminimal to the minimal state, and I would respond to them in a similar manner. Paul flatly declares, for example, that an independent association engages in a risky activity that is a violation of rights or is not. If it is a violation, the dominant association need not pay compensation. But if it is not, they must pay. But to say that independent association engages in a violation of rights, and also that they must be paid compensation, is a contradiction (see Paul 4. 70).

Wolff recognizes that the dominant association must pay compensation to independents for their loss of an ability to defend themselves against its members. But the association needs to pay only those who have the ability to enforce their rights in a proper manner, he argues, and they do not need to compensate those who enforce their rights improperly. In fact, the association employs, and presumably would accept, methods that it deems proper, and it prohibits only methods that it deems improper. Hence, no disadvantage is ever suffered, and no compensation need ever be paid (Paul 5. 82–83).

22 Mack holds that Nozick stops short. Nozick, he argues, offers a concept not of robust rights but of attenuated rights. A robust right would delineate a boundary that one is forbidden to transgress. An attenuated right delineates a boundary that one can transgress if and only if one pays compensation for crossing it (Bader and Meadowcroft 4. 100–101, 106). Nozick shifts, in other words, from a concept of a property right, which forbids a boundary crossing, to a concept of a liability right, which allows a boundary crossing if compensation is paid (108–109).

With this shift Nozick implicitly justifies not merely a minimal state but also a minimal taxing state and even a mutual advantage state, Mack continues. His argument hinges on the proposition that public goods, such as protection services, are extremely difficult to fund voluntarily because too many people will seek to be free riders. Nozick, he argues, allows a minimal taxing state because a state can deprive one of a right to defend oneself by providing compensation in the form of protective services (103–107). A mutual advantage state follows similarly for non-protective goods. A state can deprive one of a right to property by providing compensation in the form of another service. A state can even be paternalistic, he asserts (107–108).

Mack overlooks a crucial philosophical fact, I think. Nozick offers a concept of a minimal state that rests solely on the Lockean law of nature. The law of nature states merely that we ought not to suffer harm in our life, health, liberty, or possessions. This presupposition requires that a minimal state or any state restrict its services to protection only. Nozick would also deny, I think, the proposition that protective services would be difficult to fund. Without a minimal state and its protection an independent would before long face the prospect of a return to a state of nature and its endless feuds (see *Anarchy* 1. 2. 11). Except in their dealing with persons in a minimal state (e.g., *Anarchy* 1. 5. 110–111).

23 Fried argues that Nozick is a utilitarian. But she does not think him a utilitarian because he takes desire satisfaction to be our end in life. She argues that Nozick is utilitarian because he permits himself to justify the minimal state with "a comparison of the goodness or badness of the end states of anarchy and the minimal state" (Bader and Meadowcroft 9. 240–241). She would appear to take her concept of utilitarianism from Nozick himself (*Anarchy* 1. 3. 28–29; or *Anarchy* 2. 7. 153–154).

Vellentyne worries that Nozick is unclear about whether or not a right is enforceable. Nozick, he claims, seems to conceive a right to entail a duty "that others do something without it being permissible to enforce that right," and yet Nozick also seems to suggest that rights must be enforceable (Bader and Meadowcroft 6. 145–147). I would suggest that the question of enforceability for Nozick is a de facto one. A duty is enforceable only if we have sufficient power, perhaps in league with others, to enforce it.

Vellentyne, I would note, appears to rely on a generalization that is not particularly apposite. He assumes that a right entails a duty that others must either do something for us or not do something for us (145–146). But Nozick does not argue for a right that others do anything for us. He endorses the view only that others have a duty not to do something to us. They ought not to interfere with us. That is, they ought not to harm us.

24 Mack, too, notices that Nozick conceives of a state without citizens. He points out that we also find no constitution, no legislature, no political parties, and no political campaigns (Bode and Meadowcroft 4. 103–104).

25 Arneson agrees. He argues that Kant requires us to respect "the rational agency capacity" in others, and that this respect requires us to treat others in ways to which "a fully rational agent" would consent. The difference, he remarks, between rational and actual consent is "momentous" (Bader and Meadowcroft 1. 16).

Sandel puts the matter aptly. Discussing what use we may make of our bodies, he states that for Kant "we do not own ourselves and we are not at our own disposal" (*Justice* 5. 129–130, 131). Kant distinguishes, he explains, between the free act of a rational being and the consensual act of an individual. To act freely, we must regard both ourselves and others as ends in themselves and not as a mere means. Individuals are not free, contrary to contemporary views, "to choose for themselves what use to make of their own bodies" (130–132).

26 Nussbaum rightly points out that constraints against harm, though desirable, are hardly enough. She would no doubt agree, too, that we do not exhaust constraints

against harm by restraining physical aggression. She argues instead for what she calls combined capabilities. Combined capabilities include both internal and external freedoms. Internal freedom rests on developing innate abilities, especially through education and training. External freedom depends on establishing political, social, and economic conditions giving individuals opportunities to exercise their developed abilities (*Capabilities* 2. 20–23).

Nussbaum, however, does not argue in favor of happiness in the sense of a rational activity with intrinsic value. She would, indeed, argue against assuming that any rational activity ought to be a principle of political freedom. When she criticizes Rawls, for example, she disagrees with the fact that his "Kantian conception of a person is based on rationality." This Kantian concept, she states, excludes "people with severe cognitive disabilities" as well as "nonhuman animals." She wishes to include humans and other animals "with any type of agency or striving accompanied by sentience" (*Capabilities* 4. 87–88).

27 Bellah et al. would no doubt argue that Rawls and Nozick articulate what they call a "politics of interest." A politics of this kind is "the pursuit of differing interests according to agreed-upon neutral rules." It consists, they continue, "of coalitions among groups with similar interests, of conflict between groups with opposing interests, and of mediators and brokers of interests—the professional politicians." Its participants enter "for reasons of utility, to get what one or one's group needs or wants, rather than because of spontaneous involvement with others to whom one feels akin" (Bellah et al. 8. 200–201).

A politics of interest differs from small town politics and national politics, they continue. Small town politics is a "politics of community." It is a matter of reaching a moral consensus "through face-to-face communication." Its exemplar is "the New England township of legend," which, they note, Tocqueville extolled (200). A "politics of the nation" takes political activity "into the realm of statesmanship in which the high affairs of national life transcend particular interests." It especially entails leadership to unite "a disparate people for action" under a "national purpose" (201–203).

Unfortunately, neither a face-to-face community nor a national community can quite articulate a eudaimonic polity though they do attempt to offer an alternative to an expedient polity. Bellah et al. argue only that national politics bypasses the politics of special interests with an appeal to "the vision of the consensual, neighborly community" of the small town. But the small town, they note, can at times itself be subject to special interests when conducting its business (202).

Bellah et al. would likely find that Rawls and Nozick rest their politics of interest doubly on an individualistic bedrock. People today, they find, usually take their lives to consist of both success and joy. Their success rests on a utilitarian individualism. It is "the outcome of free competition among individuals in an open market." Their joy rests on an expressive individualism. It is "a union of similar individuals bound together by spontaneous ties of love" (Bellah et al. 8. 196–198; see also 2. 44–48).

But neither a utilitarian nor an expressive individualism can arrive at a moral consensus, they rightly argue. There is "no way to discuss or evaluate the relative merits of values and lifestyles in the culture of individualism." The best that one can hope for is "a generalized tolerance, dependent on strict adherence to procedural rules." They state, too, that bare tolerance is inadequate to address the conflicts and interdependences among groups within society today (203–204).

They also cite Octavio Paz. Paz points out that a hierarchical society can be better able to accept and to accommodate different groups because it "can accept and give moral meaning to different levels and degrees of wealth and power" (206–207). What "moral meaning" of this kind might be or what "levels and degrees of wealth and power" might be, they do not explain. But different abilities and functions would better serve to coordinate for the sake of the whole different groups within a society, I should think.

Chapter 4

1   The democratic principles I take up in Chapter 3.
2   The analogy between justice writ large and justice writ small has occasioned considerable contemporary controversy. Sachs is most probably the one who engendered the controversy. He argues that Plato fails to draw an analogy between a just society and a just person because he does not meet two conditions. Plato must show both that a just person will not perform an unjust action, and that a just person includes everyone who performs a just action (Kraut 1. 10–13).

I must reply that Plato draws his analogy successfully. He does meet the first condition, but he does not have to meet the second. Plato meets the first condition implicitly. A person who is just acts justly because he knows that to act justly is best for his society and for himself. A just person knows that justice requires each person to fulfill his function. Why? We find our political happiness and the political happiness of others in our functions.

However, Plato need not and cannot meet the second condition because a person who is not just can obviously perform a just action. Or, we might better say, a person who is unjust can act as a just person acts (see *Ethics* 2. 4.). He or she may act out of self-restraint or out of fear, for example. Sachs recognizes this ethical fact, but he does not fully take it into account. He rightly mentions Cephalus, for example (Kraut 1. 13).

Sachs claims that Plato commits the fallacy of irrelevance. Plato, he alleges, confuses the concept of justice within our soul with the concept of justice in our action. Socrates undertakes to show that justice in action is better than injustice, but he shows only that justice in our soul is better (Kraut 1. 1, 9–10). I am obliged to reply that Plato is not confused. Glaucon explicitly requests that Socrates explain what justice is, and what its potential in the soul is (*Republic* 2. 358b).

Sachs himself commits a fallacy, I suspect, when he requires that Plato satisfy the second condition. A person who is just does what is just, but a person who does what is just need not be just. That is, one need not be just to act as a just man acts. The fallacy is to affirm the consequent. More than one antecedent can cause a consequent.

Williams argues similarly that Plato offers an argument entailing a contradiction. For his analogy between a justice writ large and small, Plato must show, he argues, that a political society is just if and only if its citizens are just. To be just would be to have reason, spirit, and appetite each do its job. But a society has an appetitive part, and its appetitive part would be persons who act from appetite. In fact, most persons in a society would act in this way. If so, they would be citizens who are not just (Kraut 4. 50–52).

But one can see that persons just and unjust are possible within a just society. The philosophical part of a society can be just and act justly. But the appetitive part need not be just, and it can yet do what is just. This part can simply do what a just person would do, which would be to fulfill its function. Williams agrees that persons can be of these kinds, but he does not agree that Plato can allow for persons who merely do what is just. A just man, he would argue, is either a person who has attained an inner peace with harmonious passions or else, less persuasively, a person who must be vigilant and struggle to control his passions. But appetitive persons, he continues, have "to be kept in their place" (55–57).

Williams also worries that a just society presents a less than attractive picture. The philosophical class and the military class hold down and repress the working class, he concludes (Kraut 4. 52–53). Lear attempts to soften the blow. He argues that an appetitive person in a just society receives an education, and that he "will only have appetites for the bare necessities of life and for things which genuinely do him good." Because of his education, he will require no forcible restraint, apparently neither political nor psychological (Kraut 5. 71–73).

I think that Williams may be right on this point. Plato explicitly discusses education from early infancy to full maturity only for those individuals in the philosophical and martial classes. As far as I can ascertain, he does not offer any mention of education in a just society for the artisanal and agrarian class, but he does present an extended discussion of their pathologies in societies other than just. Nonetheless, Lear does have a point. One could hardly deny that education for the artisans and agrarians would remove the need for external and internal restraint.

Taylor argues that a just political society is paternalistic. Plato, he argues, cannot hold that everyone in a just society can have a harmonious soul and be happy. Why? Because not everyone has the ability to study philosophy and to know the forms of the good (Kraut 3. 40). But Plato does hold that society has the goal of making as many persons happy as possible, he continues. The guardians ought to have "the power to direct themselves and others towards the good which they alone grasp." Those who prove unable to know what is good ought "to submit to the direction of the intellect of someone else," presumably the guardians (42–43).

Taylor has a point. There is for Plato an element of paternalism in the just society. But the paternalism would apply, strictly speaking, only to the agrarians and the artisans. The guardians would be paternalistic toward those who do not understand justice and who thus cannot act justly. But toward the auxiliary guardians they need not be paternalistic. The auxiliary guardians, though without knowledge, receive an education in right opinion, and they act justly on their opinion.

I would also point out that a just society, though not democratic obviously, would be meritocratic. Plato explicitly requires that the guardians allow for both upward and downward mobility (*Republic* 3. 415a–c; *Republic* 4. 423c–d). I would add, too, that an education for the artisan and agrarian part of society would be desirable. With right opinion an auxiliary guardian can act justly and defend society. And so with right opinion, an artisan or agrarian could, I should think, act justly and provision society.

Cross and Woozley agree about the distinction between a just person and a just action. Plato, they argue, implies that very few persons will be able to be just though many can do what a just person would do. The difference turns on our "motives or reasons" for our conduct. They ask us to consider the act of keeping a promise. One man may keep a promise "out of respect for the sanctity of promises," but another many may keep a promise "because he thinks it will pay him to do so" (Cross and Woozley 6. 124–127).

We might consider a final contemporary on this topic. Annas argues that Plato equivocates between justice in a soul, which benefits us, and ordinary justice in action, which benefits others. She is right to argue that ordinary justice does not imply justice in a soul. Cephalus, she reminds us, does what is just, but he has an oligarchic soul. But she continues to argue that justice in a soul does not imply ordinary justice. Why "should a rightly ordered soul make you keep your hands off other people's property?" she asks. Plato produces no argument to support his assertion that a person with a just soul would not perform acts ordinarily thought unjust (Annas 6. 153–157).

I would argue again that a just person would act justly, but that a person who does what is just need not act justly. A just person knows or has right belief about what justice is, and he or she would do what is just for the sake of doing what is just. Recall that justice is for a person to fulfill a political function for its own sake, and to fulfill a political function for its sake is our political happiness. Do not forget, either, that our happiness is nothing other than an intelligible good, but the property of another is no more than a sensible good.

3   Annas has a good grasp of the analogy. She asserts that justice is "worth having for itself, as the ordered state of health is preferable to the disordered state of disease," and that justice is "also worth having for its consequences, because it brings happiness." She explains quite rightly that justice is worthwhile "if I do not want to deny and frustrate the human nature that I cannot help but have" (Annas 13. 321)!

I would argue that justice is our happiness, and not that it merely brings about our happiness. When we act justly, we perform an action of value for its own sake, and when we perform a just action for its own sake, we are happy. That is, we are happy in a political sense. Our happiness, after all, is itself a rational activity and not a passional passivity, and our ineluctable nature is itself rational and not passional.

4   Another paradox also arises. Not all the unlawful is unfair, but all the unfair is unlawful (*Ethics* 5. 2. 1130b12–13). "Lawfulness" in its general sense occasions this paradox. In its general sense it is simply what the law requires, and what the law requires can be lawful or fair in a specific sense.

5   Salkever agrees, if implicitly, that justice has these two senses, and that rightness is prior to fairness. He argues that justice for Aristotle ought to concern what he calls "the problem of living well" and not merely the activity of settling rights claims or economic activity (Salkever 6. 242). He is also correct to argue that justice aims at complete virtue in others. But he explains that it does so because its laws and virtues aim at human goodness, and "not because political activity is especially ennobling" (240–241).

I am obliged to respond that political activity, if just, is ennobling. I must argue that justice is itself a moral virtue, and an action morally virtuous has value for its own sake as well as for its consequences. To act justly is for us a virtuous activity. But justice does aim at virtuous activity in others, too. Their virtuous activity also includes acting justly. In other words, when we act justly we are happy, and we can help others be happy if they can act justly.

Goodman argues rightly that a statesman needs to know "the proper aims" of human beings in general and of citizens in particular. To take these aims to be "a fiscal bottom line" is to narrow perspectives and to beg questions (Goodman and Talisse 8. 133–134). He is also right to argue that a political society does not define what is good but that our nature does. A society can only determine "the broad aims laid down by our nature" and the means to them (134).

But Goodman suggests, unfortunately, that a political society has for its goal not our political happiness but our private happiness. He continues that "the state becomes the vehicle for the achievement of our own ends" (134). It exists "not just for its own good but for the good of its members, the ends they hope to achieve by enlisting one another's energies" (136).

6   Nussbaum argues that a GDP approach and a utilitarian approach to distribution both fall short. I can only agree albeit for a different reason. She rightly argues that to improve GDP growth per capita need not be to "improve quality of life in important areas such as health and education." Nor need it correlate "with the emergence and stability of political liberty." It also fails to take into account household income and labor, to overcome obvious inequalities, and to distinguish among various components in the lives of people (*Capabilities* 3. 47–50).

She criticizes the utilitarian approach in a similar manner. Utilitarianism cares about people by measuring average life quality "according to people's reported feelings about their lives." But this measure has problems. It aggregates across lives and across components of lives; it ignores "the social malleability of preferences and satisfactions"; and it "focuses on satisfaction as a goal" (*Capabilities* 3. 50–55).

Hence, she continues, utilitarianism undervalues our individual freedom to choose. She concedes that freedom has an important instrumental value. But its instrumental value is not its sole value. "Freedom to choose and to act," she argues, "is an end as well as a means." She finds "a great difference between a public policy that aims to take care of people and a public policy that aims to honor choice" (55–56).

I would add to her analysis and criticism that freedom, though public policy ought to take it for an end, is not a final end in itself. Freedom ought to be a means to our human function, political as well as personal, and our human function we ought to take to be our final end. Freedom can enable us to engage in a felicitous activity, and a felicitous activity, you may be aware, can be only a rational activity of intrinsic value.

7   Salkever argues that contemporary liberal theory, and presumably libertarian theory, is "concerned too much with just distributions and not enough with the questions of appropriately virtuous character." He explicitly mentions Hobbes and Locke and also Rawls and Nozick (Salkever 5. 205–206).

He traces this concern of modern theory to an ignorance of our moral goodness. This ignorance, he argues, "is linked with that passionate association of power and happiness which is the hidden ground of human *pleonexia*." This association is the tyrannical dream that we need only power to be happy. But all human goods, he continues insightfully, "derive their value from their effectiveness as sources of resistance to pleonectic confusion" (219–220)!

Galbraith might well add that Rawls and Nozick have a preoccupation with property because they, perhaps unwittingly, accept an unquestioned economic assumption prevalent in our era. The assumption would be that any increase in production is good and any decrease bad. It underlies almost all economic thinking today, he tells us (Galbraith 10. 115).

This assumption, however, relies on two empirical claims. The first, he explains, is that "the urgency of wants does not diminish appreciably as more of them are satisfied." "Physical needs," when satisfied, give rise to "psychologically grounded desires." These later "can never be satisfied" or, at least, "no progress can be proved." The second is that "wants originate in the personality of the consumer." The economist, in other words, assumes that our desires are a given (117).

Both claims arise, curiously, from the creation of new wants. The first obviously rests on "the fact that an almost infinite variety of goods await the consumer's attention," and "more goods will satisfy more wants than fewer goods" (Galbraith 10. 120–123). But the second overlooks what Galbraith calls the dependence effect (Galbraith 11. 129). Economic production can itself stimulate desire (124). Production can occasion emulation, for example. The satisfaction of wants in one person can create new wants in another (125–126). Production also gives rise to modern advertising and salesmanship, which designedly create new desires (127–128).

8 Wolff agrees that Nozick assumes persons to possess property when he begins with a state of nature. Nozick clearly presupposes a theory of property from the beginning, he argues (Paul 5. 79).

9 The fact that Nozick does not develop a principle for the just acquisition of property, and that he cannot accept the Lockean mixed-labor theory of property, Wolff takes to be "a fatal flaw" (Paul 5. 101–102 n9).

10 With his proviso Nozick would advocate, at least for those unable to appropriate, a return to the concept of a commons!

11 Nozick would appear to take further, if implicit, inspiration from Locke (see *Treatise* 5. 37. and 41–43.).

12 Vellentyne puts the matter succinctly. The proviso, he states, requires that "no one be worse off (in wellbeing) than she would be if the resource remained unowned" (Bader and Meadowcroft 6. 160).

O'Neill appears to overlook the fact that Nozick accepts the Lockean proviso in a weaker interpretation. She discusses only social product and its benefits. "No rights are violated," she states, if appropriation destroys a way of life, "provided there is a compensating bundle of opportunities and resources" (Paul 15. 313–314).

Scanlon raises two problems about the baseline. He worries that "the lack of natural bounds on acquisition" within a monetary system "means that others are likely to be threatened." They may not find "enough and as good left for them." But Nozick, he observes, thinks that the increase in acquisition will not outpace "the increase in the stock of goods" (Paul 6. 127).

Scanlon also asserts, quoting Locke, that acquisition "extending far beyond 'the conveniences of life' (certainly far beyond what these included in the state of nature)" makes the case for protecting this acquisition weaker. This acquisition makes more controversial the "extremely low baseline for determining whether the condition of others is worsened," he points out (127).

13 Scheffler has a similar proposal. He proposes to take a side-constraint structure and to combine it with a natural right different than that of Nozick (Paul 8. 166–167 n3). He advocates a right to property sufficient for "a decent and fulfilling life." No one, he continues, has a right "to any good… obtained by preventing someone else from having… a decent and fulfilling life" (153–154). I, of course, would take a decent and fulfilling life to be a happy one.

14 Drury agrees that Locke rests his concept of property on our animal life. He argues that "the right to property is derived from the right to life." We require property for "the preservation of life" (Drury 32). He also argues that the right to property is a consequence "of having mixed with it what is already one's own—one's labor which is part of one's life, limb, and liberty" (32).

O'Neill recognizes that Locke finds a basis for property in its use for "the best advantage of life." She points out rightly that the Lockean condition of not wasting resources also reinforces this purpose for property. This condition limits our appropriation of property because our capacities for production and consumption are both limited, she explains (Paul 15. 316–317).

But she argues that Locke offers an argument too weak to defend a mixed-labor theory of property. She sees rightly that Locke traces appropriation from consumption to the removal of resources from nature (315–316). But Locke, she goes on to claim, attempts to argue that production requires property rights of entitlement. Against him she argues that production can take place without individual holdings and even without justified holdings. Nor does production require "full capitalist property rights," which would include the right to neglect or to destroy of things (317–318).

I would respond that Locke conditions his mixed-labor theory of property on consumption not on production. Why do we gather things from nature and labor upon them? We do so because we must consume them if we are to live. Any production is ultimately for the sake of consumption. Because we have property in that which we consume, we also have property in that which we gather and improve, Locke argues. I would note that consumption for Locke does not permit us to neglect things. We cannot waste resources. But consumption does lead to the destruction of things. If we eat it, we have destroyed an apple.

Thomson does not cite Locke. But she offers in response to Nozick a similar principle for restricting property rights. What she argues is that a property right is not absolute, and that one may infringe on it without violating it (Paul 7. 135). What she means is that we may override a property right for the sake of higher right. This higher right is especially a right to animal life. We may, for example, under some circumstances take property from one person, even if they expressly deny us their consent, to save the life of another person (Paul 7. 142–143).

Scheffler would also limit property rights in a similar manner. A natural right "to insure a reasonable chance of living a decent kind of life" would curtail property rights. A right of this kind would permit transfers to insure "adequate food, clothing, shelter, or medical care" and "substantial personal liberty." These transfer do not violate any other rights because we do not have an "unlimited liberty," presumably, to dispose of our possessions as we wish (Paul 8. 154–157).

Nagel argues simply that rights are not absolute and that they do not have the same importance (Paul 10. 196, 199). Some rights are "very powerful and limit the pursuit of any goal," but some rights are "simply less serious and provide less powerful constraints" (199). We may less plausibly, he argues, claim the impermissibility of taking property from an innocent person to prevent a great evil, and we may more plausibly claim the impermissibility taking the life of an innocent person to prevent a great evil (196). Whether, he explains, we may limit individual liberty for the sake of ends deemed desirable, is "a function of the gravity of the violation and the desirability of the ends" (199).

15 Drury argues that Locke distinguishes natural and moral limitations for appropriation. A natural limit rests on self-preservation, but a moral limit rests on the preservation of mankind (Drury 32–34). A natural limit, he agrees, requires that enough and as good be left for others to appropriate and not merely to use. A moral limit, he argues, comes into play especially with the convention of money. This limit requires that "no one acquire a great deal more than he can make use of while others are left to starve in the midst of abundance" (Drury 32–36).

16 Scanlon considers an egalitarian proposal similar in some respects to my own. He argues that one might object to inequalities in life prospects caused by differences in

wealth that are "undeserved and arbitrary" (Paul 6. 112–113). He is right to point out that "control over various aspects of one's life," and presumably its prospects, has "an independent value" and can provide a basis for personal rights (115). He also argues that inequality can have a badness that is comparative. That is, being at a lower level of well-being is bad when others are at a much higher level (113).

I would argue that our life prospects are our prospects for attaining happiness, and that our happiness would provide an independent basis for political rights as well as personal rights. I could agree that our prospects for attaining happiness are comparative. But I would argue that our comparisons ought to be relative to our natural abilities and talents. Different persons have different potentials to attain happiness of different kinds and at different levels.

Scanlon draws our attention to a useful distinction in Locke. Locke distinguishes between natural and conventional property rights. Natural property rights allow less inequality. They do not require consent, and they do not exceed what Locke calls "the conveniences of life." Conventional property rights, Scanlon reports, give rise to what Locke deems the "disproportionate and unequal possession of the earth." They arise by tacit consent with the advent of money, and they permit one to amass wealth beyond life conveniences (Paul 6. 126).

This distinction is useful for our analysis because we can use a principle of happiness to account for similar consequences. A natural right would again be more egalitarian. It would permit one to acquire property sufficient for happiness. A conventional right would be less egalitarian. It would permit one to amass more wealth but on the condition that natural rights would yet have respect. One would hope, however, that persons would be less inclined to amass wealth in great excess if they were aware of and were able to appreciate a principle of happiness, which does not require excess.

17 Nozick does in fact assert that for us property comes attached to persons who, he presumes, have an entitlement over it (*Anarchy* 2.7. 159–160). Wolff suspects that with his concession Nozick has forgotten that individual property on his theory can arise only from "adequate grounding in just acts of acquisition" and from "just acts of transfer" (Paul 5. 101–102 n9).

Arneson agrees that Nozick has a weak concept of property acquisition. He argues that Nozick would better ground his concept of property acquisition in self-ownership. But he finds this ground also untenable. He sees rightly that unless resting on "rational agency capacity" a person would have no duties to help others or even to safeguard oneself. If grounded in consent alone, one could grant others a license to do whatever one might have consented to, "however grotesquely bad" (Bader and Meadowcroft 1. 23–24).

Vellentyne, too, thinks that Nozick ought to ground his theory of acquisition in self-ownership. Nozick, he claims, intends to endorse a premise of self-ownership (Bader and Meadowcroft 6. 156–157). Vellentyne points out that self-ownership in any strong sense precludes a duty to help others, and it precludes a right of another to use our person to help others (157–159).

He also argues that Nozick has a "choice-protecting conception" of rights and not an "interest-protecting conception," and that Nozick takes this conception of rights to be "almost absolute" (148–150). He continues that this concept of rights means that we have a right to transfer our self-ownership to another. We could sell ourselves into slavery, in a word. He finds with Nozick that this possibility is "unproblematic" (162–164; see *Anarchy* 3. 10. 331).

Wolff raises a radical objection to Nozick's employment of Locke. He argues that property was originally not private but social. Locke, he explains, held the view that god had property in the universe because he created it, and that he subsequent transferred the universe to mankind in common. Individual property rights, he concludes, only society can grant (Paul 5. 101–102 n9).

18 Ryan makes two insightful points about property. Nozick, he argues, overlooks the fact that property need not be private. That is, property can entail possession without ownership. One can have a right to use or to exploit property without having a right to dispose of it by selling it or by giving it away. His example is philosophy professorships. Professors hold their positions at universities, "presumably on the basis of merit or ability," but they do not have the right "to give their jobs away, exchange them for the services of others, or will them to a loved one" (Paul 16. 328–330, 340).

I would argue that the distinction between possession and ownership applies both to public property and to private. Ryan does point out that a Marxist would argue in favor of public possession of the means of production or natural resources without a right to sell them or to give them away (331). But I would take public in a large sense to include possession without ownership not only by political institutions but also by social and economic institutions even if privately held. His example of a professorship would include obviously positions in public or private universities.

Ryan also reminds us that private property can restrict personal freedom. He gives the example of enclosure movement in England. This movement transferred land from common ownership to private ownership. This transfer entailed a loss of freedom for some persons, who could no long enjoy "their freedom of access to the land, the freedom to use its soil, water, etc." (336–338).

He notes that Nozick in response would appear to allow a restriction of personal liberty in exchange for an increase in physical well-being. Citing Fourier, Nozick argues that private acquisition for those unable to acquire is "the source of long run material gain (by increasing the social product, encouraging efficiency, etc.)" (338–339).

I would add to Ryan only that private property rights can strict political freedom and also political happiness. Obviously, to reduce public funding for public institutions, such as universities, reduces both personal and political happiness for those unable to afford a private university. But Nozick would obviously permit the exchange of political happiness for physical well-being.

19 Arneson implicitly agrees that Nozick does not allow for any judgments of moral worth for transfers of property. He argues that Nozick has absolute side-constraints that do not permit us to make any comparisons of benefits and harms (Bader and Meadowcroft 1. 20–22).

20 Nagel writes in reply to Nozick that the requirement of interference to maintain a pattern is "perfectly obvious." A patterned distribution means in part that one advances "a general system of acquisition, taxation, and exchange that tends to preserve a certain pattern" (Paul 10. 201).

O'Neill agrees with Nagel. She argues that we may conclude little from our intuition that there is nothing very wrong with paying Chamberlain a premium to see him play. She finds that "other intuitions suggest nothing very wrong in a bit of pattern-restoring redistribution by the method of taxing Chamberlain's now enlarged earnings" (Paul 15. 309–310).

She argues in effect that Nozick begs the question. His example presumes that "to interfere to restore disturbed patterns" is wrong, and that any interference of this kind violates property rights. But this presumption about property rights is what needs to be demonstrated. Other theories hold that the restoration of a disturbed pattern maintains property rights. They assume that property rights have limits (Paul 15. 308–309).

Changing the example to Michael Jordan, Sandel reminds us that an assumption of self-ownership underlies this example, and that self-ownership is the basis for the mixed-labor theory of property. Taxation for Nozick is, he continues, to deprive persons of their labor as well as their property and to assert partial ownership of them. It is tantamount to slavery (*Justice* 3. 64–66).

Sandel does not offer an alternative interpretation of the example. But he does point out that self-ownership would permit some consequences "not easy to embrace." If I own myself, I should be free to do whatever I wish with myself so long as I do not harm others. Consenting adults would accordingly be free to sell body parts, to assist with suicide, and to indulge in cannibalism (69–74).

I cannot but wonder why Chamberlain or Jordan or anyone would ever wish to have so much money! Not to mention the team owners with their fortunes. The answer would appear to be that voluntary exchanges are not always for the sake of eudaimonic functions—if you will pardon the understatement. One would like to think that to have a successful athletic career entailing a more than moderately sufficient income would suffice for all concerned.

I do admit that amassing a fortune need not be unfair to others. Locke himself takes the view that it need not. He argues that money can enable one to amass property beyond what one might require for life. Why may not one "give his nuts for a piece of metal, pleased with its colour; or exchange his sheep for shells, or wool for a sparkling pebble or a diamond," he asks. But he assumes that one who accumulates money has "invaded not the right of others." One ought not, he explains, through spoilage waste "the common stock" and destroy "the goods that belonged to others" (*Treatise* 5. 46.). His assumption would appear to rest on a prior assumption that one ought to leave enough and as good in common for others (see *Treatise* 5. 36–37.).

If only it were so! Until we invade not the rights of others, we ought most likely to employ an expediency of tax and transfer with the purpose of providing resources to those persons left out so that they can have an opportunity not merely to live but to live well. But, again, the requisite resources for living well would be especially education and employment. Of course, voluntary transfers are also acceptable and admirable even. Philanthropists can be more than generous with their fortunes. But these magnanimous souls can too easily make others dependent upon them.

21 To take only one account of their plight, see *The Bottom Billion*, esp. chap. 1. Arneson takes Nozick to task for this omission. Nozick, he argues, has a concept of side-constraints that does not require an agent to promote goodness in any way. Nozick does not care to conjoin a requirement to promote goodness either in competition with these constraints or in subordination to them. Nor does he permit these constraints to have any exceptions (Bader and Meadowcroft 1. 16–18).
22 The equal liberty principle I consider in Chapter 3.
23 The introduction of the maximin rule has stimulated no little discussion. Nagel agrees with Rawls that the persons in the original position would be irresponsible not to avoid dire life prospects for themselves even if they knew their chances of ending

up in the worst position were slight. But why assume, he asks, that they would be satisfied with only a minimum guaranteed by the difference principle? He observes, I think rightly, that the persons in the original position might well eschew the maximin principle and simply decide in favor of a social minimum for all (Daniels 1. 10–12). A social minimum ought to be sufficient to enable them to pursue a minimal happiness in a eudaimonic sense, I would suggest.

Hare argues similarly that the persons in the original position could eschew a maximin strategy, and that they could easily adopt an insurance strategy. We purchase insurance for our house, for example, to avoid the calamitous outcome of having it burn down and not having money to rebuild. Once they fix a minimum to cover calamities of this sort, those in the original position would surely lose interest in a maximin strategy, he concludes. They would also lose interest in the difference principle (Daniels 4. 104–107).

Narveson argues that Rawls evinces utilitarian presuppositions when he argues for the maximin rule. That is, he makes implicit value assumptions "about the marginal utility curves for primary goods." Rawls argues in effect that good social and economic positions "don't matter as much as bad ones." In other words, the utility "diminishes for unit increases of primary goods above this hypothetical minimum," but below this minimum the utility apparently increases and is "very high for the first few units of such goods" (Narveson 137–140).

Miller offers a Marxist objection. He in effect asks us to imagine that persons in the original position have an oligarchic character. These persons would be the best-off, he argues, and they typically feel a more acute need for wealth and power than most persons do. They would be of the sort to constitute a ruling class, whom political institutions serve with coercive force, and they would be unable to come to an agreement with the worst-off (Daniels 9. 209–212).

Persons of this sort, he continues, would be especially unlikely to accept the maximin rule. They prefer "at least to have a chance" of satisfying their needs for the luxuries of life rather than to have to content themselves with "the minimum standard of living." They consider a high risk of success reasonable if the rewards of success are important enough (219–225).

24 Sandel helpfully draws our attention to the distinction between moral desert and entitlement. He points out that Rawls draws a "surprising conclusion." "Distributive justice," Rawls claims, "is not a matter of rewarding moral desert." This conclusion runs counter to our ordinary way of thinking. The Rawlsian concept of justice rejects our idea that "income and wealth" ought to be "distributed according to moral desert," or that justice is "happiness according to virtue" (*Justice* 6. 160)!

Justice, Rawls explains, is "about meeting the legitimate expectations that arise once the rules of the game are in place." The principles of justice "set the terms of social cooperation," and only then are "people entitled to the benefits they earn under the rules" (161). He distinguishes between a desert claim and an entitlement claim. A desert claim could apparently tell us how to set up the rules of the game. But an entitlement claim cannot tell us how to set up the rules. It arises only after the rules have been set up (160).

Galbraith points out that a liberal philosopher or politician is likely to favor increased production because it seems to be a panacea. Increased production appears "to ameliorate unemployment, agricultural insecurity, the threat of bankruptcy to the small businessman, the risks of investors, the financial troubles of the states and cities, even, somewhat, the overcrowding which results when people cannot afford to own or rent their own homes and must double up." It is "the nearest thing to alchemy that had ever been in the field of politics" (Galbraith 12. 138).

However, he does concede that there are mitigating factors. Among them we find, especially among the "younger generation," considerations that pertain to "the quality of life as opposed to the quantity of production." They include "racial equality," environmental quality, the role of bureaucracies, and "the honesty of artistic and intellectual expression." But these factors, he rightly asserts, are not "yet decisive" (142).

25 Feinberg agrees that Rawls does not have a theory of rightness. Feinberg distinguishes between rightness and justness. Rawls, he argues, holds that justness is always "decisively better" than rightness, and that rightness is relevant only when we choose between equally just arrangements (Daniels 5. 108–109). Rawls has "a rigid priority rule" that gives his principles of justice "absolute weight" and "a rigid ordering scheme among the various parts of his principles of justice" (111).

I agree with Feinberg. But I do so only verbally. Feinberg is a self-professed intuitionist, and he offers a concept of rightness different from mine. He questions whether any priority rules can be formulated and applied (111–116). Rightness for him can only be an "on balance" concept (109–110). This concept includes various considerations. "Conducibility to liberty, general health and happiness, perfections of character" are among them as well as "social progress, and economic growth" (108–109).

I would give priority to character and happiness, of course. The general concept of a rational activity of value for its own sake ought to have highest priority. But I am obliged to concede that conflicts between different specific concepts of happiness can arise, and that these conflicts can occasion dilemmas difficult to resolve. But liberty as well as progress and growth ought to be for the sake of our eudaimonic ends.

Fisk is rather direct. He argues that Rawls offers a false abstraction of human nature. He hypostatizes the tendencies of one class at the expense of other classes. The difference principle privileges the better-off and advances the exploitation of the worse-off. But the worse-off would prefer "not merely to get a great share of profits, but also to do away with the system of exploitation" (Daniels 3. 75–78).

I agree that Rawls offers a false abstraction of human nature, and that he hypostatizes his abstraction. His hypostatization would also appear to favor the better-off over the worse-off. But the better-off as well as the worse-off can end any exploitation of one another, I would argue, only if they come to understand that their political functions can be of great value for their own sake than for their consequences. Especially if they measure their consequences in terms of social and economic goods received.

Nagel points out that, though he claims it is, Rawls has a concept of our goodness that is not at all neutral. His concept is that we are rational to want primary goods whatever else we want. This concept shows "a very marked tolerance for individual inclinations." Rawls does not allow for other concepts that depend on the relations between the social positions of oneself and others. His concept is less useful for plans of life achievable in certain defined social structures or in societies working to realize higher human capacities or in economies of certain types (Daniels 1. 7–10).

I must agree. Rawls does not take care to distinguish different political activities from one another in any significant way. Though he incidentally mentions them, he does not consider the possibility that philosophical, martial, and artisanal and agrarian activities, for example, might each be of intrinsic as well as instrumental value or that these various activities might together make up a political society primarily of intrinsic value rather than merely of instrumental value.

Sandel also argues that Rawls does not have a morally neutral theory. Rawls takes the position that "the right is prior to the good." Our specification of rights and duties ought not, he claims, to depend on a particular concept of the good life. We cannot impose values on others and still respect them "as free and independent selves, capable of choosing their own purposes and ends." But that "persons should be free to choose their ends for themselves is itself a powerful moral idea," Sandel counters. This idea requires only that your choice respect "other people's rights to do the same."

Sandel contrasts Rawls with Aristotle. For Aristotle politics has the purpose not only of regulating economics and providing for defense. Its purpose is also "to cultivate good character and to form good citizens." Aristotle holds to the view that justice is about "realizing our nature and developing our distinctly human capacities." To think about justice, "we have to reason from the nature of a good life" (*Justice* 9. 215–217).

I would add to what Sandel has to say only that to form good citizens who lead a good life would be to cultivate citizens who perform rational activities for their own sake—even those undertaken in a political arena.

26 Mulhall and Swift attempt to put up a defense for Rawls against the objection that he offers an account of primary goods too abstract to take into account human culture. We are, the objectors argue, "culture-producing creatures" (Freeman 13. 469–470, 479). They reply to this objection that Rawls offers "an expression of the public political culture of constitutional democracies," and that the original position represents "an explicitly culture-specific shared understanding" (470).

I must ask, How cultivated is a society that acts under a principle of seeking more rather than less wealth and income and of seeking more rather than less satisfaction of desire? No matter how public their principle might be, does not a human culture entail functions other than those of material acquisition and of pleasurable indulgence? I would surely hope so.

When he extends it, Daniels brings Rawls's theory closer toward a eudaimonic principle of happiness. He argues that the theory ought to take into account "our capacities as citizens" and not only our primary goods (Freeman 6. 256–257). He uses his argument to advocate for health care. Disease and disability cause deviations from "the normal functional organization… of a species," he argues. They can reduce our opportunities to "construct or pursue 'plans of life'" (257–258).

I would add that we should also take into account our political capacities. We surely ought to mitigate political disadvantage as well as disease and disability. I would argue, too, that we ought to give precedence to our intellectual capacities for happiness rather than our capacities for fulfilling a plan to satisfy desire. Daniels does mention "cognitive and emotional functions," which enable us to pursue "our goals as social animals" (Freeman 6. 257). But he does not appear to consider that our social goals might include activities valued as eudaimonic.

Daniels rightly reminds us that our opportunities do not always find a good proxy in income and wealth. Improvement in worker health might, for example, reduce worker productivity (Freeman 6. 262). A similar observation would surely apply to opportunities for attaining or augmenting worker happiness, especially on the job.

27 Nussbaum, implicitly criticizing Rawls, argues that a program claiming to do better "the more resources it has," even if "it divides them equally (or equally enough) among all citizens," faces "formidable objections." Most importantly, income and

wealth are poor proxies "for what people are actually able to do and to be." Different functions, she rightly points out, require different abilities and different resources. She cites biological functions and needs. Adults and children have different nutritional needs, for example, and so do women who are pregnant and those who are not (*Capabilities* 3. 56–57).

She also observes that to distribute resources equally or nearly equally is to favor the status quo. If it had neglected some functions in the past, a society that distributes resources even in an egalitarian manner would continue to make an inadequate distribution of the resources to people who might wish to fulfill the neglected functions. This maldistribution could apply both to functions of some social groups, such as education for women, and to functions of all groups, such as religious freedom or freedom of speech and assembly. Those who might wish to fulfill these functions would likely require extra expenditures (57–58).

But she reminds us again that her capabilities approach, despite any similarity to a human rights approach, she grounds "not in rationality" but "in bare human birth and minimal agency." This grounding "articulates clearly the relationship between human entitlements and those of other species." She explicitly asserts that "all sentient beings have entitlements grounded in justice." Any conflicts between human and nonhuman species are to be worked out until they no longer occur (*Capabilities* 3. 62–63).

28   One could argue that the failure to distinguish rightness from fairness explains why so many attempts at domestic or foreign aid meet with failure. Consider, for example, what Easterly has to say about foreign aid. He distinguishes between planners, who would decide what aid to supply on a grand scale, and searchers, who determine what aid locals would demand.

He implies, though he does not make the distinction, that the searchers take cognizance of both rightness and fairness in their projects, but that the planners are content with what they take to be fairness. The searchers attempt to determine for what activities those whom they wish to assist require resources and to supply the appropriate resources. The planners disburse considerable moneys and other aid with little regard to the activities of those whom they hope to help (see, e.g., *Burden* 1. 1. or 4. 10–11.).

29   Piketty, a Frenchman who also visited America in his youth, gives cause for a similar fear with an analysis even more alarming. He concludes from an examination of data covering centuries that wealth inequality will continue to worsen as long as capital has a return rate greater than economic growth. His formula this increase is simply $r > g$ (see *Capital* intro. 23–27; or conclu. 571–573). He finds that the ratio of return on capital to economic growth is even higher in Europe than in America (*Capital* 2. 4. 150–155).

Piketty would advocate a return to what he calls old-fashioned political economy. Political economy, he explains, considers what role the state ought to have in the social and economic institutions of a country (*Capital* conclu. 573–575). He does not, unfortunately, take into account the intrinsic moral value of political functions fulfilled for their own sake. He recommends restraints on acquisition primarily in the form of progressive taxes on income and on wealth (*Capital* 4. 14–15.).

Galbraith also complains that inequality is increasing, and the figures that he cites are over four decades old from 1970! The tenth of Americans with the lowest income received only two percent of the total income in the country, but the tenth with the highest income receive twenty-seven percent of all income. He states that the rich have since taken an even greater share of income. He agrees with Piketty that the rich benefit from capital gains. But his point is only that their capital gains enable them to reduce their federal taxes through egregious loopholes (Galbraith 7. 70).

He contends at the same time that concern about inequality is decreasing (69-70). This decrease arises from two primary reasons, he argues. The first reason is that current inequality has not occasioned a "violent reaction." The Marxian revolution has not occurred (71). The second reason is that the rich occupy a "drastically altered political and social position." They exercise less power, indulge in fewer displays of luxury, and enjoy less prestige (71-77).

The third, and more significant, reason is apparently that increases in production present an alternative to decreases in inequality. At least, in "advanced" countries it does. Increased output "has brought the great material increase in the well-being of the average person." But this increase "leaves a self-perpetuating margin of poverty at the very base of the income pyramid." The increased benefits "are held to be comprehensive." But they only seem to be because those at the base of the pyramid are largely "a voiceless minority," he argues (78-80).

Bellah et al. take notice of what Tocqueville calls "a new form of aristocracy." They note that this aristocracy "would make owners and managers into petty despots and reduce workers to mechanically organized, dependent, operatives." The Civil War, they state, advanced the growth of an industrial aristocracy in America with its destruction of a slave aristocracy (Bellah et al. 2. 41-42).

They argue that our technological achievements, and presumably our industrial achievements, have destroyed a social ecology or a moral ecology. An ecology of this kind lies in the fact that we and our societies "are deeply interrelated, and the actions we take have enormous ramifications for the lives of others." But modernity, they continue, has led to "the destruction of the subtle ties that bind human beings to one another, leaving them frightened and alone" (Bellah et al. 11. 283-284).

What solution do Bellah and his colleague have to offer? They argue for "a reappropriation of the idea of vocation or calling, a return in a new way to the idea of work as a contribution to the good of all and not merely as a means to one's own advancement"! They would enhance vocational choices "in terms of intrinsic satisfactions" and reduce "extrinsic rewards and punishments"! We might thus reduce "the inordinate rewards of ambition and our inordinate fears of ending up as losers" (287-288).

They go so far as to recommend a revival of an artisanal class! Production generates a "social wealth" that need not be "siphoned into the hands of a few." We ought instead to use our wealth "to pay for work that is intrinsically valuable, in the form of a revival of crafts (that already flourish in supplying goods for the wealthy) and in the improvement of human services." The "satisfaction of work well done, indeed 'the pursuit of excellence,' is a permanent and positive human motive," they declare (287-289; also 294-296)!

Quoting Alan Trachtenberg, Bellah et al. would also recommend a return to original concept of a corporation. Trachtenberg reports that originally a corporation was assumed to earn "its charter by serving the public good." Its charter was not "a right available on application by any private enterprise." This older concept, they argue, would obviously change the social responsibility that a corporation has. Its responsibility would be "a constitutive structural element in the corporation itself" and no longer a public relations "whipped cream decorating the corporate pudding" (289-290).

Chapter 5

1. With a quote from George Beard, Bellah et al. suggest that the American middle class is "the most nervous people in history" (Bellah et al. 5. 120). They explain that what we deem to be the middle class has changed in concept. In the eighteenth century Americans perceived the middle class to be the "middling condition," "middling interest," or "middling rank." This condition predominated because they had neither an aristocracy nor an impoverished mass. They thought that this class "would be most apt as independent citizens to support republican institutions and to oppose both monarchy and despotism" (119).

    Americans in the nineteenth century, however, perceived the middle class "as composed of people on the rise who were 'calculating' and 'ambitious.'" This change came about in large part, Bellah and his colleagues explain, because the middle class thought their function no longer to be a calling but a career. To have a calling means "to take up a definite function in a community and to operate within the civic and civil order of that community." But to have a career means "the attainment of 'success,'" and success has a "persuasive power" in "the fact that whatever 'success' one had obtained, one could always obtain more" (119–120).

    Galbraith observes that our insecurity arises from our material possessions and, presumably, our comforts. Before we attempt to protect our fortune, we must "have some fortune to protect," he wryly asserts (Galbraith 8. 88–90). He would also suggest from an economic viewpoint that insecurity, along with inequality and poverty, is "inherent in the competitive model" of economics, and that "the orthodox view of the business cycle added a much more general sense of disquiet" (Galbraith 4. 34–39).

    He shows, nonetheless, that people do take various practical measures in an attempt to eliminate their insecurity. Businessmen form monopolies to control supply and price. "Price and production agreements or cartels, price-fixing by law, restrictions on entry of new firms, protection by tariffs or quotas," they also employ (82–83). Workers, too, make use of government interventions. These interventions include "relief and welfare funds," "unemployment insurance and old age and survivors pensions," and "price supports," among others. They also form unions to enhance bargaining power and to increase job security (85–86).

2. Adkins rightly points out that for Aristotle "human beings as such" cannot perform a human function. We can perform only a function that is specifically good. Aristotle and the ancient Greeks, he continues, prized more highly a good male and his functions, but they also speak of "a good woman, child, or even slave" (Keyt and Miller 3. 91).

3. Galbraith reminds us, if we could have forgotten, how much contemporary society neglects public goods in favor of private. We take public services, he states, to be at best "a necessary evil," and at worst "a malign tendency against which an alert community must exercise eternal vigilance" (Galbraith 9. 109). But public goods, he points out, "must be provided for everyone if they are to be provided for anyone, and they must be paid for collectively or they cannot be had at all." Public goods do not, though private goods do, "lend themselves to private production, purchase, and sale" (110–111).

    Unfortunately, Galbraith does not recognize that public goods in a broad sense can include cognitive, defensive, as well as productive functions of intrinsic value. He lists the customary modern functions, such as "clean streets and police," "mass literacy and sanitation, the control of epidemics, and the common defense." "Schools, judges, patrolmen, and municipal swimming pools," also are mentioned (Galbraith 9. 110–111).

But these functions he evidently takes to be primarily, if not exclusively, of instrumental value. The imbalance between public and private goods, he argues, is tantamount to an imbalance of production and enjoyment. Because we fail "to expand public production, we are missing opportunities for enjoyment which otherwise we might have," he states (Galbraith 17. 193).

He reminds us, too, that we decide on how much to spend on public goods by a democratic process. This process, he points out, relies on the questionable assumption of "independently determined consumer wants." But consumer wants are prey to what he calls "the dependence effect." They are "subject to the forces of advertising and emulation by which production creates its own demand" (193–194).

4 This topic I broach in Chapters 1 and 2.

5 Cross and Woozley emphasize the naïveté of this original society. They call this society an economic society, and they assert that its citizens come together because they have needs for economic goods, such as food, clothing, and shelter. Their society thinks of itself "wholly in material terms" and devotes itself "solely to production and consumption" (Cross and Woozley 4. 78–79).

Its citizens, they argue, do not make up a "high-minded community, fired by ideals of brotherly love." Each person is "still out for his own interest as much as if he were living in a state of nature." But each realizes now "that enlightened self-interest is better served by a degree of co-operation." This enlightened self-interest is that each person is willing to help others, but that each is "*thinking it better for himself to do so*" (89, their italics).

Annas also argues that the original society rests on an enlightened self-interest. The citizens in this society have a self-interest enlightened by the division of labor. Their self-interest is "far-sighted enough for them to specialize and divide their tasks" (Annas 4. 73). Each one, she also argues, gives and receives from another, "thinking that this will be best for him" (78).

She points out that in this initial society the division of labor already recognizes natural differences. The principle applies to what we find in nature and not to what we arrange by convention. It applies, in other words, to persons of "different types suited for different lives." It does not apply to individual differences "which distinguish one person from everyone else" (Annas 4. 74).

6 Annas would appear to defend the luxurious society over the bucolic society. She holds that the division of labor has plausibility only in a society "based on *need*." Plato, she argues, fails to argue for this principle "when need is not in question." He thinks that even in a just society someone who does not "co-operate as fully as possible" for the common good is "always selfish," and that someone who follows "his or her own inclinations" is "always irresponsible and immature." She herself contends against Plato that the division of labor, at least in a strict sense, is "not at all plausible where co-operating to stay alive is not at stake" (Annas 4. 75–76).

7 That there are three naïve societies most scholars overlook. Cross and Woozley do, for example. They recognize only the bucolic and the luxurious society, and they place the martial class within the luxurious society (Cross and Woozley 5. 94–95). But I think that we may recognize a third society because the martial society rests on spiritedness rather than desire.

Annas agrees with Cross and Woozley on this point. She finds that an army is a new class added to the luxurious society. She apparently concedes that the division of labor would apply to it and require that the soldiers "must be specialized much as any other trade" (*Republic* 4. 76–77).

8 Cross and Woozley ask whether a society for Plato arises from a social contract. They conclude rightly that it does not. There is no contract to establish a government in the first society, they argue (Cross and Woozley 4. 81–82). Nor, I would add, is there any contract in the succeeding societies. Plato replaces a contractual basis for politics with an educational basis. He relies on our reason and its attendant virtues instead of our passions and a restraining agreement. This reliance on education obviously marks a major division within political philosophy.

Cross and Woozley would appear to miss the key point, however. They do not see that the guardians rule best because they fulfill their function for the sake of their function itself. But they do argue that the guardians would rule better than other persons because they are passionate about and possess the appropriate knowledge, and because they accept ruling to be their responsibility. They correctly argue that the guardians have no political ambition or personal interest in ruling (Cross and Woozley 5. 101–102).

Cross and Woozley, nonetheless, recognize that Plato introduces a new principle with his natural history of political society (Cross and Woozley 5. 95). This principle is "an entirely new principle of *political* classification." This classification rests on new functions of governance and defense as well as economic functions. The classification does not turn merely on differences of social status or economic power (98–101, their italics).

They also agree that the guardians now "have the notion of working for the interests of the city as a whole," and that they no longer pursue their own interest and promote the interest of another only to advance their interest. They observe further that society now consists of three classes with their own functions and not merely of individuals with different jobs (97–98).

9 Bradley explains nicely, I think. Aristotle, he points out, takes the position that a state has a definite object for which it exists, and that it does not have an object "suggested by the chance desires of individuals." The state aims at a good, and its good is "the final object of human life, the end which alone gives value to lesser ends." Bradley implies that this good is its true end, but he notes that many men pursue false ends. They seek unworthy objects, such as wealth or pleasure (Keyt and Miller 1. 20–22).

Bradley reminds us that a state for Aristotle would be a final cause. But he hastens to add that a final cause, if natural presumably, arises from within and is not imposed from without. He argues that man realizes his final cause when he develops his potential nature into his actual nature. "His final cause is to be himself," he states aphoristically (Keyt and Miller 1. 25).

Bradley also claims that we cannot find in Aristotle "our own ideas of the individual." We view man, he explains, "as having a nature of his own and objects of his own, independent of society." We see the state "as a contrivance for securing to him the enjoyment of his liberty and the opportunity of pursuing his end" (Keyt and Miller 1. 18–19).

I agree that our idea of the individual is not present in correct constitutions, which Bradley appears to have in mind. But our idea of the individual is present in corrupt constitutions, I would submit. Individuals in democracies and oligarchies, for example, surely pursue their own ends. Their ends are the false ends that Bradley mentions—those of wealth and pleasure.

But Keyt demurs, and my reader might share his reasons for hesitation. Keyt argues that Aristotle in his philosophy carefully distinguishes reason and its products from nature and its products. A "product of reason is not a product of nature," he asserts plainly. A political society, if it is a product of practical reason, cannot, he concludes, be a product of nature. He speculates that the *Politics* might be "fatally flawed" with "a contradiction at its very root" (Keyt and Miller 5. 118–119).

I would submit that Keyt has neglected to take into account a key tenet of Aristotelian philosophy. The tenet in question is the very definition of a human being. We are, Aristotle argues repeatedly and insistently, animals that are rational. That is, our nature is our rationality. Hence, a natural product for us is a rational product. Our rational nature, I would hasten to add, can occasion cognition and action as well as production.

Keyt continues that a political society originates in the same way as a poem. A society "originates in a natural immanent impulse," but it is "brought to completion by the art of politics" (119–120). He does note, rightly I think, that by calling man a political animal Aristotle would mean that "nature endows man with a latent capacity for civic virtue (*politikê aretê*) and an impulse to live in a polis" (124–125). But, he argues, this impulse need not bring about a product that exists by nature. A natural impulse can cause poetry, but poetry is not a natural product (126).

I reply that Aristotle would agree in part with the last point. He clearly distinguishes between moral virtue and art, and he would argue that politics is a moral virtue and not an art. An impulse, whether habitual or not, can issue either in action or in production. A moral virtue, say justice, results in an action that is an end in itself—if eudaimonic, and an art results in a product distinct from action—a poem or perhaps a play (see *Ethics* 6. 5. 1140b6–7). Nonetheless, both an action and a product, Aristotle would assert, do exist by nature. We do, after all, have a rational nature.

Keyt, finally, objects that by nature a producer and a product are the same in form (120–121). But he argues that a household, a village, and a political society differ in form. And so the one cannot produce the other by nature. Only when one society establishes a colony do the producer and the product have the same form. Or when one household generates another, he claims (122).

My reply is that Aristotle distinguishes between a potential form and an actual form (*Physics* 3. 1. 201a9–15, e.g.). A political animal has the potential form of a political society in a family or a village, but he realizes the actual form in a political society itself. Similarly, a man and a woman, when single, are a potential family, but they are an actual family when they couple and have children. And so does an acorn become an oak tree.

10 Nussbaum is quite right to remind us that for Aristotle politicians ought not merely "to make everyone perform desirable activities." They ought rather "to aim at producing capabilities or opportunities." Aristotle thought, she claims, that "satisfaction achieved without choice is unworthy of the dignity of human beings." By enabling one to reflect and to inform oneself, education can remove impediments to meaningful choice (*Capabilities* 7. 125–126).

Aristotle could agree with Nussbaum that an education can enable one to reflect and to make meaningful choices. But he would surely argue also that a meaningful choice would be a eudaimonic choice, and that a eudaimonic choice would be to choose an action not a satisfaction, and that it would be, among other considerations, to choose an action for its own sake (see *Ethics* 2. 4.).

11 Bradley explains that the state is "a moral organism." Man is not confined to perception and desire as an animal is, nor is he limited to nutrition and growth as is a plant. Man has a soul that is "intelligence and rational will." He not only has "a law of his life," but he "is capable of knowing the law of his life," and he "is capable of living by it" (Keyt and Miller 1. 33–34; see also 26–27).

Miller puts the matter nicely. Human beings "must engage in cooperative forms of social and political organization in order to fulfill their nature and these forms of cooperation require a conception of justice." Because it makes nothing in vain, nature endows us alone with speech, and speech enables us to form our conception of justice (Keyt and Miller 12. 293–294).

A political society, he continues, requires "two cooperating factors: the natural potential of a given population for the political life, and lawgivers and politicians applying the science of politics" and fashioning "the legal structure" (295–298).

Sandel reminds us that for Aristotle only "in politics do we fully realize our nature as human beings." We do so because we have language, he argues, and with language comes our ability to declare "what is just and what is unjust," and to distinguish "right from wrong" (*Justice* 8. 195–196). Do we have a rational and political nature, then? Apparently we do not in the sense that we can pursue a rational and political activity of value for itself. But only in the sense that in society we can realize our ability to deliberate. When we are separate, we cannot "develop our capacity for language and moral deliberation" (196).

12 Halper agrees that a political society for Aristotle advances a good essentially political, and that this good consists in participating "in mutually beneficial activities." These beneficial activities especially include "the governance and administration of the state itself." For Aristotle these political activities provide citizens "with opportunities to cultivate and exercise their human capacities." The state, in other words, "opens up possibilities for virtue" and, presumably, for happiness (Goodman and Talisse 2. 33).

That citizens can find their happiness in these activities, Halper argues explicitly. Political activity for Aristotle is an activity in accordance with virtue. A person fulfills his human potential and leads the best life that he can when he performs activities that constitute the state (35–36). I would add only that these political activities would also include, besides political functions in a narrow sense, military and artisanal functions (but see 36–37).

Halper argues by contrast that the liberal state allows for "mutually beneficial activities," but that these activities fall "under the rubric of individual choices." If they share interests, people find no obstacle to pursuing their shared interests together. But government service they take to be "the forsaking of one's private interest to serve others' needs." A person engaged in public service is "motivated by a noble personal self-sacrifice" (33–34).

13 Annas agrees that Plato offers an educational system applicable today. She argues in fact that the contemporary system most resembling the Platonic is the American. She cites the National Educational Association and its objectives set forth in the early twentieth century. These objectives include the development of ethical character and of citizenship (Annas 4. 86). Perhaps the American education system does resemble the Platonic. But I would urge that we ought not to forget to ask a prior question or two. Ethical character of what kind does the American system inculcate? And citizenship for what kind of society does it instill?

14   Keyt argues that aristocracy faces "a formidable obstacle." A more virtuous person ought to have more political power in an aristocratic constitution, he rightly asserts. But he also argues that there is no basis for inferring that one person has more virtue than another, and that he or she ought to have more power than another. Virtue is "an intensive rather than an extensive quality," he asserts. One cannot say that one person is x times as virtuous as another and deserves x times as much power (Keyt and Miller 11. 247).

    I cannot but think that this proposition is a slip of the pen. Virtue especially differs in quality, and Aristotle assigns different offices to persons in accordance with their different virtues. Rule is appropriate for those who have practical wisdom, for example, and military service for those who, presumably, have courage.

    Keyt himself recognizes this fact. He states that "the value of the authority assigned to one person stands to the value of the authority assigned to another as the political virtue and wealth of the one stands to the political virtue and wealth of the other" (264–266). With this assertion he also reminds us that property is necessary for carrying out a political function.

15   Aristotle does deny the people individual offices. But he does so precisely because they separately would make partial judgments (*Politics* 3. 11. 1281b21–1282a17).

    That Aristotle chooses the term "practical wisdom" suggests that the people have not knowledge proper but right opinion (again *Ethics* 6. 1. 1138b35–1139a15; or *Ethics* 6. 5. 1140b24–28). His analogy of practical wisdom to judgment would carry the same implication (see *Ethics* 6. 11. 1143a19–32).

    Bradley states that with these arguments Aristotle presents his version of "the sovereignty of the people." He would add some explanations and cautions. He rightly points out, for example, that people ought to have sovereignty not because of their consent, nor their equality, nor their majority. Their sovereignty arises because their rule "is more likely to realize the government of intelligence and character than any other arrangement."

    He also observes that Aristotle would subject the people and their sovereignty to the rule of law. He cautions, however, that Aristotle has a concept of the people that is more limited than ours. The people would not include even the male population in its entirety, and that it would not include aliens and slaves. Nor would sovereignty be appropriate for all peoples (Keyt and Miller 1. 32–33).

    I would reply to this caution that the people could have a sovereignty that includes more persons, male and female, provided that they have an appropriate education. The people must consist of persons, Aristotle argues, who have a portion of practical wisdom and virtue. Aristotle himself thought, Bradley reminds us, that women ought to be educated (Keyt and Miller 1. 40).

    An education of this kind a society would also require, would it not, for their artisans and agrarians though, uneducated, they seem to Aristotle no better than ignorant migrants or slaves. I am assuming, of course, that the persons in question are by nature rational and, hence, educable.

16   Keyt takes Aristotle to support sovereignty for the people in democracy. Aristotle, he claims, shows that "democracy would seem to be absolutely just in some circumstance and not a deviant constitution at all" (Keyt and Miller 11. 270–272). Keyt would thus overlook the qualification that Aristotle finds necessary. A people worthy of sovereignty must have an education in virtue and practical wisdom. But not all peoples do. Democratic peoples, in fact, prefer freedom and even license to virtue (see *Politics* 6. 2. 1317a40–1317b17).

Salkever would also take the people to rule in a democracy. He recognizes that the people best rule together and not separately, and that not every people is able to rule better than the few. But he does not appear to attach sufficient importance to the requirement that a people worthy of rule are those who have practical wisdom and moral virtue though he mentions this qualification (Salkever 5. 223). He argues instead that the rule of the people rests on good law, and he explains that the many are more open to rule of law and less open to corruption than the few (223–224).

Salkever does, however, observe that a democracy requires civic opinion "committed to the maintenance of the rule of law" and to the conservation of "familial prosperity." This opinion public education "supportive of the regime" best secures. An education of this kind would instill the belief that to be free consists "in ruling and being ruled in turn" and not in "living as one likes," he explains (225–226). I would note that the one belief as well as the other are hallmarks of democracy (see *Politics* 6. 2. 1317a40–1317b17).

17   Miller apparently recommends a mixed polity for contemporary society. A state of this kind is a minimal state, which he calls "laissez-faire capitalism" or "democratic capitalism" (Goodman and Talisse 1. 24, 30). He makes his recommendation because he finds Aristotle to be an "approximist" (17–18). Aristotle provides the lawgiver with three functions, he argues (15–17). These functions, he continues, serve for levels of approximation to establish a minimal state. One ought to identify an ideal for a minimal state, to recognize population and resource limitations, and to work incrementally to reform an actual society (23–29).

But Miller modifies the functions of a lawgiver to arrive at his concept of approximation. He states that a lawgiver has functions that serve to establish a constitution with "distinctive levels of application" (Goodman and Talisse 1. 23–24). Aristotle argues that a lawgiver has functions that establish constitutions of different kinds. He thinks that an ideal constitution is either a monarchy or an aristocracy. He would likely hold that a minimal state is a constitution best only in given circumstances or under a given hypothesis. In other words, a constitution of this kind could be the best for a society given its limited resources, or it could even be less than the best given its resources (*Politics* 4. 1. 1288b24–33).

Miller overlooks the fact that Aristotle gives the lawgiver a fourth function. A lawgiver also ought to be able to establish a constitution most suitable for any society (*Politics* 4. 1. 1288b33–39). A constitution of this kind is a eudaimonic polity in which the ancient hoplites rule (*Politics* 4. 11. 1295a25–1295b1; *Politics* 3. 7. 1279a37–1279b4). Miller, consequently, does not consider the possibility of a eudaimonic polity in which the artisans and agrarians might rule. His analysis would appear to rest on an assumption, shared with Plato and Aristotle, that the oligarchic and democratic classes need not have an education or are uneducable.

Mulgan would agree that oligarchy and democracy are more similar than usually thought. He argues that both oligarchs and democrats "aim at material economic advantage," and that they both do so "in order to gratify their desires." Oligarchs seek "a life of luxury and license," he explains, and democrats seek simply to live as they please (Keyt and Miller 13. 320).

18   Halper argues that the Founding Fathers conceived the American constitution to be a eudaimonic polity. The founders thought that an Aristotelian polity would ease their concerns about preventing faction. He cites James Madison in *Federalist* No. 10. The founders, he explains, thought that the constitution ought to promote positive ends, and that the state ought to have a positive role. He also asserts that the Declaration

of Independence "accepts some positive end for the state" (Goodman and Talisse 2. 40–41 and n5).

Halper concludes, rightly I should think, that we need not make any radical changes in our institutions to effect an instauration of a polity. We need only to recognize that the scientist, the politician, and the businessman can realize their talents for a public good. And, presumably, the military man can, too. We would require, he states rather eloquently, "only the simplest and the most difficult of changes: to think of ourselves differently" (41–42)!

Nussbaum would agree that the working class ought to receive an education. She discusses at length what Adam Smith has to say about their education. Smith argues that government ought to provide "free compulsory public education" (*Capabilities* 7. 134–135). His concern was that the division of labor without education "has a very pernicious effect on human abilities," but that the common person has little time or money free to invest in an education (135–136).

Unfortunately, Smith proposes only that the state provide workers with an education in reading, writing, and arithmetic. He is partial to "useful subjects, such a geometry and mechanics," but he would omit "frivolous subjects such as Latin" (136–137). One cannot but wish that Smith might have advocated for his curriculum a tincture of philosophy, frivolous though it might perhaps appear. But we are surely obliged to commend him for not thinking the workers uneducable.

Bradley addresses the matter rather directly. He finds that Aristotle has a concept of citizenship "too exalted" for us and not even "plausible" given the increased size of contemporary states. He argues that, if we were to adopt his concept, we, too, would have to exclude from citizenship those who are "the labouring classes." They do not possess the qualities requisite for citizenship even if they had the leisure for political and military duties (Keyt and Miller 1. 37).

Yet he does observe that we today find "no shame in labour." He argues that labor can develop moral character, and that this character can lead to happiness (37–38)! He even recognizes that work done for pay can yet be done for its own sake! Citing *Politics* 7. 4. 1333a6–11 and *Politics* 8. 2. 1337b17–21, he reminds us that Aristotle himself argues that "menial services" need not be servile (38–39).

If only Bradley would take one more step! He apparently does not recognize that the artisans and agrarians have a function to fulfill within political society even though he sees that they can become virtuous and can attain happiness. He need concede only that a citizenship includes not only political and martial functions but also artisanal and agrarian functions. The artisans and agrarians, if educated, need not be unenfranchised conditions of society.

19 I omit a discussion of "the democracy most in accordance with equality." But I would say only that this constitution appears most likely to be a polity of the mixed variety leaning toward a rule of the poor (*Politics* 4. 4. 1291b30–39).

Halper agrees that a democracy of the first species closely resembles a eudaimonic polity of artisans and agrarians. This constitution is a mixed one with a democratic population of farmers and an oligarchic property requirement albeit a low one, he points out (Goodman and Talisse 2. 43 n6). Jefferson especially, he reminds us, thought that the new American constitution ought to aim at a public good of agriculture. Its farmer citizens would also be law-abiding and able to participate in their legislature for only short periods (40–41).

Salkever also agrees that democracy is best when "composed of farmers or herdsmen of middling wealth." A democracy of this kind rests on an opinion about the best life that gives the "highest marks to industrious and law-abiding people." This opinion it secures less "by direct instruction" than "by economic regulations that favor farming, limit the amount of property which may be held, reduce poverty, and separate political office from financial reward" (Salkever 5. 224–225).

20 Sandel argues rightly that we need a "political discourse" that "involves reasoning together about the good life." Its purpose would be to take "moral and spiritual question seriously" and to bring them "to bear on broad economic and civic concerns." He offers the example of Robert F. Kennedy, who attempted to appeal "to a sense of community" that goes beyond mere material prosperity. And the example of Barack Obama, who "articulated a politics of moral and spiritual aspiration" (*Justice* 10. 261–263).

But Sandel himself does not advance a concept of the good life. He offers instead four "possible themes" for public discourse. The first theme is "to cultivate in citizens a concern for the whole." This one can achieve through "common institutions," in which "young people of different economic classes, religious backgrounds, and ethnic communities come together." These institutions have included public schools and military service.

The second theme concerns "the moral limits of markets." He reminds us that "marketizing social practices may corrupt or degrade the norms that define them." These practices include, among others, hiring mercenaries, outsourcing pregnancies, and buying and selling organs. We accordingly ought to consider "what non-market norms" we would "want to protect from market intrusion."

Thirdly, economic inequality "undermines the solidarity that democratic citizenship requires." One can overcome the corrosiveness of inequality with "the reconstruction of the infrastructure of civic life." This reconstruction would include investments in public schools, public transportation, public health clinics, playgrounds, parks, recreation centers, libraries, and museums. These investments would draw people "into the common spaces of a shared democratic citizenship."

Finally, we ought to attend to "the moral and religious convictions that our fellow citizens bring to public life." Sometimes we might challenge them and contest them, but we might also sometimes listen to and learn from them, he states (263–269).

Sandel surely offers important themes that we ought to address in American democracy and in contemporary democracies generally. But a question yet remains. What would be the goal of addressing these themes? Ought we to take them up with the purpose of creating a community with primarily intrinsic value for its own public ends? Or ought we to take them up and create a society with primarily instrumental value for our private ends?

21 Salkever follows Tocqueville and argues that education ought to aim at "virtue or excellence as self-interest properly understood" (Salkever 6. 237, 249). He agrees with Tocqueville that modern democracy presents the problem of individualism. Individualism is for each person to isolate himself from larger society within a smaller society of family and friends (Salkever 6. 245–246).

He also agrees with Tocqueville that the solution to this problem is an "education in liberty" arising from equal participation in economics and politics. He quotes from Tocqueville an example of public works. Participation in a local project, such as cutting a new canal or opening up a new road, can inspire a "love of the common motherland." Why? Because these local improvements can give one a hope of enriching oneself (249–251).

Galbraith, too, favors education. He finds an imbalance between investment in personal and in material capital. We underfund education because almost all "investment in individuals is in the public domain." The states provide most of the funding for primary and secondary schools and for colleges and universities. Hence, investment in education falters on an "active discrimination against investment in the public domain" (Galbraith 18. 202–204).

But he argues also that education has an independent justification higher than an increase in human capital. He all but concludes that education ought to be for a rational activity of intrinsic value. He distinguishes humans from other animals by "the desire to know, understand and reason" in addition to desires for material and psychological comforts. Education, he suggests, ought to be "for human satisfaction and fulfillment" as well as for production (206–207).

Galbraith agrees that education would undermine "the want-creating power which is indispensable to the modern economy" by widening taste and inducing a critical attitude. The consequence is that "the preoccupation with production" would also be undermined. He explains that "education enables people to see how they are managed in the interest of the mechanism that is assumed to serve them" (208).

But he notes that the modern youth have their interest deflected from public education by private production. "Motion pictures, television, automobiles and the vast opportunities which go with the mobility they provide" all compete for the interest of the young (Galbraith 17. 190–191). I would add that we now have personal computers, mobile phones, and the internet.

Bellah et al. find in contemporary America a veritable taxonomy of individuals who act with enlightened self-interest. Persons whom they call town fathers appear most enlightened. They "think of their love for their community as intertwined with what Tocqueville would have called 'self-interest properly understood.'" This person is a member various service clubs, such as the Rotary Club, the Lions, and the Kiwanis. He joins these clubs for "the satisfaction from giving the effort," he reports. But he also believes that "his business success depends on the support of his community" (Bellah et al. 7. 170–175).

But persons whom they call the cosmopolitan professionals are less clearly enlightened. They seek primarily to further their individual ambitions through community service. They accordingly are not committed to their community though they participate in it. They provide "a kind of service to others by doing well the very things that will make them a success," and they are committed "to a career path that entails moving from job to job and from place to place" (185–187).

Between the town father and the cosmopolitan are the concerned citizen and the volunteer citizen. A concerned citizen exhibits enlightened self-interest, but his community involvement is for the most part defensive. He wishes to restrain strangers. He gets involved "to protect one's hearth and home and one's decent friends and neighbors from the evils of a mysterious, threatening, complicated society composed of shadowy, sinister, immoral strangers" (181–185).

The volunteer citizen pursues self-restraint. This person believes that we cannot simply serve ourselves, but that we must recognize our debt to society. We must see that "the public good is based on the responsibility of one generation to the next." The public good is "a pie, a limited pie, and when you take all the pieces out of it, then it all will be gone." We have to forsake our "short-term interests" for the sake of "the long-term public good" (192–195).

Bellah et al. agree that all these persons have difficulty conceiving "of a common good or a public interest that recognizes economic, social, and cultural differences between people but sees them all as parts of a single society on which they all depend" (191–192). An exception would seem to be the volunteer citizen who realizes that "respect for the dignity of others and concern for the welfare of society as a whole are more important than selfish interests" (192–193). But the welfare of society as a whole turns out to be an unspecified "generosity of spirit" that acknowledges "an interconnectedness—one's 'debts to society'—that binds one to others whether one wants to accept it or not" (194–195).

22 Freeman offers a solution to the congruence problem that links the Kantian interpretation with the Aristotelian principle. He first reformulates the problem. Are the principles of justice "compatible with a human good that affirms our nature," he asks (Freeman 7. 288–289). His answer is that they are. Everyone, he explains, accepts the principles of justice under Kantian conditions that "characterize them as 'free and moral persons' (or 'free and equal rational beings'…)." The Aristotelian principle in turn establishes "that it is intrinsic to people's good to realize their nature (as free and equal rational beings)" (292–294).

Freeman, unfortunately, offers an argument, cogent though it may be, that is beside the point. He recognizes that his argument requires, and he explicitly asserts, that our rationality for Rawls be "an intrinsic good," and that a just action be "worth doing for its own sake" (290–291). But Rawls holds quite clearly that our free and equal rationality is not of value for itself but of value for its consequences, and, by implication, that a just action is instrumental. That we have only a rationality, "standard in economic theory, of taking the most efficient means to ends," he explicitly assumes (*Theory* 1. 3. 12).

Nussbaum apparently endorses the Rawlsian congruence problem and its solution though she differs on specifics. She argues that we must articulate "in a calculatedly 'thin' way" political principles concerning "some definite values, such as impartiality and equal respect for human dignity." She proposes in particular that this articulation endorse her capabilities approach but "*for political purposes only.*" This approach would enable citizens to be free, she implies with a reference to Rawls, to pursue "a plurality of religious and secular views of the meaning and purpose of human life" (*Capabilities* 4. 89–90, her emphasis).

Halper agrees in general that Aristotle offers a conception of political society that is a public good, and that the contemporary liberal conception advances only a private good. He would, however, appear to hold that the contemporary concept aims at a private good that is less distributive than rectificative. That is, it aims at the prevention of interference (Goodman and Talisse 2. 33).

He finds three salient differences between an Aristotelian state and a liberal state. An Aristotelian state creates a political good "that individuals would not have on their own," but a liberal state preserves a preexisting individual good. An Aristotelian state "is itself a fulfillment of human nature," but a liberal state is "an artifice" and "serves merely to preserve individual nature." Finally, an Aristotelian state requires "a real insight into the state's end and the ability to advance it," but a liberal state requires only "some ability to act collectively" and "without interference from others" (Goodman and Talisse 2. 35).

Halper rightly observes that a contemporary political society rests on what Aristotle would take to be a false assumption. Aristotle argues that a person finds self-sufficiency and happiness not in isolation from others but in "working together with family, friends, and fellow citizens." But a liberal state assumes that a person is self-sufficient and can pursue happiness individually (Goodman and Talisse 2. 37–38).

A political society today harbors an ironic incongruity, he wryly continues. A liberal state has the purpose of enabling persons to pursue individual happiness because it is indifferent about their happiness. When engaging in a political activity, then, individuals who might choose "to pursue large ends" are only facilitating their own happiness, which is insignificant. They are precluded from engaging in any activity, political or not, of "real significance" (38–40).

23 Nagel would seem to accept at face value Rawls's claim that a well-ordered society is of worth for its own sake. He argues that Rawls offers a concept of rights that is "not instrumental." Rights are "good in themselves" and are not good "because of the results that they will bring about," he states (Freeman 1. 65–66). He argues, again, that for Rawls respect for rights "should be valued for itself" and "the highest value in the sphere of political institutions" (83).

But Nagel argues earlier that Rawls has a concept of goodness that is less social than it is individual. He explains that the common good for Rawls "is measured in terms of a very restricted, basic set of benefits to individuals" (Daniels 1. 3). He reminds us that goodness for Rawls is that we are rational to want primary goods whatever else we want. But goodness of this kind "implies a very marked tolerance for individual inclinations," he continues. It exhibits a strong bias toward an individual and "the unimpeded pursuit of his own path" (7–10).

He does, however, attempt to explain in his essay that a desire for primary goods is not a motive for obeying the principles of justice "in real life," presumably in a well-ordered society, but that this desire is a motive only for choosing the principles of justice in the original position (4 n3). I have to agree that persons in a well-ordered society could have a motivation different from persons in the original position. But Rawls explicitly rests his theory on the persons in the original position and their motivation. That is precisely why he takes up the congruence question.

Nagel is not the only philosopher to accept naïvely Rawls's claim about a social union and its value. Other philosophers also assume that a well-ordered society is essentially of intrinsic value. For example, Mulhall and Swift argue, citing Rawls, that a political society is a "social union of social unions." Citizens in a political society accordingly establish and maintain just institutions "as good in themselves" (Freeman 13. 469). A society is thus not merely "a cooperative venture for the pursuit of individual advantage," they purport to explain (467).

Parijs, however, agrees with my analysis. He observes that "individual opportunistic behavior" and "self-seeking individual conduct" could undermine a well-ordered society and its just institutions, especially in a "secular and globalized society" (Freeman 5. 228–230). But he continues that "an ethos of solidarity, of work, indeed of patriotism" could stabilize political institutions. This ethos, he continues, would not be one "of the intrinsic goodness of a life inspired" by it but rather one of "crucial instrumental value in the service of boosting the lifelong prospects of the incumbents" in the worst-off position (230–231).

Sandel argues that "the liberal concept of freedom" entails a weakness despite its appeal. If we think of ourselves "as free and independent selves, unbound by moral ties that we have not chosen," then we cannot explain "a range of moral and political obligations that we commonly recognize, even prize." These moral ties, he continues, "arise from communities and traditions that shape our identity." Among them are "obligations of solidarity and loyalty, historic memory and religious faith" (*Justice* 9. 220; also 240–241).

    He aligns himself with Alasdair MacIntyre. He finds in MacIntyre an account of these obligations not chosen. This account rests on "a narrative conception." We are "storytelling beings." Only if we ask ourselves what story we live out can we determine what obligations we have, he continues. The stories that we live out have a form projected into the future. My moral deliberation is thus "more about interpreting my life story than exerting my will" (221–222). He presents extended examples of this sort in family, community, religious, and national obligations (225–234).

    I am obliged to suggest that we might live out stories that are less than veracious and that entail claims of loyalty and solidarity less than moral. Robert E. Lee, whom Sandel discusses, surely failed to act morally when he sided with Virginia against the Union. He himself opposed both secession and slavery, Sandel points out. And yet he chose to side with his family and with his home State.

    Sandel does question whether loyalty might be merely "an emotional tug that beclouds our moral judgment and makes it hard to do the right thing." But he answers simply that loyalty is "a claim with moral import." What we admire in Lee is "the disposition to see and bear one's life circumstance as a reflectively situated being." Otherwise, Lee would be simply experiencing "a conflict between morality on the one hand and mere feeling or prejudice on the other" (236–237; also 234–235).

24 Scanlon puts the matter succinctly. A well-ordered society has principles of justice "to provide a common bond for cooperation between persons with disparate aims and purposes." The principles set "limiting conditions on the pursuit of these other ends" (Daniels 8. 170–171). Institutions can be just, he adds, only if defensible to an individual "on the basis of the contribution they make to his good as assessed from his point of view" (172–173). The difference principle, more specifically, applies to persons "engaged in a cooperative enterprise," and it determines "how *the benefits of their cooperation* are to be shared" (202, his italics).

    Fisk argues, rightly I think, that a social union would require individuals to have capacities "inexplicable apart from reference to the roles they would play in society." Even in the original position "mutual interestedness," he nicely phrases it, rather than mutual disinterestedness would be a condition of sustaining and supporting these social roles and their social structure (Daniels 3. 64).

    Rawls, unfortunately, cannot establish a social union. Persons in a well-ordered society, Fisk explains, would view their institutions neither as shared ends nor as good in themselves. Why? Because they are atomistic individuals. They have the goal not of realizing a community but only of realizing themselves "as self-interested," and they consider their institutions good "because they interfere least with the realization of self-interest" (65–67).

25 Fisk argues from a Marxist perspective that a social contract establishes a state at once diversionary and coercive. A state of this kind is diversionary because self-interested individuals establish it to maximize their interests. This state is coercive, he argues, because it must use force to prevent even the suspicion that others might cheat and violate the contract "to get greater benefits for themselves." It must, though, expend more resources "against conflicts arising from memberships in antagonistic groups" than on "freeloading by random individuals" (Daniels 3. 61–62).

    He continues that only on the assumption that individuals are atomistic can one construct a contract. On the assumption that individuals are members of groups, no one could agree to a contract. To do so would be to accept "coercive mechanisms" to maintain social stability and to prevent one from defending his or her group interests "by fundamentally altering the structure of society." Especially if one considers that we are more likely than not to be a member of a historically disadvantaged group (62–63).

I would respond that one can rest a social contract on a group conception of an individual. Groups within society can act in concert with one another and need not be in continual conflict. They can do so if each recognizes its position and function within the whole of society and does not attempt to usurp the position and function of another group. There need not be diversion, but coercion would remain. The state would need to restrain groups within society, whether oligarchic or democratic, who might attempt to gain dominance and to oppress others.

Miller also contends that Rawls "has a relatively low estimate of the extent and consequences of social conflict." A Marxist account of social conflict would, he argues, preclude persons in the original position from working toward a commitment to the difference principle. If, that is, these persons are presumed to know the general facts of human society and history of conflict (Daniels 9. 206–207). But, again, my reply would be that a society need not entail conflict if only its parts can accept their diverse functions and reject any temptation to usurp political rule for the sake of their exclusive advantage.

26 Rawls, of course, would not allow the upper and the lower classes to despoil the middle class. He assumes Pareto optimality, which requires that a distribution cannot make any class worse off (*Theory* 2. 12. 58).

27 One might wonder whether chain connections and close knittings would not render the difference principle superfluous. But Rawls would likely reply that, even if it is empirically true, we still ought to affirm our commitment to the principle with an express public announcement. This response he makes to utilitarianism and its appeal to empirical assumptions about rights (*Theory* 3. 27. 138–139).

28 One may fairly say, I think, that contemporary American society will enjoy neither chain-connections nor close-knittings as long as corporate executives can with impunity permit themselves whatever salaries and bonuses they might wish.

Carville and Greenberg offer an analysis, if polemical, to show how the middle class in American society is indeed whipsawed. Their analysis includes on overview of data concerning several current factors (see Carville and Greenberg 3–4., esp.).

More recently *Fortune Magazine* also published an extensive article on the middle class and its present plight (see Staff).

Sandel is quite right to assert simply that the difference principle presumes egalitarian effects that are difficult to determine. Wage and salary differences have an effect that "depends on social and economic circumstances." Higher salaries for doctors might lead to better "health services in Appalachia," but the higher salaries might lead instead to "more cosmetic surgeons in Beverly Hills" (*Justice* 6. 152).

Fisk sounds a rather pessimistic note. He does not think that one could ever take the viewpoint of society as a whole. He argues that society constitutes "an interrelation of roles," but that this interrelation sets "groups in conflict." Hence, for one to take a view of society as a whole "will not be natural." A view of this kind will be "an artificially induced ability" (Daniels 3. 69–70).

I wonder if we need be so pessimistic. If we value our political roles as good in themselves, and if our political roles naturally harmonize with one another, may we not then take a view of society as a whole without class conflict? Education ought to have the purpose of helping us attain this view. Our political roles, so-called, can obviously conflict and occlude a view of society as a whole if we take them to be of value primarily for their consequences, most often taken to be possession and enjoyment of material resources.

29 One might well say that the persons in a well-ordered society do not have a social desire but merely a common desire for more rather than fewer primary goods (see *Theory* 9. 79. 460–461).

30 Wolff decries what he calls the weirdness of applying game theory in this sphere of activity. He argues that this application is "inhuman." It presupposes "homogeneity, continuity, and substitutivity," and "is a proposal to dehumanize much of our experience." It is "the rationalization of a sphere of human experience" historically left to religion, politics, and family and personal life (97–100). And to moral theory, I might add.

31 I cannot but observe that Nozickian utopias bear an uncanny resemblance to contemporary suburbia with their homeowner associations and their covenants and restrictions.

32 One might wonder whether the difference principle would not have a similar effect of coopting the worse-off. Not that Rawls intended any such effect, of course.

33 Indeed, the Duchy of Bavaria in the sixteenth century with its purity law specified rather austere parameters for the brewing of beer.

34 Galbraith all but reaches our conclusion. He appears to arrive at the concept of a function with intrinsic value. He argues that there is what he calls a new class of workers. This class takes it for granted that its work will be "enjoyable." If not enjoyable, its work is "a legitimate source of dissatisfaction, even frustration." The members of this class find their pay "not unimportant," but they also "expect to contribute their best regardless of compensation" (Galbraith 23. 249–250). He urges that to expand this class "ought to be a major, and perhaps next to peaceful survival itself, *the* major social goal" (252 his emphasis).

But he does not see that this new class could take work of this kind to be their political happiness. He is, alas, unaware of the ancient Greek concept of happiness. He finds that the pursuit of happiness is "admirable as a social goal," but that the concept of happiness lacks "philosophical exactitude." He states, quoting Bertrand Russell, that happiness is "a profound and instinctive union with the stream of life." But this definition is "too vague," he rightly asserts. We do not know what is united with what (Galbraith 24. 255).

Galbraith would seek to dampen unfettered overproduction by finding "reasonably satisfactory substitutes for production as a source of income." Production and employment have an obvious connection, he states. Even products "of slight consequence" provide individuals with income "of great consequence to them" (Galbraith 20. 217–218). "The obvious device," he continues, "for breaking the nexus between production and income" would be "unemployment compensation." He suggests that unemployment benefits ought "to approach the level of the weekly wage" (218–219).

But I would argue that this remedy neglects to take into account the fact that people can find intrinsic value in their work. Their work can be an activity of their rational and political nature, and an activity that is an end in itself. Galbraith himself implies that people find unemployment to be less than desirable even when compensated. "The aversion to idleness is remarkably strong," he asserts. Unemployment compensation close to a weekly wage, he argues, would hardly be likely to increase "malingering." The workers who exercise this option have historically been "negligible" (Galbraith 20. 218–219).

Bellah et al. come even closer to recognizing a eudaimonic function. They find an ambiguity in the middle class attitude toward their work. The middle class professionals, they argue, can find "intrinsic validity" in their work. This validity lies in "the correct solution of a problem or, even more, an innovative solution to a problem." If they act "in the service of the public good—as, for example, in medical practice at its best," their work "expresses an individualism that has social value" (Bellah et al. 6. 149).

But they are quick to note that the middle class can become caught up in their careers. Their "concern for rational problem solving (not to speak of social contribution) becomes subordinated to standards of success measured only by income and consumption." This concern can lead to "doubts about the intrinsic value of the work itself." These doubts become amplified "in the context of a large public or private bureaucracy where much ingenuity must be spent, not on solving external problems, but on manipulating the bureaucratic rules and roles, both in order to get anything done and in order to move ahead in one's career" (149).

Americans, Bellah and his colleagues also remark, often "make a rather sharp distinction between private and public life." They tend to think that their fulfillment is found in themselves alone. When they do, they take "negative view of public life," and they feel a need to protect themselves against "impersonal forces of the economic and political worlds." This view "often ends in emptiness" (163).

But Americans sometimes find, they continue, that "private fulfillment and public involvement are not antithetical." Those who do evince a life "that is not empty but is full of content drawn from an active identification with communities and traditions." Perhaps the private and the public "are so deeply involved with each other that the impoverishment of one entails the impoverishment of the other," they tentatively conclude (163).

Chapter 6

1. In another dialogue Plato argues explicitly that a physicist is obliged to accept a theory that is literally "a probable myth" (τὸν εἰκὸτα μῦθον) (*Timaeus* 29c–d).

    Cross and Woozley think that we ought not to make too much of the analogy between a philosopher and a painter. The analogy "is introduced in a fairly incidental way and without discussion," they argue (Cross and Woozley 7. 136–137).

2. Incidentally, Socrates also remarks to Glaucon and Adeimantus that they are, as if in a myth, making up a myth (ὥσπερ ἐν μύθῳ μυθολογοῦντές) about educating the guardians (*Republic* 2. 376d).

3. The cubist painters are perhaps instructive. They attempt to capture a sensible object in its entirety by imitating more than one perspective at a time. But despite their efforts they cannot successfully imitate an object. They can only paint more perspectives.

4. The cubists also imitate intelligible objects, I would argue. As if to emphasize their intent, they at times distort sensible objects in their paintings almost beyond recognition. I have in mind Pablo Picasso, especially his portraits.

Annas apparently does not see that the term "imitation" is ambiguous. She holds to a narrow definition that "imitation" can refer only to "recited poetry" in which someone acts out a role. A recital, she reminds us, can be an imitation, or a narrative, or a mix of the two. She asks herself "how can we carry over the distinction between narration and role-acting to the other arts," such as painting (Annas 4. 94–96)?

I would respond that Plato makes the distinction of what is imitated prior to the distinction of how it is imitated. I would further note that the term "imitation" is a homonymic genus. The genus includes imitation of intelligible objects and imitation of sensible objects. A poet or a painter can imitate an object of either kind, and a narrator or an actor can also imitate an object of either kind. But a good imitation is of an ideal reality, and a poor imitation of a sensible reality or, worse, of its appearance. In his analysis Plato focuses on an imitation of an appearance.

Urmson agrees that Plato offers a definition of imitation that is broader than playacting. Socrates initially states, Urmson points out, that he yet needs to define imitation, and he eventually shows that his definition applies as much to narrative poetry as to dramatic poetry (Kraut 13. 225–226). Plato wishes to argue, he continues, that a poet has no understanding of the world, and that he portrays the world not as it is but as it appears. Homer, for example, did not gain fame for his ability in the fields that he wrote about, such as warfare or medicine, but only for his ability to write his poetry (226–229).

5 Annas denies that painting and poetry are similar. Plato, she argues, takes painting to be "the literal copying of one visual aspect of a particular thing." He takes into account only *trompe-l'œil* painting, and he states explicitly that painting is "like holding a mirror up to reflect things." But poetry does nothing comparable "to holding up a mirror to particular things," she claims, or to capturing the way a thing looks "from one angle of vision" (Annas 14. 336–338).

I would reply that the point of the mirror analogy does not appear to be that a painter is a copyist. The point is rather that a painter captures only an appearance of particular things, and that the appearance captured is illusory. Plato states that a painter makes only the appearance of a couch, for example (*Republic* 10. 596e; also see 598a–c). By playing on our emotions, poetry also can surely capture an appearance of things that is illusory. Our emotions can make events appear more important than they are. Pity does, and, presumably, so does fear (see *Republic* 10. 606a–b).

Annas goes on to ask, "How can the strength and importunate nature of one's desires have anything to do with one's being taken in by optical illusions?" She states rightly that reason is not taken in by an optical illusion, but an inferior part of the soul, presumably vision, is taken in. Plato wishes to argue that poetry presents a similar illusion, she continues. Our reason is not taken in by tragedy, but a "lower, desiring part of the soul," is taken in. But the analogy cannot hold, she asserts, because the inferior parts of the soul are "not the same in both case" (Annas 14. 338–339).

I must agree that painting and poetry appeal to inferior parts of the soul that are indeed not the same. But I must also argue that both inferior parts of the soul, vision and passion, are yet vulnerable to similar illusions. Plato wishes to make the point that as the visual effects of an object need not reflect what a thing truly is, so the emotional affects of an object can similarly distort what a thing really is. Vision can make things appear to be larger or smaller than they are, so passion can make things appear to be more or less desirable than they are (see *Republic* 10. 602c–605c).

Urmson argues simply that a poet is especially "ignorant of the nature of moral excellence," and he represents "people who are supposed to be heroes as behaving in a theatrical and intemperate manner." Homer portrays Achilles grieving frenetically at the death of Patroclus in a manner that "a man of good character would be ashamed to exhibit" (Kraut 13. 229).

6 The Greek is literally "sympathizing" (ξυμπάσχοντες).

Cross and Woozley agree. They argue that we can "surrender ourselves to the performance and share in the feelings of the characters." We can accordingly "identify ourselves with, and thus imitate, characters whom we would ordinarily condemn" (Cross and Woozley 12. 275–277).

Annas expresses what is today a rather common view that to identify with a tragic character is not always bad. She does concede that to put oneself in the place of someone doing "a callous or revolting or treacherous deed" can expand our "horizons for the worse." She also acknowledges that imitation can have a tendency "to undermine unity of character." But against Plato she argues that to lack unity of character need not be bad. She finds "an awareness of a plurality of moral outlooks" to be healthy. Finally, she argues that the value of tragedy "lies in the moral conflict embodied in what happens." Tragedy leaves us with a feeling that "there is no single statement of moral truth."

Annas concludes, then, that Plato is "wrong, and dangerously wrong," to deny "the impossibility of giving a single finally right moral appraisal of certain situations." She finds fault with him for condemning poetry because it can lead us to live "a confused life instead of a well-organized one" and because it can "frustrate the intellectual search for a single rational answer to moral problems" (Annas 4. 96–98).

7 Cross and Woozley recognize that Plato would welcome poetry back if it can show why it ought to exist in an ideal society. They also recognize that hymns and praises are permitted (Cross and Woozley 12. 275–277).

Citing Tate, Cross and Woozley accept the possibility that Plato would appear to allow poetry and painting of a kind that "imitates the ideal world." Imitation of this kind would express the ideas of beauty or of justice, for example. They also point out that a poet who imitates in this way "would have the same education in mathematics and dialectic" as a philosopher.

But they are not entirely confident in this view. They find that Tate presents evidence that "scarcely supports the positive view of good imitative art." Tate apparently rests his position on the analogy between the politician and the painter of an ideal of beauty. This analogy, they reiterate, is "incidental" (Cross and Woozley 12. 279–281).

Annas accuses Plato of paternalism. He does not distinguish between an immature character and a mature character, she argues, and he does not consider the possibility "of censoring children's reading but leaving educated adults to choose for themselves." But "treating adults as though they were children" is paternalism (Annas 4. 85–86).

The question of paternalism is complex. Though I cannot now decide it, I would suggest, albeit briefly, that the question concerns, in part at least, what basis morality ought to provide for censorship. We tend today to think that the moral basis for censorship of imitation ought to be less to sustain good character in an audience than to prevent harm to those engaged in a performance.

But Plato has a point, I think. He reminds us that an imitation of unsavory characters presents a danger because we can become sympathetic toward them.

Even educated adults can identify with a protagonist decidedly immoral. I would also note that with our permissiveness we still do not permit some actions not causing harm to be presented or represented in the theater or in the cinema. Nor on television or even on the internet.

8   Annas contends that the forms "do not fit into the picture at all" because they are not objects of use. The contrast, she argues, is "not between levels of reality but different ways of relating to things on a single level of reality." A consumer, a producer, and an imitator all concern themselves with a thing of the same kind, which is a bit or a flute (Annas 14. 337).

One surely needs knowledge, I would think, to grasp what a thing is and what its function is. But to have knowledge is to grasp the form of a thing and to distinguish its form from its many particulars (see *Republic* 5. 476c–d). This knowledge would provide a paradigm with which a consumer can instruct a producer about the making of a particular thing (see *Republic* 6. 500b–501c). An imitator does not have knowledge of a form, does not have an ability to distinguish a form from its particulars, and likely has a false opinion about its particulars.

Yet I could hardly deny that consumers or producers could also be without knowledge or right opinion. Indeed, consumers or producers who are ignorant, we are about to see, can be a source of tragedy for a political society. They can constitute a society of imitators who are susceptible, one might say, to the contagion of fashion and fad!

9   Cross and Woozley contend that the arguments about the equestrian and the flautist are an addition "which has no direct connection with the theory of the Forms." The philosopher and not the consumer, they argue, has knowledge (Cross and Woozley 12. 284–289).

I would respond that the philosopher is obviously, at least on occasion, a consumer who has understanding and reasoning though we may forget this fact when we are absorbed in philosophy. But I would also point out that a consumer need not be a full-fledged philosopher with both understanding and reasoning. Indeed, a consumer can be nescient.

10 Cross and Woozley worry about how to reconcile the carpenter and his knowledge with the bronzesmith and his opinion (Cross and Woozley 12. 284–287). Perhaps the reconciliation lies in the fact a consumer can have knowledge of a product and its function, and that a producer need have only right opinion. A carpenter would obviously use a couch, for example, and not only make it. He would thus know, or at least reason about, its function. But a bronzesmith would not likely have a use for a bridle. He thus could not reason about its function but would rely on right opinion.

11 Galbraith would very likely be amenable to my argument. He argues in effect that contemporary theory of the economic variety is myth. Economic theory he calls conventional wisdom. He implies, though not with a philosophical but with a popular argument, that wisdom of this sort is myth because it is anachronistic. We devised our economic theory in an era of poverty, but we still cling to our theory in an era of affluence. Our theory has not changed, he contends, but the facts have (Galbraith 1. 1–2). In one passage he actually states that the central tenet of current economic theory, that the production of goods is paramount, is mere myth (Galbraith 19. 209).

We keep to our outdated economic theory less because it is right than because it is "most agreeable," he continues. The truth can create consensus, but the agreeable can also create consensus. We often construct a theory out of what is acceptable to us, and what is acceptable may be merely what we best understand (Galbraith 2. 6–8). Both liberals and conservatives exhibit this epistemological malady, he continues. A conservative prefers the old theory out of a desire, "not unmixed with pecuniary self-interest, to adhere to the familiar and the established." Liberals exhibit a "moral fervor and passion, even a sense of righteousness" for the familiar old ideas (8).

He compares "the articulation of the conventional wisdom" to "a religious rite," such as "reading aloud from the Scriptures." A businessman who listens to an address on free enterprise is "already secure in his convictions," but he appeases the gods with his attendance, his attention, and his applause. Academics, similarly, attend their scholarly meetings "not to convey knowledge but to beatify learning and the learned" (Galbraith 2. 10).

We have, he states, instituted "a respected secular priesthood." Its function is "to rise above questions of religious ethics, kindness, and compassion and show how these might have to be sacrificed on the alter of the larger good." The larger good, unfortunately, is "more efficient production" (Galbraith 19. 215–216). This secular priesthood, he suggests, rests on "a system of morality," which arose from the economic circumstance of carving our country out of the wilderness. Succinctly put, "The world owed no man a living. Unless he worked, he did not eat" (214–215).

Galbraith only briefly speaks of tragedy. Our sacrifice in the name of more efficient production has tragic implications, he argues, which "the rejection of scarcity and the acceptance of affluence involve." But our sacrifice "loses some of its point if it is on behalf of the more efficient production of goods for the satisfaction of wants of which people are not yet aware." The sacrifice is even more tenuous philosophically "if it is to permit more efficient contriving of wants of which people are not yet aware" (215–216).

He reminds us that our social existence is precarious. In our unprecedented affluence we guide our conduct "with rules of another and poorer age," and "in misunderstanding itself" an affluent age runs the risk of proscribing for itself "the wrong remedies." But our affluence is rather precarious. "Western man," he states, "has escaped for the moment the poverty which was for so long his all-embracing fate. The unearthly light of a handful of nuclear explosions would signal his return to utter deprivation if, indeed, he survived at all" (Galbraith 1. 4–5).

Bellah et al. would also very likely agree that our view of society is a myth. But they, too, present not philosophical but popular arguments. They argue that "the larger dependences in which people live, geographically, occupationally, and politically, are neither clearly understood nor easily encompassed by an effective sympathy." The complexity of society today is "elusive and almost invisible" (Bellah et al. 10. 250–251).

What we do, they argue, is rely on nostalgic notions of an earlier time. We wish "to transform the roughness of utilitarian dealings in the marketplace, the courts, and government administration into the neighborly conciliation" of "the idealized 'small town'" in our New England past. But "the rules of the competitive market" in our day overpower "the practices of the town meeting or the fellowship of the church." They, nonetheless, express the hope that these practices, resting on "habits of the heart," can help us "to construct a common future" (Bellah et al. 10. 251–252; see also 6. 152–155, e.g.; or 11. 281–283).

Bellah and his colleagues conclude that our quest for an understanding of the public good is incomplete. They remind us that the Founding Fathers of the American democracy all agreed that a government ought to be "animated by a spirit of virtue and concern for the public good," and that it ought not to be merely "an area within which various interests could compete" (252–254). But this new democracy soon left "the weak and distant national government in the hands of a new breed of professional politicians who specialized in the accommodation of interest rather than in civic virtue" (Bellah et al. 10. 255–256).

We find ourselves in an "unresolved tension" summed up with "the oxymoron 'private citizen.'" They cite Ronald Reagan. He asserts that the people are "a special interest group." This assertion implies that what alone holds us together is "our concern for the economy." They conclude, "The citizen has been swallowed up in 'economic man'" (270–271).

12 Wolff suggests, rightly I think, that Nozick offers "a rational reconstruction of libertarian consciousness." He does not argue that Nozick rests his arguments on assumptions that are emotive, but he argues instead that Nozick develops his arguments with specifics that are "nothing more than a reconstruction or systemization of a set of moral intuitions" (Paul 5. 79–80).

13 Gaus applauds Nozick for his invisible hand explanation. He claims that Nozick provides "a powerful account" of the political realm and demonstrates "its moral permissibility and justifiability independent of collective choice or actual history" (Bader and Meadowcroft 5. 116–117).

Nozick offers, Gaus argues, a successful account because the invisible hand works under the moral constraint that "people are assumed to act out of good-faith concern for the rights of others" (129 and 130). Or, more specifically, Nozick shows that "a just and legitimate state… would emerge from the prosaic actions of rational and reasonable Lockeans" (132–133, also 130–131).

My reply must be that we can attain political happiness only by acting consciously and intentionally for the sake of functions both rational and political. A Lockean, even if deemed rational and reasonable, does not aim at political happiness but only at what seems to him to be desirable, and he has a concern for the rights of others only to the extent that he does them no harm. Or, perhaps, that they do him no harm.

14 Scanlon puts the matter succinctly and approvingly. He argues that Rawls requires "no controversial empirical or metaphysical presuppositions." Presuppositions about justice do not have to be "the results of our causal interaction with independently existing moral properties or entities." These presuppositions are not theoretical but practical, he continues. Their objectivity is a method of reasoning "that all reasonable individuals have good reason to regard as authoritative and normally overriding." It is "a way of reasoning about what to do that is distinct from any given individual's point of view" (Freeman 3. 146–147).

15 Rawls also draws an analogy between our intuitions about morality and our intuitions about grammar. Our sense of justice is analogous to our "sense of grammaticalness." A moral theory formulates principles that characterize, presumably, our ability to make correct moral judgments as a grammatical theory expresses principles that characterize our ability to make correctly formed sentences (*Theory* 1. 9. 41–42).

Nagel is correct to argue against this analogy between morality and grammar. He points out that "the intuitions of native speakers are decisive about grammar." English, for example, is what we agree on. But what we agree on morally condemning "is not necessarily wrong," he argues (Daniels 1. 2 and n2). Nor is what we agree on morally commending necessarily right, I would add.

Dworkin helpfully distinguishes between two models of reflective equilibrium. One model is natural, and it rests on objective moral intuitions. The other model is constructive or, I would say, conventional, and it rests on stipulated moral intuitions (Daniels 2. 27-29). Rawls favors the constructive model, he rightly argues. This model relies not on a moral ontology but on "consistency with conviction." It rests on the assumption that officials ought to act "on the basis of a general public theory" (30-31). But to achieve a theoretical consistency we may have to discard some stipulated intuitions (31-33).

The natural model takes moral intuitions to be observational data. It relies on the assumption that officials ought to be able to explain all "clear observational data." But it accepts the possibility that a current theory may not be able to account for a given intuition though another theory may eventually be able to take it into account (29).

I obviously favor a natural model for political theory. What would my objective moral intuitions be? That we are rational animals, and that we are happy when we engage in a rational activity for its own sake!

Other philosophers have their reservations about reflective equilibrium. Hare, for example, charges Rawls with "advocating a kind of subjectivism, in the narrowest and most old-fashioned sense." This subjectivism is one in which the author and the reader agree about their considered judgments. The result is that they find "a cosy unanimity in their considered judgments," they think that "they adequately represent 'people generally,' " and they "congratulate themselves on having attained the truth" (Daniels 4. 82).

Hare also remarks that any analogy to linguistics or mathematics is "vitiated by the fact that they do not yield substantive conclusions." Linguist intuitions are authoritative for correct language use, and only anthropological theories about moral judgments could be checked "against actual moral judgments," he argues. A moral theory analogous to mathematics would only "elucidate the meanings of moral judgments." After all, mathematics is "purely formal" (85-86).

Scanlon, however, defends reflective equilibrium. He argues that it constitutes a justification of the original position (Freeman 3. 153-154). That the principles of justice are to be chosen in the original position is "at best a plausible hypothesis," he concedes (154-156). But he finds confirmation for this hypothesis in the fact that its principles confirm "judgments that were already fixed points in our thinking," and that they most often require us to "modify or abandon the judgments that seem to conflict" with its principles. For example, we must reject the idea that claims of justice ought to be "proportional to moral desert," or "individuals' marginal contributions to society" (155-157).

I must respond that Scanlon offers a defense of the original position that proves my point. Indeed, his argument shows that the question is begged at the level of principle. Are not the judgments that moral merit provides a basis for claims of justice, or that market demands provide a basis for claims, essentially principles opposed to those of the original position? Rawls simply asks us in effect to accept his own principles and to give up other principles.

Nussbaum, too, accepts reflective equilibrium. She agrees with Rawls that we ought to find a fit between our "theoretical principles" and "ethical judgments about justice." This reflective process she takes to be a "debate among Socratically deliberating individuals." "Nothing is held fixed," she asserts. We may find that "an initially attractive theory" may fall to considered judgments, or that a theory may require modification of "an initially compelling judgment." But the goal is to find "a stable fit" between theory and judgments (*Capabilities* 4. 77–78).

She advises that we focus our reflection on the idea of a life of human dignity and her list of ten central capabilities. She rightly observes that her approach avoids a comment to any particular religious or metaphysical tenets (78–79). But she would apparently omit from consideration that we are potentially eudaimonic creatures, who can live a rational life with intrinsic value. Or perhaps she holds the principle that we are rational animals to be somehow religious or metaphysical.

Sandel would appear to advocate reflective equilibrium of a sort. He presents many examples to show that we cannot avoid moral values in thinking about moral puzzles. Consider what he has to say about the famous runaway trolley car. This dilemma, he argues, pressures us to sort out our moral convictions and to figure out "what we believe and why." But he declines to offer any resolution for the dilemma. He states only that hypothetical examples "help us to isolate the moral principles at stake and examine their force" (*Justice* 1. 21–24).

He argues instead that we can arrive at what amounts to a reflective equilibrium between our principles and our judgments. We arrive at an equilibrium apparently by revising our judgments and principles "each in light of the other." Our reflection does not result in "a self-consistent skein of prejudice," he informs us, because it is "not a solitary pursuit but a pubic endeavor." He claims that a philosopher who ascends to the sun and its light in the allegory of the cave can offer only "a sterile utopia." The allegory fails to give due consideration to "opinions and convictions, however partial and untutored" (28–29).

I would reply that in our reflections, whether private or public, we ought to seek out a moral truth and not merely an equilibrium. A society that has discovered a truth, if only hypothetical, would most likely attain an equilibrium, but a society that has attained an equilibrium need not have discovered any truth. I hardly need cite examples. A moral truth, Plato would argue, is an object of knowledge and not of opinion. That is to say, a truth truly true, if we could but grasp it, would be an intelligible entity and not a sensible one. But he is quick to point out that we also need opinion to grasp the sensible approximations of these truths in a situation requiring action.

16 Nagel makes what might seem to be a useful distinction. He distinguishes two camps within the liberal tradition. His distinction stems from Rawls's statement to the effect that our natural abilities are a common asset, and that we ought to share in their benefits. There are, Nagel asserts, "those who identify justice with the fight against any kind of undeserved inequality" that society can address, and "those who believe... that society is exempt from responsibility for certain forms of 'natural' difference" (Freeman 1. 79–80).

This division of liberal philosophers misses the point, I am afraid. We no doubt ought to regard our natural abilities as a common asset. But I would argue that we ought to do so in order to determine who can best make what contribution to political society, whether theoretical, practical, or poetical. Only then can we apportion the material benefits of living in society to those who would make the best use of them.

Nagel is quite right to assert further that, because the state, law, and property conventions make possible extraordinary production and accumulation, we "bear a collective responsibility for the general shape of what results from the sum of individual choices within that framework." We are "responsible for large scale inequalities that would not have arisen in an alternative framework" (80–81). But is not the answer to these extraordinary inequalities to devote our attention and our action toward promoting political and rational functions of intrinsic value and not simply to divvy up the spoils in a manner deemed to be more equitable?

17   Schmidtz agrees. He argues that skilled workers for Rawls would view themselves "as undeserving winners in a genetic and social lottery," and they would see "the distribution of skill as a common asset." Yet they would not, he continues, see themselves as making a contribution to society, but instead they would view themselves as having an interest in taking away a "bundle of primary goods" from society (Bader and Meadowcroft 8. 200–201).

18   Schmidtz points out that Rawls would agree with the general proposition that how our institutions deal with the natural distribution of our abilities determines its justice or injustice (Bader and Meadowcroft 9. 219).

Recently, political philosophers have argued against Rawls that we ought to take into account our capabilities to use primary goods when we distribute them. But these philosophers evidently accept the Rawlsian concept of our goodness. They argue that we ought to take into account capabilities that enable us to pursue our plan of life (see Brighouse and Robeyns for an anthology offering a spectrum of views on this topic).

With the general proposition that we ought to take our capabilities into account when we distribute resources, I can obviously agree. But I would argue more specifically that we ought to take into account our capabilities to pursue political happiness in one form or another and not our capabilities to pursue a plan of life.

Sandel also argues against Rawls. Discussing affirmative action, he cites Dworkin to imply that Rawls would not take moral desert into account for admission to institutions of higher education. Dworkin argues that admission to a university depends on contributions "to the social purpose the university serves" and not on "merit or virtue." An applicant has no right to be admitted on the basis of "academic criteria alone" (*Justice* 7. 173–174).

Sandel replies to Dworkin and Rawls that we may not be able, "politically or philosophically, to detach arguments about justice from debates about desert." He offers two arguments to show that we may not. First, there is an "honorific aspect." A distribution recognizes "what qualities are worthy of honor and reward." Second, "schools, universities, occupations, professions, public offices" are social institutions that "are not free to define their missions just any way they please." We define these institutions "by the distinctive goods they promote" (178–179).

I would concur, and I would add that an honor bestowed upon a moral quality is closely aligned with the mission of a social institution. And we rightly recognize those moral qualities that contribute to the mission of a social institution, whether educational or professional or political.

19   Schmidtz lends Nozick support. He argues that "arbitrary" is ambiguous. A natural distribution can be arbitrary in the sense of being random or capricious. Randomness does not arise from choice, but capriciousness arises from an unfair choice. And so a random distribution cannot be unfair (Bader and Meadowcroft 9. 218).

Schmidtz also argues that we speak of the talents belonging to a person "as *their* talents" because a person is "a self-owner." But he does not see that the theory of mixed labor can apply to the talents of a person. He applies the theory only to the acquisition of external objects (Bader and Meadowcroft 9. 208–209, his italics).

20 Schmidtz suggests succinctly that Nozick places an emphasis "on our separateness as producers," and Rawls places on accent "on our separateness as consumers" (Bader and Meadowcroft 8. 200–201).

21 Lear puts the matter nicely. He states that a false myth is a falsehood in words. It contains a truth, and its truth is a reflection of a truth in the soul. Therefore, it is "not completely untrue." A falsehood in the soul is ignorance, and its expression in words is an unacceptable myth (Kraut 5. 67).

Cross and Woozley, perhaps mislead by Adams, do not seem to attach due importance to the fact that a lie in words can contain in its kernel a truth about what is. The philosopher guardians are truthful in the sense that they will not tolerate a falsehood in the soul, they argue. But the philosopher guardians will tolerate a falsehood in words if not purely unadulterated. The philosopher guardians, they conclude simply, "may use deception as an instrument of government" (Cross and Woozley 9. 196–97).

Annas concurs with Cross and Woozley. She argues that Plato makes "an odd attempt to distinguish two kinds of lie." What she calls a real lie is "a lie in the soul," which is intolerable, but a lie apparently less than real, an image of a lie, is a lie in words, which "can be quite useful sometimes." She explains that "as long one takes care not to be deceived oneself, telling falsehoods to others is not really lying" (Annas 4. 106–107).

22 Cross and Woozley find the noble lie "little less than insulting" because it may be told to the guardians and not only to the artisans and agrarians. They cannot conceive why the most intelligent citizens would have any difficulty grasping a literal proposition together with its evidence. But they do concede that the lie might be effective for the young guardians, who are not knowledgeable (Cross and Woozley 5. 103).

Annas rightly points out that every society has its identity myth. But she thinks that the noble lie is simply false. She argues that Plato is ready "to legitimize the telling of lies in the interest of some higher end." He is ready "to revise the content of morality in the interests of establishing morality" (Annas 4. 107–108). She explains that the guardians can lie because "they are just." What "they see fit to do, will be right, even if it is also a case of lying." We ought, she adds, "not to worry about their breaking the rules, because when just people do this, the rules ought to be broken" (Annas 6. 166–167).

23 Bellah and his colleague adroitly capture the dilemma. "The American dream," they state, "is often a very private dream of being the star, the uniquely successful and admirable one, the one who stands out from the crowd of ordinary folk who don't know how." This dream we find hard to give up "even though it contradicts another dream that we have—that of living in a society that would really be worth living in."

We fail to see, they continue, "that what is best in our separation and individuation, our sense of dignity and autonomy as persons, requires a new integration if it is to be sustained." We fear instead that "we will be abandoning our separation and individuation, collapsing into dependence and tyranny" (Bella et al. 11. 285–286).

Select Bibliography

Of Works Cited or Consulted

Annas, Julia. *An Introduction to Plato's Republic*. Oxford: Clarendon Press, 1981.
Anscombe, G. E. M. "Thought and Action in Aristotle." In Renford Bambrough, ed. *New Essays on Plato and Aristotle*, pp. 143–158. London: Routledge & Kegan Paul, 1965.
Aristotelis. *De Arte Poetica Liber*. I. Bywater, ed. Oxford: Clarendon Press, 1898.
Aristotelis. *Ethica Nicomachea*. I. Bywater, ed. Oxford: Clarendon Press, 1894.
Aristotelis. *Physica*. W. D. Ross, ed. Oxford: Clarendon Press, 1950.
Aristotelis. *Politica*. W. D. Ross, ed. Oxford: Clarendon Press, 1957.
Bader, Ralf M. and John Meadowcroft, eds. *The Cambridge Companion to Nozick's Anarchy, State, and Utopia*. Cambridge: Cambridge University Press, 2011.
Bellah, Robert N., Richard Madsen, William M. Sullivan, Ann Swidler, and Steven M. Tipton. *Habits of the Heart: Individualism and Commitment in American Life*. Updated ed. Berkeley: University of California Press, 1996.
Benoni, Francesco. "Βασανίζειν: Practical Experience as the Touchstone of Platonic Education." Paper presented at the annual meeting of the Society for Ancient Philosophy, Baylor University, April, 2017.
Brighouse, Harry, and Ingrid Robeyns, eds. *Measuring Justice: Primary Goods and Capabilities*. Cambridge: Cambridge University Press, 2010.
Carville, James, and Stan Greenberg. *It's the Middle Class, Stupid!* New York: Blue Rider Press, 2012.
Collier, Paul. *The Bottom Billion: Why the Poorest Countries are Failing and What Can Be Done About It*. New York: Oxford University Press, 2007.
Cooper, John M., ed., and D. S. Hutchinson, assoc. ed. *Plato: Complete Works*. Indianapolis, IN: Hackett Publishing Company, Inc., 1997.
Crane, Gregory R., ed. *Perseus Digital Library*. http://www.perseus.tufts.edu/hopper/.
Cross, R. C., and A. D. Woozley. *Plato's Republic: A Philosophical Commentary*. New York: Macmillan & Co., Ltd., 1964.
Daniels, Norman, ed. *Reading Rawls: Critical Studies on Rawls' A Theory of Justice*. 1975 ed. Stanford, CA: Stanford University Press, 1989.
Drury, S. B. "Locke and Nozick on Property." *Political Studies*, vol. 30 (1982), pp. 28–41.
Easterly, William. *The White Man's Burden: Why the West's Efforts to Aid the Rest Have Done So Much Ill and So Little Good*. New York: The Penguin Press, 2006.
Ferguson, A. S. "Plato's Simile of Light." Part I. *Classical Quarterly*, vol. 15 (1921), pp. 131–152.
Ferguson, A. S. "Plato's Simile of Light." Part II. *Classical Quarterly*, vol. 16 (1922), pp. 15–28.
Ferguson, A. S. "Plato's Simile of Light Again." *Classical Quarterly*, vol. 28 (1934), pp. 190–210.
Freeman, Samuel, ed. *The Cambridge Companion to Rawls*. Cambridge: Cambridge University Press, 2003.

Galbraith, John Kenneth. *The Affluent Society*. 40th anniversary ed. New York: Houghton Mifflin Company, 1998.

Goodman, Lenn E. and Robert B. Talisse, eds. *Aristotle's Politics Today*. Albany: State University of New York Press, 2008.

Helliwell, John, Richard Layard, and Jeffery Sachs, eds. *World Happiness Report* 2018. http://worldhappiness.report/.

Hobbes, Thomas. *Leviathan*. Edwin Curley, ed. Indianapolis, IN: Hackett Publishing Company, Inc., 1994.

Hume, David. *Enquiries concerning Human Understanding and concerning the Principles of Morals*. L. A. Selby-Bigge, ed. 3rd ed., P. H. Nidditch, ed. Oxford: Clarendon Press, 1975.

Hume, David. *A Treatise of Human Nature*. L. A. Selby-Bigge, ed. 2nd ed., P. H. Nidditch, ed. Oxford: Clarendon Press, 1978.

Kant, Immanuel. *Grounding for the Metaphysics of Morals*. James W. Ellington, trans. Indianapolis, IN: Hackett Publishing Company, Inc., 1981.

Keyt, David, and Fred D. Miller, eds. *A Companion to Aristotle's Politics*. Cambridge: Basil Blackwell, Inc., 1991.

Kraut, Richard, ed. *Plato's Republic: Critical Essays*. New York: Rowman & Littlefield Publishers, Inc., 1997.

Locke, John. *Second Treatise of Government*. C. B. Macpherson, ed. Indianapolis, IN: Hackett Publishing Company, Inc., 1980.

McKeon, Richard, ed. *The Basic Works of Aristotle*. Modern Library, ed. New York: Random House, 2001.

Narveson, Jan. "Rawls and Utilitarianism." In Harlan B. Miller and William H. Williams, eds. *The Limits of Utilitarianism*, pp. 128–143. Minneapolis: University of Minnesota Press, 1982.

Nozick, Robert. *Anarchy, State, and Utopia*. New York: Basic Books, Inc., 1974.

Nussbaum, Martha C. *Creating Capabilities: The Human Development Approach*. Cambridge: Harvard University Press, 2011.

Paul, Jeffery, ed. *Reading Nozick: Essays on Anarchy, State, and Utopia*. Totowa, NJ: Rowman & Allanheld, 1981.

Piketty, Thomas. *Capital in the Twenty-First Century*. Arthur Goldhammer, trans. Cambridge: Belknap Press, 2014.

Platonis. *Gorgias*. In John Burnet, ed. *Opera*, vol. 3. Oxford: Clarendon Press, 1903.

Platonis. *Res Publica*. In John Burnet, ed. *Opera*, vol. 4. Oxford: Clarendon Press, 1902.

Rawls, John. *A Theory of Justice*. Rev. ed. Cambridge: Harvard University Press, 1991.

Salkever, Stephen G. *Finding the Mean: Theory and Practice in Aristotelian Political Philosophy*. Princeton, NJ: Princeton University Press, 1990.

Sandel, Michael J. *Justice: What's the Right Thing to Do?* New York: Farrar, Strauss and Giroux, 2009.

Shorrocks, Anthony, Jim Davies, and Rodrigo Lluberas. *Global Wealth* 2017. https://www.credit-suisse.com/corporate/en/research/research-institute/global-wealth-report.html.

Smith, Nicholas D. "How the Prisoners in Plato's Cave are 'Like Us.'" *Proceedings of the Boston Area Colloquium in Ancient Philosophy*, vol. 13 (1997), pp. 187–204.

Smith, Nicholas D. "Plato's Divided Line." *Ancient Philosophy*, vol. 16 (1996), pp. 25–46.

Staff. "The Shrinking Middle Class." *Fortune Magazine*, December, 2018. http://fortune.com/longform/shrinking-middle-class/.

Tocqueville, Alexis de. *Democracy in America and Two Essays on America*. Gerald E. Bevan, trans. New York: Penguin Books, 2003.

Index

abilities, natural 134–7
Adkins, A. W. H. 178 n.2
agrarians. *See* artisans and agrarians
akrasia 68
America xv–xvi, 122
animals
　greedy 43, 78 (*see also* greed)
　poetical 122, 139
　rational and passional xi, 21, 24–5, 29, 35, 44, 53, 68, 73–4, 81, 82, 84, 87, 89, 94
　rational and political xi, 35, 43–4, 95, 100, 105, 139
Annas, Julia 140–1 n.1, 141 n.2, 144 n.6, 144–5 n.8, 145 n.9, 145 n.11, 146 n.13, 147 n.1, 148 n.4, 149 n.5, 152 n.17, 166 n.2, 166 n.3, 179 n.5, 179 n.6, 180 n.7, 182 n.13, 194 nn.4–5, 195–6 nn.6–8, 202 n.22
Anscombe, G. E. M. 155 n.10
Aristotle
　artisans and agrarians 41–2, 102
　community, political 99–100, 102
　desire 99–100
　division of labor (*see* non-self-sufficiency and division of labor)
　education 38, 42, 96, 99–100, 102–3
　happiness 37–9, 54, 76–7, 99–100, 102–4, 108, 115
　justice 76–7, 93, 96, 99–100
　liberty 50, 53–4, 61
　middle class 102–3, 104
　myth 121
　non-self-sufficiency and division of labor 100
　oligarchy and democracy 93, 103–4
　people, the 38, 102–3
　polity 38–9, 66, 103–4
　production 41–2, 54, 100
　property 77, 102, 103
　rightness and fairness 76–7

society, natural history of 99–100
Arneson, Richard J. 162 n.25, 170 n.17, 171 n.19, 172 n.21
artisans and agrarians 19–20, 22, 36, 39–41, 42, 42–3, 101, 103, 104, 115, 130. *See also* Aristotle; Plato

Bellah, Robert N., et al.
　aristocracy, industrial 177 n.29
　community, politics of 163 n.27
　despotism, danger of 154–5 n.8
　dream, American 202 n.23
　interest, politics of 163 n.27
　middle class 178 n.1
　myth 197–8 n.11
　self-interest, enlightened 187–8 n.21
　work 193 n.34
Benoni, Francesco 149 n.7
Bradley, A. C. 151 n.14, 153 n.19, 180 n.9, 182 n.11, 183 n.15, 185 n.18

Callicles xii, 71–2, 74, 78, 91–2, 133–4
Carville, James, and Stan Greenberg 191 n.28
cave, allegory of. *See* Plato
cavemen 112, 116
Chamberlain, Wilt 83
choice, fundamental 35, 40, 122–3, 127
Collier, Paul 147 n.3
community, political x, 35, 40, 51, 76, 82, 95, 96, 115, 116, 117, 130. *See also* Aristotle; Nozick; Rawls
Cooper, John M. 152 n.17, 153 nn.2–3
Cross, R. C., and A. D. Woozley 140 n.1, 141 n.2, 141–2 n.3, 143 n.5, 143 n.6, 145 n.9, 145–6 n.12, 146 nn.14–15, 147 n.1, 147 n.2, 148–9 n.4, 149 n.6, 152 n.16, 152–3 n.18, 153 n.2, 165 n.2, 179 n.5, 179 n.7, 180 n.8, 193 n.1, 195 n.6, 195 n.7, 196 nn.9–10, 202 n.21, 202 n.22

Daniels, Norman 159–60 n.17, 175 n.26
democracy. *See* oligarchy and democracy
deus ex machina 138
divided line, figure of. *See* Plato
division of labor. *See* Aristotle; Nozick; Plato; Rawls; Tocqueville
Dream, American 122, 139
Drury, S. B. 168 n.14, 169 n.15
Dworkin, Gerald 155–6 n.11, 199 n.15

Easterly, William 176 n.28
education 20–1, 40–1, 42, 73, 83, 84, 96, 104, 130. *See also* Aristotle; Plato; Tocqueville
equality 90–1
eudaimonocracy 42

fairness. *See* rightness and fairness
Feinberg, Joel 174 n.25
Ferguson, A. S. 140 n.1, 141 n.2, 142–3 n.5, 143 n.6, 147 n.1, 148 n.4, 153 n.19
Fisk, Milton 156–7 n.13, 174 n.25, 190 n.24, 190 n.25, 191–2 n.28
fraternity 116
freedom. *See* liberty
Freeman, Samuel 188 n.22
Fried, Barbara 160–1 n.20, 162 n.23

Galbraith, John Kenneth
  education 187 n.21
  inequality 176–7 n.29
  insecurity 178 n.1
  myth 196–7 n.11
  production 167–8 n.7, 173–4 n.24
  public goods 178–9 n.3
  work 192–3 n.34
game, zero-sum 96
Gauss, Gerald 198 n.13
Glaucon 4, 22, 31, 32, 43, 74–5, 76, 97
Goodman, Lenn E. 166–7 n.5
greed 22, 74, 91–2. *See also* animals, greedy
Greenberg, Stan *See* Carville, James., and Stan Greenberg
Gutmann, Amy 157–8 n.15

Halper, Edward C. 154 n.6, 157 n.15, 182 n.12, 184–5 n.18, 185 n.19, 188–9 n.22
happiness, political. *See also* Aristotle; Nozick; Plato; Rawls

artisanal 39–42
and community 95–6
feasibility of 36–9
and justice 72, 73–4, 77, 82, 85, 91
and liberty 51, 54, 55, 56–7, 67–8
and lies 139
natural 35
not absolute 68–9
and oligarchy and democracy 93–4
pluralistic 115
and polity 49–50, 61–2, 67–8, 123
and production 127
and property 17
rational and passional (hedonic) ix–x, xiv–xv, 43, 49–50, 104
and tragedy 131
Hare, R. M. 155 n.11, 173 n.23
Helliwell, John, et al. 140 n.2
Hobbes, Thomas 3, 22, 29, 43–4
Holmes, Robert L. 161 n.21
Homer 26–8, 31–2, 123, 125, 126
hoplite 38, 39, 54, 103
hubris 117
Hume, David 87, 88–90, 91, 92

illusion 23, 24
invisible hand 122, 138. *See also* Nozick

justice. *See also* Aristotle; Callicles; Glaucon; Hobbes; Nozick; Plato; Rawls
  artisanal 19–20, 43, 101
  feasibility of 36–9
  natural 72–3
  and passion 34
  rightness and fairness 73–4, 77–8, 90–1
  and state, establishment of 132
  and tragedy 126, 130–1
  value of 21, 76, 95, 96, 116

Kant, Immanuel 54–5, 61, 67, 106, 108
Keyt, David 181 n.9, 183 n.14, 183 n.16
Kraut, Richard 147–8 n.4

Lear, Jonathan 150–1 n.13, 152 n.17, 202 n.21
liberty 49–50, 51–2, 54, 55, 56–7, 67–8. *See also* Aristotle; Nozick; Plato; Rawls
license. *See* liberty

lies 121, 123, 138–9
Locke, John 63, 64, 78, 79, 80, 81–2, 83–4, 91, 92, 113, 114, 131, 136

Mack, Eric 161–2 n.22, 162 n.24
media, mass 8, 9, 24
middle class xiv, 100–4, 109–10, 114–15
Miller, Fred D., Jr. 150 n.11, 182 n.11, 184 n.17
Miller, Richard 173 n.23, 191 n.25
minuteman 39
mixed-labor theory 81–2. *See also* Locke; Nozick
Mulgan, Richard 150 n.11, 184 n.17
Mulhall, Stephen, and Adam Swift 156 n.13, 159 n.17, 175 n.26
myth 121–2, 122–4, 126, 127, 131–4, 137, 138–9

Nagel, Thomas 156 n.12, 157 n.13, 159 n.17, 160 n.18, 169 n.14, 171 n.20, 172–3 n.23, 174–5 n.25, 189 n.23, 198 n.15, 200–1 n.16
naïveté, state of 3–4, 4–6, 8–9, 12, 13, 21–2, 23–4, 24–5, 43, 49, 96
Narveson, Jan 173 n.23
nature, state of 3–4, 4, 21–2, 23, 43, 81–2, 89, 122. *See also* Nozick; Rawls
non-self-sufficiency. *See* Aristotle; Plato
Nozick, Robert. *See also* Kant; Locke
  abilities, natural 136–7
  association, protective 64–5, 112–14
  association, utopian 105, 111–14, 115
  community, political 106, 111, 112, 114, 116
  desire 62–3, 66, 68, 91, 112, 131, 132, 134, 137
  division of labor 137
  happiness xii–xiii, xiv, 57–9, 62, 63–4, 65–7, 68, 78, 111, 115–16
  invisible hand 132
  justice 72, 79–81, 83–4, 116–17
  liberty 50, 57, 62–7, 68
  merit, moral 82–4
  middle class 114–15
  mixed-labor theory 79–80, 81–2
  myth 131–2, 134, 137
  nature, state of 63–5, 67, 72, 78–80, 111–15, 117, 131–2
  oligarchy and democracy 50, 57, 62, 105, 111, 114, 115

  plan of life xii, 57, 62–3, 63–4
  polity 49–50, 57, 61–2, 67, 68, 91, 105, 110, 114–15
  principle, difference 115
  principles, entitlement 78, 79–80, 81
  production 80–1, 116, 136, 137
  property 72, 78–81, 82–5, 88, 91–2, 110, 136
  proviso, Lockean 78, 80–1, 83, 84–5, 136
  rightness and fairness 78, 84–5, 91–2
  self-sufficiency 134–5, 135, 137
  social union 111–12, 114, 117
  sophistry xii–xiii, 72, 91–2, 115, 117
  state, minimal (night-watchman) and ultraminimal 65, 65–6, 66–7, 114, 115
  tragic 131, 134, 136, 137
  utilitarianism xii–xiii, 140 n.3
  utopia (*see* association, utopian)
  veil of ignorance 62–3
Nussbaum, Martha C.
  capabilities 158 n.16, 181 n.10
  congruence problem 188 n.22
  constraints 162–3 n.26
  distribution 175–6 n.27
  education 185 n.18
  pluralism 160 n.17
  reflective equilibrium 199–200 n.15
  utilitarianism 167 n.6

oligarchy and democracy xiv–xv, 18, 22, 34, 39–40, 49–50, 74, 77, 91, 93–4, 104. *See also* Aristotle; Callicles; Nozick; Plato; Rawls
O'Neill, Onora 168 n.12, 168–9 n.14, 171–2 n.20

Parijs, Philippe Van 189 n.23
Paul, Jeffery 161 n.21
people, the 19–20, 39, 93. *See also* Aristotle; Plato
Piketty, Thomas 176 n.29
plan of life. *See* Nozick; Rawls
Plato. *See also* Callicles; Glaucon; Protagoras; Socrates
  abilities, natural 134
  artisan and agrarians 16, 17, 20–1, 22, 28, 29, 33, 34, 41, 44, 53, 75, 76, 101, 127–8, 130, 138

cave, allegory of 5–13, 13–15, 19, 21, 23–4, 26–7, 30–1, 122, 123, 126, 137–8
desire 17–18, 26–9, 30–5, 41, 97–9, 101, 129–30, 134
divided line, figure of 7–8, 10–12, 26, 30, 124–5, 127, 128
division of labor (*see* non-self-sufficiency and division of labor)
education 5–6, 7–8, 9–11, 12, 13, 14–15, 27, 32, 33, 42, 44, 75, 96, 98–9, 101, 123, 128, 128–9, 130, 131
good, the 11, 14–15, 30, 98, 122
good, idea of 15, 30, 98, 122
happiness 31–2, 52–3, 74, 75–6, 98, 115, 129
justice 14, 15, 16–19, 31–4, 36, 43, 44, 52, 75–6, 96–9, 124, 126, 128, 129–30, 137
liberty 52–3
middle class 100–1
myth 123–4, 127, 138
nature, state of 4
non-self-sufficiency and division of labor 20, 43, 45, 97, 129–30, 134, 138
oligarchy and democracy 17–18, 19, 22, 28, 34, 37, 44
people, the 28
poetry 123–6
principles (*see* divided line; non-self-sufficiency and division of labor)
production 97, 101, 124–5, 127–8, 129, 130, 137
property 75, 99, 110
rightness and fairness 74–6
society, natural history of 97–9, 126, 128–30
soul, tripartite 31–2, 125–6
tragedy 125–6
polity. *See also* Aristotle; Nozick; Rawls
artisanal and agrarian xiii–xiv, xiv–xv, 39–42, 61–2, 77, 93, 103–4, 115–16
Calliclean 91–2
eudaimonic and expedient (mixed) xiii–xv, 49–50, 57, 61–2, 67–8, 74, 109, 115–16, 123
and middle class 100, 103–4, 109
production and products xiii–xiv, 19–20, 31, 36, 39–42, 73–4, 85, 95–6, 127,
130. *See also* Aristotle; Nozick; Plato; Rawls
property 29, 71, 81, 82, 82–5, 91, 92, 103, 112. *See also* Aristotle; Callicles; Hume; Locke; Nozick; Plato; Rawls
Protagoras xii

Rawls, John. *See also* Aristotle; Hume; Kant
abilities, natural 134–6
community, political 106, 108
desire 58–61, 62, 68, 88, 90, 91, 106–8, 110, 131, 135–6, 137
division of labor 106, 135
goodness, full and thin theory of 107–9, 111
happiness xii–xiii, xiv, 57–9, 68, 78, 87, 88, 90, 107–9, 110
justice 58–61, 72, 85–8, 90, 91, 106–9, 109–11, 116–17, 133–4, 136
liberty 50, 57–62, 68
maximin rule 86
middle class 109–10
myth 131, 133–4, 137
nature, state of 85
oligarchy and democracy 50, 57, 62, 105, 110
original position 58–9, 85, 88–9, 90, 116–17, 133
plan of life xii, 57–8, 60–1
polity 49–50, 57, 62, 67, 68, 91, 105, 109–10
principle, difference 59, 78, 86–7, 90, 110, 115, 135
principle, equal liberty 59–60, 61, 67, 86
production 137
property 72, 78, 86–7, 88, 91–2, 110, 135
reflective equilibrium 133–4
rightness and fairness 78, 85–6, 87–8, 91–2
self-sufficiency 134–5, 135
social union 106–9, 110–11, 116–17
sophistry xii–xiii, 72, 91–2, 117
tragic 131, 134, 135–6, 136, 137
utilitarianism xii–xiii, 140 n.3
veil of ignorance 58–9, 60–1, 85, 87–8, 88, 90

well-ordered society 105, 106–9
rightness and fairness. *See also* Hobbes;
  Locke; Nozick; Rawls
  and equality 90–1
  and happiness 77, 85
  paradox of 73–4
Ryan, Cheyney C. 171 n.18

Sachs, David 164 n.2
Salkever, Stephen G.
  aristocracy 149 n.9
  democracy 184 n.16, 185–6 n.19
  education 186 n.21
  internal cause of action 153–4 n.5
  pleonexia 167 n.7
  political life 149–50 n.10
Sandel, Michael J.
  constraints 162 n.25
  dessert and entitlement 173 n.24
  difference principle 191 n.28
  freedom, Kantian 154 n.7
  good life, a 151–2 n.15, 175 n.25, 186 n.20
  justice 166 n.5
  language 182 n.11
  moral desert 201 n.18
  practical wisdom 151 n.14
  reflective equilibrium 200 n.15
  self-ownership 172 n.20
  ties, moral 189–90 n.23
Scanlon, T. M. 155 n.11, 159 n.17, 168 n.12, 169–70 n.16, 190 n.24, 198 n.14, 199 n.15
Scheffler, Samuel 159 n.17, 168 n.13, 169 n.14
Schmidtz, David 201 nn.17, 18, and 19, 202 n.20
self-sufficiency. *See* Nozick; Rawls
sensibility, external and internal 25, 30, 34
Shorrocks, Anthony, et al. 140 n.1
slavery, political 55, 68
Smith, Nicholas D. 142 n.4, 144 n.8, 146 n.12

social union 116, 134. *See also* Nozick; Rawls
society, cancerous 45
society, dual 28–9, 110
Socrates 11, 15, 16, 20, 28, 31, 33, 72, 74–5, 76, 96, 98, 101, 122, 123, 125, 128, 129, 130, 133
sophistry xi–xiii, 72, 91–2. *See also* Nozick; Rawls
status quo ix
Swift, Adam *See* Mulhall, Stephen, and Adam Swift

Taylor, C. C. W. 165 n.2
theatrocracy 9, 13, 126
Thomson, Judith Jarvis 169 n.14
Tocqueville, Alexis de
  America xvi
  anxiety 94–5
  aristocracy, industrial 92
  division of labor 92
  education 105
  enslavement 55–6
  liberty 51, 68
  self-love, proper 105
  virtue 94, 105
tragedy 123–4, 125–6, 127, 128–9, 130–1, 131, 134, 135–6, 137, 139. *See also* Nozick; Plato; Rawls

unrestraint, restrained 58, 66
Urmson, James O. 194 n.4, 195 n.5
utilitarians xii–xiii

Vellentyne, Peter 162 n.23, 168 n.12, 170 n.17

Williams, Bernard 164–5 n.2
Wolff, Robert Paul 161 n.21, 168 nn.8–9, 170 n.17, 171 n.17, 192 n.30, 198 n.12
Woozley, A. D. *See* Cross, R. C., and A. D. Woozley
working class 19–20, 39

www.ingramcontent.com/pod-product-compliance
Lightning Source LLC
Chambersburg PA
CBHW052040300426
44117CB00012B/1907